The Handbook
of 5GW
A Fifth Generation
of War?

Edited by Daniel H. Abbott

NIMBLE BOOKS LLC

NIMBLE BOOKS LLC

Nimble Books LLC

2846 S. Knightsbridge Cir

Ann Arbor, MI, USA 48103

http://www.NimbleBooks.com

wfz@nimblebooks.com

Version 1.1; last saved 2021-01-06

Printed in the United States of America

ISBN-13: 9781608882243

∞ The paper used in this publication meets the minimum requirements of the American National Standard for Information Sciences—Permanence of Paper for Printed Library Materials, ANSI Z39.48-1992. The paper is acid-free and lignin-free.

DEDICATION

To the Militant, the Suffering, and the Triumphant.

NIMBLE BOOKS LLC

EPIGRAPH

Matthew 25:32

NIMBLE BOOKS LLC

Contents (including Figures)

A HANDBOOK OF 5GW (DANIEL H. ABBOTT)

This volume is a Handbook of Fifth-Generation Warfare (5GW). It discusses 5GW in the context of the xGW framework and in terms of other conceptions of 5GW, presents examples of 5GW, provides source documents in the emergence of 5GW and xGW, presents two lists for further reading, and ends with a conclusion. In other words, this volume expresses 5GW theory as it is now known and discussed.

There are many other books about 5GW that remain to be written.[1] For example:

- An introduction to 5GW that would be appropriate for use in 100- or 200-level college courses on military history, strategy, or counterinsurgency. No vocabulary lists or review sheets appear in this volume, and no Instructor's Edition is available. There are no quizzes and no tests. A pedagogically sound approach to teaching 5GW to warfighters is needed. This volume does not fulfill that need.
- A Field Manual for 5GW, designed to be used by the warfighter in tactical, grand tactical, operational, strategic, or grand strategic campaigns. While examples of 5GWs are included in this volume, practitioners who read this book hoping to wage and win a 5GW will be disappointed. A work along the lines of the *U.S. Army/Marine Corps Counterinsurgency Field Manual* (Nagl 2007) is needed to avoid defeats in 5GW campaigns. This volume does not fulfill that need.
- A briefing of 5GW. It does not convey the main points of 5GW and xGW theory within thirty minutes, in PowerPoint format, or with theatrical enunciation. While the discourse around 5GW provides methods for testing the theory, provides summaries of actual 5GWs, and outlines 5GW

---

[1] If you are interested in doing so, please visit NimbleBooks.com and use the Contact form to submit a proposal!

1

theory, this book will not win over a skeptical audience with the efficiency of a celebrity speaker or a tireless believer. An evangelistic summary of 5GW similar to John Boyd's famous briefings is needed to make sure that 5GW theory is known. This volume does not fulfill that need.

- A history of 5GW that carefully documents the streams of research and thought that converged to form the xGW framework with source documents and citations.. Colonel Frans Osinga's *Science, Strategy, and War,* his recently published history of the theories that helped build John Boyd's OODA loop, is an example of what is needed.

This volume is a Handbook of 5GW. It outlines 5GW and the xGW framework as they exist now. This volume is an atlas that pieces together smaller maps to form a coherent outline of a continent of warfare. 5GW is not new. It is not revolutionary. It is not an invention. It is part of the human experience, and warfighters have always been familiar with it. It is time that academics, researchers, and analysts knew about it as well.

If you need a Handbook of 5GW, a central published repository of thinking on that subject, this book is for you. This book is aimed at the analyst who needs a theoretical justification for his views, an academic who requires a published literature to work from, a journalist who needs a vocabulary to describe the fighting he sees, or a layman interested in this subject. After you read this volume, you will be ready to start.

ABOUT THE AUTHORS

Dr. Daniel H. Abbott is an educational psychologist with a doctorate from the University of Nebraska–Lincoln. He previously earned graduate degrees in Computer Science and Educational Psychology (Cognition, Learning, and Development). Daniel lives in Bellevue, Washington, with his wife. He can be reached at danhabbott@gmail.com.

David Axe is a journalist based in Columbia, S.C., and the author of *War Bots*. He blogs at www.warisboring.com.

Shane Deichman has spent most of his adult life thinking about the influence of information and perception on military operations. He has worked for the military-industrial complex for nearly two decades, and blogs at www.oz.deichman.net, antilibrarium.wordpress.com and—for book roundtables like the *John Boyd Roundtable* (Nimble Books, 2008) at www.chicagoboyz.net .

Patrick Dugan is a game designer living and working in Buenos Aires, Argentina.

Brent Grace is a political science major at Capital University in Columbus, Ohio. He plans to attend graduate school after he finishes his BA.

Adam Herring is a 1998 graduate of the College of Communications, Information and Media at Ball State University with a degree in Broadcast Telecommunications. Adam writes under the handle Arherring at the blog *Red Herrings,* which can be found at www.arherring.wordpress.com. He resides in Indiana.

Chad Kohalyk is a Canadian who has lived most of his adult life in Japan, where he currently works in the tech industry. He holds a master's degree in War Studies from the Royal Military College of Canada and an undergraduate degree in theoretical linguistics from the University of British Columbia. His research interests are primarily communications technology and social network theory, and their relationship in terms of international relations theory.

Dr. Samuel Liles is an associate professor of computer information technology at Purdue University Calumet researching cyber warfare and cyber terrorism. His research agenda follows the spectrum of information operations and how cyber warfare realistically impacts the kinetic effects of conflict. Samuel is a Web 2.0 proponent and maintains a blog (www.selil.com) with his spouse, Sydney (also a professor). It has archives dating back to 1993 (before it was called blogging).

Dr. Daniel McIntosh is an Associate Professor of Political Science at Slippery Rock University. He blogs at http://secureliberty.blogspot.com.

Stephen Pampinella is a graduate student in the Department of Political Science, State University of New York at Albany. His research interests include IR constructivism, counterinsurgency, and military theory. He blogs at www.stephenpampinella. wordpress.com.

L. C. Rees is a software engineer. He has been a student of military science and history since the Reagan Administration.

Mark Safranski is the editor of *The John Boyd Roundtable* and a contributing author to *Threats in the Age of Obama*. An educator and freelance writer, he has written for *Small Wars Journal*, *HNN* and *Pajamas Media*. He blogs at www.Zenpoundit.com.

Purpleslog is the pseudonym of a US citizen living in Milwaukee, Wisconsin, working as a private-sector network/security engineer. He has interests in IT, information security, cyberwar, national security, fifth generation/gradient warfare (5GW), history, public policy, entrepreneurship, economics, pop culture and the future. He blogs at http://purpleslog.wordpress.. He tweets as http://twitter.com/purpleslog. He originally came to explore 5GW in response to the 9/11/2001 attacks and his interest in finding a subtle way to counter 4GW.

Curtis Gale Weeks blogs at www.dreaming5gw.com.

Sir Francis Edward Younghusband (1863-1942) was a British explorer, army officer, military-political officer, and foreign correspondent born in India who led expeditions into Manchuria, Kashgar, and Tibet. He three times tried and failed to scale Mt. Everest and journeyed from China to India, crossing the Gobi desert and the Karakoram mountain range in modern day Pakistan. **"Younghusband"** is a contributor to ComingAnarchy.com, a blog on issues of world affairs and politics.

INTRODUCTION

The successful application of the Fifth Generation of Warfare (5GW) is "indistinguishable from magic" (Rees 2009, following in the spirit of Clarke's Law, propounded by the author of *2001: A Space Odyssey*) "any sufficiently advanced technology is indistinguishable from magic"). The Fifth-Generation warrior hides in the shadows, or in the static. So, then, how can analysts and researchers study and discuss 5GW?

Other questions also demand answers:

- What is the xGW framework, which many theorists use to describe 5GW?
- What alternatives to the xGW framework exist?
- What 5GWs have been observed?
- What are the source documents for the xGW framework?
- What is the universe of discourse that the xGW framework emerged from?
- Why bother trying to understand 5GW?

This handbook attempts to provide systematic answers to these questions in several major sections, each of which is written by many contributors. While this handbook records many different voices of 5GW research, it speaks with one voice on the need to understand 5GW, the fifth gradient of warfare.

5GW AND THE xGW FRAMEWORK

Most discussions of 5GW take place within the context of the xGW framework. This framework began as an attempt to clarify and rationalize earlier views of 5GW, specifically Lind's (2004) idea of a yet-to-emerge generation of warfare and Hammes's (2004) hints of a future generation in his work *The Sling and the Stone*. The approaches associated with Lind and Hammes include a *theory of sequential emergence*, as each generation of warfare is thought to emerge from previous generations of war in the same way that each human generation emerges from a previous human generation.

The xGW framework rejects the *theory of sequential emergence*, and the *Generations of Modern War* (GMW) school that is associated with it. While some theorists in the xGW framework still use the term *generation*, the elements of the taxonomy are now generally known as *gradients*. The gradients of war, like gradients we see in other elements of social organization (wealth, height, skin color, and so on) flow indefinitely into each other, and their emergence pre-dates written history. The first 0GW occurred thousands of years ago. According to the xGW framework, the first 5GW was fought and lost before the dawn of time.

THE xGW FRAMEWORK (DANIEL H. ABBOTT)

An earlier version of this chapter appeared as "Chapter 2. The Generations of Modern War," in Revolutionary Strategies in Early Christianity(Abbott 2008).

According to the xGW framework, warfare exists along a gradient of violence, which is more focused on one end and more diffused on another. Militant forces that better focus their violence can overcome less-focused militant forces many times their size. At the fifth gradient of warfare (5GW), violence is so diffuse that only a single murder or outrage may separate it from politics.

The Zeroth Gradient of War, or 0GW

At the zeroth gradient of warfare (0GW), war is a genocide and a holocaust. In 0GW, the entire able population fights. As such, there is no difference between civilians and soldiers. Likewise, as there is no distinct army to destroy, 0GWs are genocidal. Ant colonies regularly engage in 0GWs. The Holocaust is another example. Because 0GWs are total wars, counterinsurgency (COIN) in 0GW typically involves ethnic cleansing in kind. Thus, the Great Sioux Uprising that temporarily removed all whites from what is now South Dakota, for instance, was rapidly followed by the removal of most Sioux Indians onto reservations.

The First Gradient of War, or 1GW

1GW is characterized by concentration of labor, or the attempt to win by selecting those most able to fight and concentrating them in one place for battle. Chimpanzees are capable of 1GW, with rival troops forming insertion teams, engaging in pitch battles, and other civilized behaviors. Many European conflicts around the time of Napoleon were also 1GWs.

The Second Gradient of War, or 2GW

The concentration of firepower describes 2GW. If the majority of fighters are armed only with spears and swords (as in medieval Europe), or powerful forearms (as with chimps), 2GW is impossible. However, from bands of archers to the powerful artillery guns of the First World War, 2GW allows victory through producing deadly goods and aiming them at the same place at the same time. More of the fighting society is now involved in essentially economic or technical roles, taking men away from the front lines while keeping them in the fight.

The Third Gradient of War, or 3GW

While 0GW relies on wiping out the enemy, 1GW on defeating him with larger numbers, and 2GW on defeating him with better machines, victory in 3GW comes from better minds. The most famous 3GW was the German Blitzkrieg against France in 1940. Contrary to myth, the French had better fortifications, better equipment, and even better tanks. However, the Germans had a better trained officer corps that knew how to create uncertainty by maneuvering inside and out of the French lines, preventing any meaningful counterattack and paralyzing the French. The "Shock and Awe" defeat of Saddam Hussein's Iraq in 2003 relied heavily on 3GW, as did the 100-hour campaign during the first Gulf War.

The Fourth Gradient of War, or 4GW

4GW is more complex and subtle yet. As in 0GW, the boundary between war and peace breaks down, but the reason is different: while in 0GW peace is so violent that the bureaucrat becomes a killer, in 4GW war is so peaceful that the warfighter becomes a criminal. The wars America has lost, including Vietnam, Lebanon, and Somalia, have all been 4GWs (Hammes 2004). Defeat in Vietnam so broke America's will to fight that America's institutional knowledge of occupation warfare was eliminated, and would

9

not be restored until years into the Iraq War. COIN in 4GW often involves either degrading the opponent into an earlier generation of warfare that can be defeated conventionally, or else providing incentives for some part of the 4GW force to turn on their comrades. Proponents of 4GW, such as Paul of Tarsus in the Christian revolt against the Senate and People of Rome (Abbott, Revolutionary Strategies in Early Christianity 2008) and the Chinese Communists in their wars against Japan and the KMT (Mao 1961), accept a more violent path to power than in 5GW as the cost of not being able to blind the enemy to the existence of a war.

The Fifth Gradient of War, or 5GW

In 5GW, violence is so dispersed that the losing side may never realize that it has been conquered. The very secrecy of 5GW makes it the hardest generation of war to study. Because 5GW attacks occur below the threshold of observation, COIN in 5GW is the preemptive, system-wide, automatic degeneration of 5GW forces into more primitive gradients of warfare. The 5GW warfighter hides in the static, and *the most successful 5GWs are those that are never identified.*

BATTLING FOR PERCEPTION: INTO THE 5TH GENERATION? (SHANE DEICHMAN)

What is the role of perception in modern conflict and how has the evolution of technology changed its importance?

In 1989, Bill Lind et al. published a seminal article in the *Marine Corps Gazette* entitled "The Changing Face of War: Into the Fourth Generation" (Lind, Nightengale, et al. 1989). The article identified "three distinct generations" in "the development of warfare in the modern era," sounding a clarion cry to alert us to the emergence of a "4th Generation." Specifically, Lind et al. warned of widely dispersed and undefined conflict without a clear distinction between "civilian" and "military." Lind's "Generations of Modern War" (GMW) model has elicited a number of follow-on theories and revisions. In many revisions, an additional level focusing on information and perception—"5th Generation War"— is introduced.

Adam Herring (Searching for 5GW 2009) includes taxonomies of both the Generations of Modern Warfare and xGW frameworks in his chapter in this volume. In a similar vein, I define the *generations* of warfare, or what others describe as *gradients*, as follows:

1GW: Marked by regimental structure and strict discipline. Noted historians Keegan and van Crevald have attributed this to the advent of firearms, which create a need for more rigorous safety mechanisms.

2GW: In response to 1GW rank-and-file formations, fires (i.e., explosive and kinetic energy delivered by a variety of means, such as artillery) are massed to shatter their cohesion.

3GW: Massed fires are countered by maneuverability.

4GW: Maneuver forces are proved inadequate in the face of an asymmetric adversary who exploits the full breadth of the maneuver space (not only military but also civil) by denying sanctuary to 3GW units.

5GW: Moral and cultural warfare is fought through manipulating perceptions and altering the context by which the world is perceived.

Rather than defend the Generations of Modern Warfare framework, or attempt to discriminate between 4GW (culture-based asymmetrical warfare focused on the "rage of the people") and 5GW (perception-based warfare focused on the context of conflict), I will instead use this model to illustrate the importance of command, information and human cognition in the conduct—and resolution—of conflict.

Foundation

The foundational theories of modern war are described in Carl von Clausewitz's magnum opus, *On War*. In addition to defining the nature of war (a "duel on a larger scale") and its purpose ("a continuation of politics by other means"), Clausewitz also provided the three core elements of any campaign:

- Rationality (of the state)
- Probability (in military command)
- Rage (of the population).

Much of the "Cold War" ethos of warfighting was vested in the first premise: the rationality of the state (q.v., "Mutually Assured Destruction" doctrine in nuclear warfare). Similarly, insurgencies like the U.S. faced in Vietnam forty years ago—and in Iraq today—are driven by the third premise: the rage of the people. Mark Safranski (2009) provides us with an excellent analysis of several case studies on the impact such insurgencies have had on *regimes of paranoid character* in his essay "5GW: Into the Heart of Darkness," which appears later in this volume.

Could 5th Generation Warfare (where perception and context are key) be described as a fusion of popular rage with political rationality, where the very idea of "conflict" is altered in order to create conditions favorable to the 5th Generation warrior? Such a feat would logically factor the second premise (the probabilistic calculus of the military commander) out of the equation—or at least reduce its relevance in the larger battle of ideas.

Context

In the first chapter, "Muhammad the Enemy," of a biography of the Prophet, *Muhammad,* Karen Armstrong (1993) describes the 9th century CE monk Perfectus of Cordova, in Andalusia (formerly the capital of the Muslim state of al-Andalus). Perfectus's diatribe against the Prophet of Islam warranted a death sentence, and inspired dozens of others from all levels of society to similarly insult Muhammad—and receive similar fates from the Qadi.

Perfectus, his contemporaries Eulogio and Alvaro, and the many other "Cordovan martyrs" were influenced by an apocalyptic biography of Muhammad that (with extensive artistic liberties) linked the Prophet of Islam to the "Great Deceiver" predicted in the Apostle Paul's second epistle to the Thessalonians. The association of Muhammad with the "rebel [who] would establish his rule in the Temple of Jerusalem and mislead many Christians with his plausible doctrines,"[1] and with John's Book of Revelation through "selective addition" (claiming Muhammad died in the year 666 CE—even though he lived another 38 years), were what we may call a "5th generation war": a secret war that exploited cultural icons in order to diminish and defeat an opponent.

My personal epiphany while reading Armstrong is that none of the "generational" models is necessarily exclusive—nor, for that matter, are they strategic. Rather, they are simply tactical methods that one may choose to apply in the achievement of an objective or the fulfillment of a task.

Whether a commander chooses to align his forces in columns (a staple of "close order drill," one of the most basic elements of modern-day "Basic Training" in the armed services), or to mass fires, or to exploit maneuver, or to focus on "creating political support among the population" as General Petraeus has done with "the Surge" in Iraq, the fact of the matter is that ALL of these are valid tactics at some point. In fact, I submit that the methods are force structure neutral in many respects. Whether a given force is comprised of professional soldiers, ragtag irregulars or an enraged mob, each has the capacity to apply destructive force (though obviously some force structures are optimized for certain methods).The crux of the matter is that warfare is no longer the sole purview of the nation-state. The proliferation of information technologies and ready access to design "best practices" is collapsing the barriers to entry in the bazaar of violence, as author and blogger John Robb has been telling us for some time.[2] Even seemingly advanced weapon systems like cruise missiles (the "rich man's IED") will soon become accessible to self-subsidized organizations with Do-It-Yourself ingenuity, GPS-enabled cell phones and a modicum of propellant and guidance. And we have all seen the power of networks for manipulating and influencing perceptions.

While the nation-state is optimized for the first of the late Col. John Boyd's three "Categories of Conflict" (Attrition, Maneuver and Moral),[3] the latter two have very low barriers to entry and are readily accessible for nearly any size of organization.

On Command

Command and Control (C2) theory is very well developed for 1GW, 2GW and 3GW campaigns. Joint Publication (JP) 6-0: Joint

Communications Systems lays a solid foundation for communications between different elements of a joint force, and each uniformed service has well-developed doctrine with respect to C2.

In 4GW contests, C2 becomes more problematic. Lines of authority are often blurred, and effective 4th-generation warriors rely on mission-type orders (*Auftragstaktik*) and operational empowerment seldom seen in more strictly regimented militaries. Similarly, 4GW's reliance on "Mass"—one of the nine principles of war in conventional military thought—is also dramatically different, allowing them to exploit a very small signal-to-noise ratio through dispersion in the general populace and leveraging commercial communications (mobile phones, IM, Internet) to convey "intent" or "objectives."

In addition to 4GW being primarily a moral conflict, there is something else—something deeper that can be manipulated, influenced and exploited to achieve desired objectives. The morality of a 4GW campaign is not the most fundamental force that drives people and shapes their support for, or opposition to, or acquiescence to, a campaign.

That distinction belongs to the context by which we perceive the world. By altering how the world is perceived, one can achieve what Sun Tzu called the "acme of skill": victory without fighting.

This raises some interesting questions. For instance, does a 5GW force require cohesion and unity of effort? (I have argued in the past that it does not—rather, that a 5GW force becomes increasingly effective the more disparate its efforts become.)

But what does this do to the notion of "command"? There's a stream of American thought that loves hierarchies—rigid, singular command structures with no doubt as to who is "in charge." But is such a command structure valid for a 5GW campaign?

Or could a 5GW opponent be "commanded" simply through the naturally emergent behavior of complex systems? Is "self-synchronization" valid as a method of C2 for a 5GW campaign? And is the notion of a "campaign" even relevant in this context? Or is our lexicon lacking in describing emergent methods of influencing thought—and, by extension, limiting our actions to those that a faceless adversary allows? Prof. Sam Liles (2009), in his essay "Unified Generational Warfare," decouples innovation from technology and shows its immutability in conflict.

Epistemology

Command, Control, Communications, Computers, Intelligence, Surveillance and Reconnaissance ("C4ISR," or, as Admiral Giambastiani liked to refer to it during his tour as my boss at US Joint Forces Command, "C2 + C2ISR") is simply a tool. The technology only provides a medium by which information can be shared, the same way that Roman signal towers allowed information to be conveyed rapidly across great distances millennia ago.

Our modern technology, though impressive, has not ushered in a unique "Information Age." In fact, today's technologies have not created wholly new capabilities; they have simply enriched capabilities that have existed for centuries. Rather than living in "The Information Age," I believe we are actually living in the fifth "information age":

1st: Verbal exchange of information (oral communication)

2nd: Physical representation of information (Sumerian writing)

3rd: Portability of information and popular literacy (papyrus; fourth century BCE Greece)

4th: Mass-production of information (Gutenberg's movable type press)

5th: Information freed from constraints of physical space (telegraph, Internet)

A significant effect of proliferating information technology and communications capabilities has been to neuter the initiative and empowerment of subordinates—stunting the audacity that makes (or breaks) battles. For many important applications, rigid hierarchies coupled with pervasive communications grids—with "Net-Centricity"—are demonstrably less effective than ones with "weak" links (Barabási 2002).

Consider the "Operational Level of War"—the level between "Tactics" and "Strategy," known as "Grand Tactics" during the nineteenth century. Many organizations of the US Department of Defense invest inordinate numbers of labor hours in developing an idea that peaked in Napoleon's time, but is not as relevant today.

Napoleon's logic was simple: he commanded an army so vast that its interior lines could exceed the distance of daily information propagation. (Information in the late eighteenth/early nineteenth century could propagate at approximately 100 miles per day.) But while technology increased the bandwidth of information transfer (as well as the speed, thanks to decoupling it from physical form and allowing velocity = c), the intermediate layer that once served as a proxy for the Imperial edict (i.e., empowerment of the on-scene commander to act on behalf of the Emperor) has remain entrenched.

Modern C4ISR tools have served to perpetuate this folly, giving today's commanders a beguiling sense of "Situational Awareness." MIL STD 2525: Common Warfighting Symbology, the military standard for unit icons and symbols, merged with theater-scale maps can give a commander a "real-time snapshot" of the entire physical battlespace. As the scale increases (since warfare is not scale invariant[4]), though, the trade-off between "relevance" and "intelligibility" becomes akin to Heisenberg's Uncertainty Prin-

17

ciple: as one becomes more precise, the other becomes dangerously less so. Later in this book, Stephen Pampinella (2009) provides a lucid analysis of *identity construction* and *misperception* as insurgent goals.

"Quo Vadis"

The temptation to treat warfare like a game of chess (with its ordinal moves and perfect battlefield intelligence) is fallacious. Clausewitz's description of "Genius" in battle is the antithesis of a reductionist thinker who seeks the unique solution to a given problem. Complex adaptive environments can have multiple solutions—but an even larger number of incorrect options.[5]

If Clausewitz was correct that war is a "duel on a larger scale," then it would follow that the intent is to use the threat of violence to shape the will of the adversary. For the unified, loyalist state, only the leader need be influenced. But in more diffuse command structures, this influence must be far more widespread.

This is the challenge of our day: how do we influence a large, disparate population distributed across multiple states? It is clear that the ubiquity of information access, coupled with the increased prosperity of individuals across all socioeconomic strata, creates a value structure incompatible with a rigid hierarchy.

Therefore, perhaps a better description of an effective leader is not simply "charisma," but "network fitness": per Barabási, the ability to "attract" links in order to influence their perceptions. A message not heard is akin to the tree that falls in the forest with nobody around: though it may create spherically propagating pressure fluctuations in the surrounding air, it does not make a "sound." And a leader who cannot attract followers is destined to fail.

Barabási's description of analysis by Ginestra Bianconi shows that network fitness models do not correlate well to power law (i.e., scale invariant) models. Rather, they are more similar to the properties of Bose-Einstein condensates (where all "nodes" collapse into one shared state—a "winner-take-all" model). The end result is the "fittest" node grabs all the links, shaping the network into a star topology.

This applies not only to quantum fluids, but also to counterinsurgencies (COIN), Information Warfare, Public Diplomacy and the fermenting clash of civilizations between a globalized free-market economy and a nomadic, tribally organized world. Chad Kohalyk (2009) delves deeper into the applicability of social networks in another chapter of this book.

Conclusion

Technology has significantly enhanced our awareness of the world, both as individuals and collectively as an interconnected, globalized society. It has also made the tools of violence far more accessible to organizations with limited means. "War" is no longer the sole purview of the nation-state. The convergence of ubiquitous networks with pervasive sensors can elicit tectonic shifts in geopolitics.

While Lind et al. (1989) underscored the expansion of the battlespace beyond professional militaries serving a rational state, the nature of perception in conflict deserves our attention. The ability to shape the perception—and therefore the opinions—of a target audience is far more important than the ability to deliver kinetic energy, and will determine the ultimate victor in tomorrow's wars.

THE END OF THE RAINBOW: IMPLICATIONS OF 5GW FOR A GENERAL THEORY OF WAR (L. C. REES)

> For we wrestle not against flesh and blood, but against principalities, against powers, against the rulers of the darkness of this world, against spiritual wickedness in high places. (Ephesians 6:12)

Three implications of 5GW are particularly significant for a general theory of war:

- War is more than the threat and use of violence.
- The major features of the power used to wage war are energy and visibility.
- War is a spectrum of power that falls between an absolute concentration of power at one extreme and an absolute absence of power at the other extreme.

5GW is the deliberate manipulation of an observer's context in order to achieve a desired outcome (Herring 2009). This implies that *war is more than the threat and use of violence*. While, to paraphrase LTG James Mattis, it is true that sometimes the best way to manipulate the context of the enemy commander is to put a bullet in it, violence is not the only way to manipulate context. Other tools are available. Yet violence is war's most obvious feature. Indeed, the simplest definition of war is that *war is violence*. If pressed for more detail, we might expand this definition a bit:

War is nothing but a duel on a large scale. Countless duels go to make up war, but a picture of the whole can be formed by imagining a pair of wrestlers. Each tries through physical force to compel the other to do his will; his immediate aim is to throw his opponent in order to make him incapable of further resistance.

War is thus an act of force to compel our enemy to do our will. (Clausewitz 1989)

While this definition covers some forms of war, it misses other, more subtle forms of war. A more expansive definition of war is needed, a definition that emphasizes the second part of Clausewitz's formulation, "compelling the enemy to do our will" (the goal of war) more than the first part, the "act of force" (the means of war). The goal of war is essential in defining the nature of war. The means of war are not. Making the enemy do our will is essential to war. An act of force is not. 5GW is the manipulation of observational context in order to make the enemy do our will. Since an act of force is not required to manipulate observational context, force is not required to wage 5GW. Since 5GW is undoubtedly war, war must be more than a mere act of force. However, making the enemy do our will remains an essential part of 5GW and, by extension, war. Since "our will" is critical to defining what war is, we have to include the critical dimension of politics since it is through politics that we arrive at "our will." Clausewitz observes:

> When whole communities go to war—whole peoples, and especially civilized peoples—the reason always lies in some political situation, and the occasion is always due to some political object.

Politics, however, cannot be divorced from the dimension of culture. The nature of politics is heavily shaped by the nature of the culture that employs it: the strengths and flaws of culture become the strengths and flaws of politics. Culture is the realm where information about the world is structured, where, as Adam Eklus has remarked, "the values, norms, and goals of organizations, societies, and nations are defined." It is also where the desires of a human community, its values, norms, and goals, are prioritized. Most of this process is completely unconscious: culture is the art of the unspoken assumption. However, unconsciousness is a feature, not a bug. Once desire is entrenched in unconsciousness, it's difficult to dislodge. The height of cultural achievement is embedding a desire so deeply in the human mind that the conscious mind

21

is completely unaware of either its presence or its potency. Desires that attain maximum priority will achieve maximum unconsciousness. Only then will they be safe from the whims of fickle fashion. All that a desire needs to achieve priority is power, and to achieve that power, desire needs politics.

Politics is the division of power between cultural desires. The amount of power available at any one time is finite. There will never be enough power to give every cultural desire the priority it is clamoring for. What power there is, therefore, must be divided between a clamoring multitude of cultural desires. The process of dividing power is both an internal and an external process. Externally, power is divided between the competing cultural desires of different political communities. Internally, power is divided between the competing cultural desires within a political community. Once a desire becomes associated with a particular division of power, it becomes a *political desire*.

The division of power within a political community heavily shapes the division of power between political communities. The division of power between political communities in turn heavily influences the division of power within a political community. Due to the finite nature of power, the process of political division will usually degenerate into a struggle for power. To prevail in this virtuous political cycle, each side must employ strategy. Strategy is the reconciliation of the quantity and quality of cultural desire with the quality and quantity of the power available to achieve that cultural desire. While politics is the instrument of culture, strategy is the instrument of politics: its nature is a direct reflection of the politics that employs it. Since war is a strategy, its nature is highly dependent on the politics that employs it. The nature of politics, more specifically the nature of the internal division of power and the internal struggle for power, determines the nature of war. The strengths and flaws of politics become the strength and flaws of war. Healthy politics makes healthy war. Unhealthy politics makes unhealthy war.

Adding the critical dimension of politics gives us our definition of war: war is a strategy intended to make the enemy conform to our political desires when doing so is contrary to what they would do if they possessed both the power to resist us and sufficient knowledge about our true political desires.

This definition of war captures several aspects of war that are not immediately obvious:

- Since war, as a strategy, is an instrument of politics, the intentions of war, as *strategic* intentions, should remain subordinate to *political* intentions.
- War is intended to satisfy political desires. There is no guarantee, however, that what is *intended* will significantly correspond to what *actually happens*.
- The enemy may know enough about our true political intentions to want to resist our efforts to achieve them, but may be powerless to do so. On the other hand, the enemy may have the power to resist us but they may accede to our activities because they believe we're motivated by something else. If they knew enough about our true political motives, they might contest our efforts to satisfy them.

War is a mixture of two forms of strategic power: *violence* and *influence*:

Violence is the strategic form of power used to physically deny the enemy the power to resist our efforts to satisfy our desires.

Influence is the strategic form of power used to shape the enemy's knowledge in ways that help us satisfy our desires.

Influence takes many forms: diplomacy, propaganda, subversion, commerce, agitation, intelligence, education. However, the most elemental form of influence in war is deception, *the strategic form of power used to distort enemy perceptions in ways that help us satisfy our desires.* Since 5GW is a war of deception, it's almost entirely a war of influence. This doesn't mean 5GW is violence-free. However, most of the violence it incites will be committed by third parties whose observational context is manipulated through a war of influence. 5GW doesn't need to dirty its hands with violence. Its aspirations lie beyond violence. As T. E. Lawrence (1920) wrote:

> [S]uppose we were an influence...an idea, a thing invulnerable, intangible, without front or back, drifting about like a gas? Armies were like plants, immobile as a whole, firm-rooted, nourished through long stems to the head, we might be a vapour, blowing where we listed. Our kingdoms lay in each man's mind, as we wanted nothing material to live on, so perhaps we offered nothing material to the killing. It seemed a regular soldier might be helpless without a target. He would own the ground he sat on, and what he could poke his rifle at.

If influence and violence are in harmony, they reinforce each other and make the war effort stronger. If influence and violence are in disarray, the war effort will become weak and ineffective. The nature of the politics that blends violence and influence determines how harmonious or how conflicted the mixture will be. The second implication of 5GW, that *the major features of the power used to wage war are energy and visibility*, will shape what portion of influence and what portion of violence get mixed in to a war.

Energy is how much power it takes to make the enemy conform to our political desires while visibility is how easy it is for the enemy to gather knowledge we don't want them to have. There's a trade-off between visibility and energy. The more energy that's concentrated into a form of strategic power, the more visible it is. The smaller the amount of energy that's concentrated into a form of strategic power, the less visible a form of strategic power is.

Influence has low visibility and low energy while violence has high visibility and high energy. It's hard to hide the energy of an atom bomb and it's hard to light a city with invisible ink.

To become "an influence...an idea, a thing invulnerable, intangible, without front or back, drifting about like a gas," 5GW must become a true war of influence. It must influence others to expend energy on its behalf rather than expending energy itself. Any visibility caused by energy expenditure is death to its political desires. To wage a 5GW campaign, 5GW politics must have low energy and low visibility. It must become invisible politics. Only then will 5GW become a war of influence instead of a feeble war of violence. High energy and high visibility 5GW is not 5GW. The possibility that 5GW could degenerate into other forms of war characterized by greater visibility and greater energy leads us to the third implication of 5GW: war is a spectrum of power that falls between an absolute concentration of power at one extreme and an absolute absence of power at the other extreme.

Clausewitz provides many examples of the spectrum of war. From Book 1 Chapter 1 of On War:

> Generally speaking, a military objective that matches the political object in scale will, if the latter is reduced, be reduced in proportion; this will be all the more so as the political object increases its predominance. Thus it follows that without any inconsistency wars can have all degrees of importance and intensity, ranging from a war of extermination down to simple armed observation.

Here's another example from book 1 chapter 2 of *On War*:

> We now see that in war many roads lead to success,
> and that they do not all involve the opponent's outright
> defeat. They range from the destruction of the enemy's
> forces, the conquest of his territory, to a temporary oc-
> cupation or invasion, to projects with an immediate po-
> litical purpose, and finally to passively awaiting the
> enemy's attacks.

The use of a spectrum to represent war is useful because it presents war as a range of strategies from which politics can pick and choose. Since politics can choose to pursue a wide variety of desires, war, to be a useful political instrument, must be equally varied. Clausewitz observes:

> To think of [political goals] as rare exceptions, or to
> minimize the differences they can make to the conduct
> of war, would be to underrate them. To avoid that we
> need only bear in mind how wide a range of political in-
> terests can lead to war, or think for a moment of the gulf
> that separates a war of annihilation, a struggle for politi-
> cal existence, from a war reluctantly declared in conse-
> quence of political pressure or of an alliance that no
> longer seems to reflect the state's true interests. Be-
> tween these two extremes lie numerous gradations. If
> we reject a single one of them on theoretical grounds,
> we may as well reject them all, and lose contact with the
> real world.

Following Clausewitz's own logic, we must look beyond his narrower spectrum of war to discover *all* of the ways that politics can wage war. What separates one form of war from another on Clausewitz's spectrum is energy: for example, a war of annihilation involves more energy than simple armed observation. However, as 5GW implies, energy is only one feature of the power used to wage war. For a spectrum of war that includes both energy *and* visibility, we need to turn to the Indian strategist Kautilya. His spectrum of war has three wavelengths (Kautilya, 1992):

- **Open war:** waging war where the war, political desires, combatants, and the strategic forms of power used in the war are visible, energetic, and lean towards violence over influence.
- **Secret war:** waging war where the war and political desires are visible but the combatants and strategic forms of power used in the war are invisible, moderately energetic, and lean towards a balance of violence and influence.
- **Silent war:** waging war where the war, political desires, combatants, and the strategic forms of power used in the war are invisible, not very energetic, and lean towards influence.

Though Clausewitz described elements of secret war, he mostly dealt with open war. This means that he mostly dealt with energy and violence. However, Kautilya's two other forms of war can only be understood if the spectrum of war covers energy *and* visibility, violence *and* influence. This is particularly true of silent war, the form of Kautilyan war closest to 5GW. Roger Boesche comments:

> [S]ilent war is a kind of fighting that no other thinker I know of has discussed. Silent war is a kind of warfare with another kingdom in which the king and his ministers—and unknowingly, the people—all act publicly as if they were at peace with the opposing kingdom, but all the while secret agents and spies are assassinating important leaders in the other kingdom, creating divisions among key ministers and classes, and spreading propaganda and disinformation....In silent warfare, secrecy is paramount, and, from a passage quoted earlier, the king can prevail only by "maintaining secrecy when striking again and again." This entire concept of [silent] war was apparently original with Kautilya. (Boesche 2003)

Contemporary war is shifting from the more violent, energetic, and visible end of Kautilya's spectrum (open war) to the less violent, less energetic, and invisible end (silent war). Existing general theories of war must adapt to this shift in order to remain useful. This adaption was unnecessary for most of human history.

Movement along the spectrum of war was usually in the opposite direction, towards more violence, more energy, and more visibility. However, after Hiroshima and Nagasaki, war achieved its most violent, energetic, and visible extreme. The desires that could be satisfied through thermonuclear violence were sharply limited. After the hydrogen bomb, there were sporadic outbreaks of open war but there was a pullback from more violent, energetic, and visible forms of war. Most wars were fought with less violent, less energetic, and less visible forms of war. Wars of influence became more common while wars of violence became less common.

5GW is valuable because it forces us to pay attention to the unseen wavelengths of the spectrum of war. It forces us to see war as more than violence. It forces us to see war as a spectrum that is constantly shifting between extremes of energy and visibility. It forces us to develop a definition of war that is broader than the definitions found in most contemporary general theories of war. The problem with using a narrower definition of war is that the enemy may fight you with a form of war that you not only can't see, but, even worse, don't even believe in. If the enemy uses a broader definition of war than you, any attack on that portion of the spectrum where you are defenseless may inflict a decisive defeat. The worst part of such a defeat may be that:

- You never knew you were at war.
- You never saw what hit you.
- You never knew there was a chance for victory.
- You never knew that you were defeated.
- You don't believe in any of the above.

In discussing silent war, the progenitor of 5GW, Kautilya includes a chapter on how to use black magic and other occult practices against the enemy. This is strangely appropriate: any sufficiently advanced 5GW is indistinguishable from magic.

5GW AS NETWAR 2.0 (CHAD KOHALYK)

Towards a New Military Theory of Social Networks

The term "netwar" was coined in the early 1990s by John Arquilla and David Ronfeldt, who felt that the information revolution was going to have an unprecedented impact on the way conflict is carried out (Arquilla & Ronfeldt 1996). Since its inception, the concept of netwar has been confused with war waged on or through computerized platforms on the Internet. Though Internet and communications technologies (ICT) can be an important ingredient for netwar, the more profound attribute of netwar is the organizational design of its protagonists. In netwar one or more sides display a dispersed organization—a widely cast social network without the centralized command structure found in today's military hierarchies. Although the World Wide Web has acted as a catalyst for increased awareness of networks due to its capabilities for maintaining relatively cohesive groups on a global scale, netwar is more about social organization than technological revolution.

In 2001, Arquilla and Ronfeldt released a collection of essays that explored in depth the impact of social networks on netwar (Arquilla and Ronfeldt, Networks and Netwars 2001). The book covered a wide breadth of topics from terror and crime to activism and social movements. During that time Albert-Lásló Barabási, a physicist from the University of Notre Dame, was making immense headway in the study of networks (Barabási 2002). His discovery of the scale-free quality of real networks has had resounding impact in the fields of computer science, theoretical physics and biology. Due to the timing, Barabási's findings were not incorporated into the updated concept of netwar.

There is great potential for the fields of netwar and network theory in a military context to be revolutionized due to these recent breakthroughs. A better understanding of the underlying structure of networks will also aid in the discovery of historical analogues. Though the concept of netwar was established in the early 1990s, the actual practice of netwar could possibly date back to the earliest social networks of humankind. Recent advances in social network analysis may aid historical researchers searching for antecedents to modern-day netwar. In the same manner, theories about future forms of netwar may also be conceived.

Previously unknown types of networked organization are being realized that could prove to be the threat of tomorrow.

It is beyond the scope of this chapter to answer these difficult questions definitively. But through examining the present, past, and possible future of social network theory in the context of netwar, paths for future study will be illuminated in an attempt to provoke a reexamination of the network-based warfare concept, which accounts for recent advances in other fields.

Historical Antecedents

From the current military perspective, netwar is associated with asymmetric threats, pitting non-state actors against a state who holds conventional military dominance. Thus networked conflict is not the stuff of modern traditional warfare. With the unchallenged dominance of the American military today, the networks of terrorist groups and insurgents have come to the forefront of current military strategic inquiry. Ten examples of netwars since 1994 are listed in *Networks and Netwars* (Arquilla and Ronfeldt, Networks and Netwars 2001). The American invasion of Afghanistan in 2001 saw US Special Forces deployed in a distributed network on the ground. But is netwar truly a newly discovered form of war?

The advent of the telegraph and the railway was an information revolution in itself, allowing commanders far from the front to exert control over men in the trenches. In fact the type of "total war" that World War I represented—requiring the efforts of the people and industry to be subordinate to military goals— galvanized the organizational design of the hierarchy for the rest of the twentieth century. (In fact, the twentieth century corporation, born out of the factories of the industrial revolution, is another example of the dominance of hierarchies in the last century.) Prior to the Great War, limitations on communication technology required distant units to act semiautonomously. The Royal British Navy would receive extremely simple orders (i.e., "Find French ships and sink them") that they would act on during months at sea between port calls and their next mission.

This is not to say that there were no forms of netwar after the invention of modern industrial warfare. Even during the heyday of hierarchy militaries experimented with decentralized forms of control. The German concept of *Auftragstaktik*, or "mission tactics," allowed each officer and NCO to do what they thought needed to be done in order to achieve the mission goal. Decision-making was devolved to the lowest levels. The Israeli Defense Force utilized "optional control," allowing field commanders to make their own tactical decisions regardless of whether or not they had orders. Furthermore, during World War I, T. E. Lawrence (of Arabia) masterfully navigated tribal politics to organize a network of irregulars with a single mission: harass Turkish lines of communication (Lawrence, Seven pillars of wisdom: A triumph 1991).

Yet not all guerilla movements relied upon eyes of netwar. Mao (1961) and Trinquier (1964), both influential tracts in guerilla warfare, outline extremely hierarchical forms of organization. Mao's *On Guerilla Warfare* contains very specific personnel and arms requirements in a strict hierarchy dividing divisions into regiments, battalions, and companies. Trinquier's diagrams of the military organization of the National Liberation Army (ALN) in

Algiers during the 1950s show a hierarchical command and control structure sitting atop isolated three-man cells: each discrete armed group consisted of thirty-five armed men. Trinquier charted the ALN's bomb-throwing network as well, which was "kept apart from other elements of the organization...broken down into a number of quite distinct and compartmented branches, in communication only with the network chief through a system of letter boxes."

The guerilla networks of successful revolutionary wars during the middle of the twentieth century exhibit a surprisingly rigid hierarchical structure from the perspective of today's current challenges in fighting insurgency and terrorism worldwide. Despite a community of prominent theoreticians trying to come to terms with postcolonial "people's wars," the notion of a resistance movement divorcing itself from hierarchy and organizing along the lines of a distributed network seems to have remained unexplored. This could be due to culture. Mao's revolution was steeped in Leninist doctrine, which required strict socialization. Yet he did say that "command must be centralized for strategical purposes and decentralized for tactical purposes" (p. 114).

There are also possibilities for investigating primitive netwar from an age even earlier than Westphalia. In fact, Arquilla and Ronfeldt (1997) use the Mongols of the twelfth and thirteenth centuries as an example of cyberwar and netwar (pp. 34-37). Ancient tribes, one of the earliest forms of human organization, display many characteristics similar to the kind of distributed networks current militaries face. Tribes are relatively horizontal organizations, with each member roughly equal. Clans represent the various segments of tribes, and can operate autonomously. Lastly, tribes are *leaderless,* in that elders are advisors or facilitators, and their roles change due to circumstances. One of the most important netwar-like characteristic of tribes is their mastery over the tactic of swarming. Ancient tribes offer interesting historical analogues to netwar.

Possible historical examples of netwar seem to be plentiful throughout history. Upon further investigation a pattern might emerge, such as the ostensible correlation between the rise of industrial warfare and de-emphasis on decentralized, networked organizational designs. But in order to search out precise analogues we need an accurate model of when an organization is a network. Until recently, no such model existed.

Network Theory Today

The study of social networks in conflict was pioneered by John Arquilla and David Ronfeldt in a number of essays during the 1990s (Arquilla and Ronfeldt, In Athena's Camp: Preparing for conflicts in this information rage 1997). The *information age* provided a new paradigm for conflict, particularly in the face of military dominance by the post-Cold War victor, America. Arquilla and Ronfeldt proposed three different types of networks—the chain, the star or hub network, and the all-channel network—that could be used to categorize network-based threats. These three topologies could also be used together, or form a hybrid with a hierarchical organization. For example, some actors have a "hierar-chical organization overall but use network designs for tactical operations; or other actors may have an all-channel network design overall but use hierarchical teams for tactical operations." Needless to say, the possible configurations are numerous, which represents a challenge to analysts seeking to map a particular network.

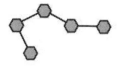  

Chain network   Star or hub network   All-channel network

Figure 1. Reproduced from Arquilla and Ronfeldt (2001) at 8.

Real-world examples, such as the nineteen hijackers involved in the September 11 attacks of 2001, don't fall neatly into the categories described by Arquilla and Ronfeldt. Even a cursory visual comparison shows that the 9/11 terrorist network falls somewhere in between a star network and an all-channel network (c.f. Krebs 2008). An all-channel network of 19 nodes would render 361 links, with each hijacker linked with all 18 other hijackers. Only 112 total connections exist, less than a third of the predicted amount. And yet there is no central hub, maintaining links with all other nodes. The best-connected node has only 11 links, the least-connected only 2. The four best-connected nodes (with 9, 10 or 11 links) account for nearly half of the total links (51, or 46%). The three basic network models do not capture the sprawling complexity of the 9/11 hijackers.

The reason is that Arquilla and Ronfeldt based their models on an idealized form of social network, one that is not evidenced in the real world.

The roots of network theory date back to the mid-twentieth century and the work of the Swiss mathematician Leonhard Euler, who solved the problem of the Seven Bridges of Königsberg in 1736 (Barabási 2002). This was one of the first publications to use graph theory, a subfield of mathematics, and the ancestor of modern-day network theory.

Königsberg, modern-day Kaliningrad, is located on the Pregolya River, which contains two large islands connected to each other and the mainland by seven bridges. The people of Königsberg passed the time trying to solve the puzzle: was it possible to walk a path across the seven bridges never crossing the same one twice? Such a path was never found, and in 1736 Euler devised a mathematical solution proving that it was impossible. He did so through abstraction, replacing each of the land masses with a node, and each bridge with a link. By doing this he realized that the problem could be solved by looking at the degree of each node, or number of links each node possessed. Euler discovered that the only way a path could be completed without crossing a node twice was for each node to have an even number of degrees. This became known as an Eulerian path. Since the Königsberg puzzle had three nodes with 3 links, and one node with 5 links, it was mathematically impossible to complete a circuit crossing each bridge only once.

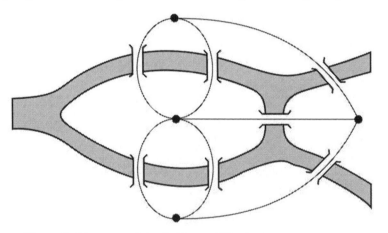

Figure 2. Diagram of the Bridges of Königsberg

One hundred fifty years later, in 1875, a new bridge was built in Königsberg, making such a path possible. The importance of Euler's discovery is that graphs, or networks, have certain properties "that limit or enhance our ability to do things with them" (p. 14).

More than two hundred years later, two Hungarian mathematicians, Paul Erdos and Alfréd Rényi, made the next leap in graph theory by asking the question: how do networks form? Erdos and Rényi argued that the simplest solution nature could follow was to connect each node randomly. Take for instance the example of a cocktail party with 100 strangers, where each guest is a node and each encounter is a social link.

As each guest moves around the room, randomly mingling and collecting social links, small clusters of two and three guests will form. Soon these clusters will connect with one another. Inevitably, at some point, each guest will have at least one link. This is the turning point: we now have one massive cluster. Starting from any node, one can reach any other node within the network. To sociologists, this is a community. To physicists, this is called "phase transition" (like when water forms ice). Erdos and Rényi calculated that it would take only thirty minutes for the entire room of guests to become connected in an all-encompassing social web (p. 16).

This is known as the theory of random networks, which dominated thoughts on networks after 1959. But this theory did not accurately explain networks in the real world. Nodes in nature tend to have many more than the one link necessary to be part of the whole. It is estimated that we know between 200 and 5,000 people by name. Also, random network theory says that the more links added to a network, the more difficult it is to find a node that is relatively isolated. Most nodes will have approximately the same number of links. The result is a distribution of links represented by a bell curve. Yet in nature it is entirely possible to find nodes that have only a very few links, and other nodes with a massive number of links.

Erdos and Rényi could not explain this complexity, and substituted it with randomness. This concept of random networks has dominated thought on complex networks until the late 1990s. It is evident in Arquilla and Ronfeldt's three models of networks, each with perfectly symmetrical distribution of links.

In 1998, Barabási and Eric Bonabeau with Hawoong Jeong and Réka Albert of the University of Notre Dame used a web crawler to trawl the World Wide Web and map the links between Web pages (Barabasi and Bonabeau 2003). They were surprised to find that the World Wide Web is not very democratic in its placement of links; in fact, a few highly connected Web pages were holding the entire network of the Web together. Most of the Web pages, 80%, had fewer than four links, while a tiny minority of 0.01% of nodes had over 1,000 links. This distribution of links is not explained by a bell curve, but by a power law.

A power law predicts that most nodes have only a few links, and a few nodes have a great many links. These nodes with an anomalously large number of links are the hubs that keep the network from flying apart into smaller, isolated mini-networks. In a random network the peak of distribution represents the "average node" in a system, which retains the same number of links as a majority of nodes within the system. Thus a random network is said to have a scale. Networks with a power law distribution don't have a peak, and therefore there is no "average node." These types of networks are called "scale-free."

Examples of scale-free networks are found throughout nature, including molecules involved in burning food for energy, the router connections that make up the Internet, and collaborations and sexual relations between people (p. 54). They are represented by a topology somewhere in between the all-channel and star or hub network of Arquilla and Ronfeldt.

Barabási and his team have continued their study of scale-free networks and have made some intriguing discoveries beneficial to the field of military studies. For example, scale-free networks are extremely robust against accidental failures. The number of nodes with few links far outweighs the number of hubs, so any random attack against a network is far more likely to hit a relatively isolated node, without any serious repercussions to the entire system. Barabási et al. found that up to 80%of randomly selected routers could fail and the Internet would still be able to function. But a network's reliance on hubs means that it is highly vulnerable to coordinated attacks on the relatively few hubs. The question remains: how many hubs need to be neutralized to crash a system? Recent research suggests that somewhere between 5 to 15% of all hubs need to be eliminated to destroy a network.

In the case of the War on Terror, randomly stopping individual terrorists at the border will have little negative impact on a terrorist network. But, as hubs in a social network are the relay points for many communications, we should be able to identify and destroy these leader hubs and inflict real damage on the network (Sageman 2004).

Barabási's work on the way scale-free networks form could also be a boon to current link analysis techniques. As each new node enters a system, it prefers to attach to an existing node that already has many other connections. As time goes on, the system becomes dominated by hubs with a massive number of links. Applying these principles to social network analysis used in mapping terrorist or insurgent networks may help to identify nodes where preferential attachment is high, where recruitment and growth occur.

Netwar 3.0?

In an attempt to deduce the next type of netwar we can extrapolate from a combination of John Boyd's concept of the observe, orient, decide, and act (OODA) loop and William Lind's model of generational warfare (Abbott, Orientation and action, part I: The OODA Loop 2009).

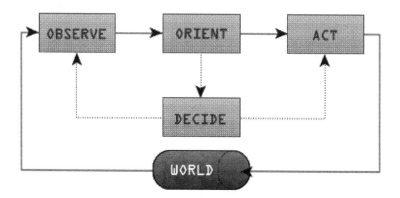

Figure 3. Abbott's Depiction of Boyd's OODA Loop

US Air Force Colonel John Boyd conceived a decision cycle made up of four elementary processes: observe, orient, decide and act. Boyd was a fighter pilot, and argues that in a dogfight the first combatant to make it to the end of his decision cycle would be victorious. The pilot observes his opponent, orients himself, makes a decision and then acts (Abbott, A history of the OODA loop 2008). The ideal process is to skip the decision process, to be able to act on reflex, from the gut. This is what the Germans call *fingertip feeling* or *Fingerspitzengefuhl*. Thus the decision process is ideally a secondary process.

Lind's framework of generational warfare is not without controversy, but when combined with Boyd's OODA loop, we can extrapolate a type of warfare that has yet to be defined. The four generations of war are generally considered to begin at the dawn of the modern state. The first generation was that of line and column, fought by massing infantry at a focal point, or *Schwerpunkt* in Clausewitz's terms. This was war during Napoleon's time. The second generation developed as improvements were made in

40

weapons and massed firepower, including the rifled musket, breechloaders, the machine gun, and indirect fire. World War I is an example of 2nd-generation warfare. The third generation, as evinced in the blitzkrieg tactics of World War II, is that of maneuver warfare (Hammes 2004). Fourth-generation warfare, commonly referred to as 4GW, is a departure from the first three generations in that it is not reliant on technology. In fact, it is in a way a regression, to a style of warfare from before the age of the modern state.

> [W]hat changes in the Fourth Generation is who fights and what they fight for....Fourth Generation war focuses on the moral level, where it works to convince all parties, neutrals as well as belligerents, that the cause for which a Fourth Generation entity is fighting is morally superior. It turns its state enemies inward against themselves on the moral level, making the political calculations of the mental level irrelevant. (Lind, On War #90: The Sling and the Stone 2004)

4GW is fought on a moral level, without regard to the nation-state, and usually through asymmetric means. It is much like our concept of netwar.

First-generation warfare is characterized by massed armies, which moved wherever their feet would take them, and fought with commanders on the battlefield. The objective was to destroy the enemy's army, hopefully gaining advantage by deciding which battlefield to fight on. Thus, 1GW was centered around the enemy's ability to DECIDE and ACT. Thanks to the telegraph, railway, and other modern communications, the second generation of warfare saw the influx of massive amounts of information to commanders far behind the line of battle. Decisions had to be made based on this information about where and when to make the big push. 2GW moves further into the OODA loop and centers around the ability to ORIENT and DECIDE. 3GW moves further in still, attacking an enemy's ability to ORIENT himself by unleashing lightning maneuver attacks at unexpected points. Finally, 4GW, which is an asymmetrical battle over the moral superiority of the population, attacks the enemy's civil society, and his ability to OBSERVE and ORIENT himself toward his enemy, which he himself becomes. Each generation moves deeper and deeper into the OODA loop. Thus we must ask, what will 5GW look like?

By extrapolating from generational warfare's progression deeper into the OODA loop we can deduce that 5GW will attack an enemy's ability to OBSERVE. The enemy could be blind, unaware to the true identity of the adversary he is engaging with, or maybe oblivious to the fact he is fighting a war at all. But assuming that a war requires two or more sides to actually be aware of engagement, let us explore the puzzle of being unable to observe one's enemy. Indeed, Abbott (Orientation and action, part I: The OODA Loop 2009) has argued that the gradients of warfare can be differentiated based on what part of the enemy's OODA loop is the target of military operations.

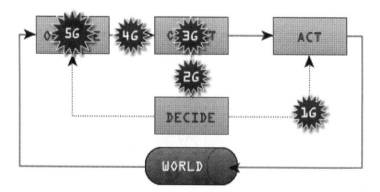

Figure 4. The Gradients of War Superimposed on the OODA Loop

The distributed networks of both 4GW and netwar have proven resilient to the identification of a center of gravity that may be attacked, destroying the enemy. But what if even those nebulous leaderhubs were to disappear? One idea comes from a former Grand Dragon of the Knights of the Ku Klux Klan through the article "Leaderless Resistance," which attempted to outline a new organizational design to fight against perceived state tyranny (Beam 1992). Beam calls for the abolition of a pyramid-style organization because "nothing is more desirable" for federal agencies than opposing groups who are "unified in their command structure." He advises using a cell structure, but to defend against attacks by the federal government the structure must be deeply decentralized with no headquarters giving command or direction. He dubbed these "phantom cells." Arguing that "in any movement, all persons involved have the same general outlook, are acquainted with the same philosophy, and generally react to given situations in similar ways" Beam put the onus on the individual to acquire the necessary skills and intelligence to carry out missions for the "cause." Coordinating attacks will be possible because:

> Organs of information distribution such as newspapers, leaflets, computers, etc., which are widely available to all, keep each person informed of events, allowing for a planned response that will take many variations. No one need issue an order to anyone. Those idealist [sic] truly committed to the cause of freedom will act when they feel the time is ripe, or will take their cue from others who precede them.

Beam credits the idea of the phantom cells to one Col. Ulius Louis Amoss, who apparently first wrote of leaderless resistance in 1962, thirty years before Arquilla and Ronfeldt conceived of netwar.

The type of organization described by Beam is known as an "emergent network." Emergence is a phenomenon that is evidenced in many places, from multicellular biological organisms, to metropolitan zoning, to no-limit poker. Emergence is a dynamic process of self-organization where nodes behave individually under a set of simple rules, and yet as a whole render a complex pattern. Johnson explains:

> Emergence is what happens when the whole is smar-
> ter than the sum of its parts. It's what happens when you
> have a system of relatively simpleminded component
> parts—often there are thousands or millions of them—
> and they interact in relatively simple ways. And yet
> somehow out of all this interaction some higher level
> structure or intelligence appears, usually without any
> master planner calling the shots. These kinds of systems
> tend to evolve from the ground up. (Johnson 2005)

Emergence is unpredictable at the lowest levels of operations. Thus it is a very difficult to define phenomenon. Further research is currently being conducted into the properties of emerging networks.

How this could affect security can be seen in today's headlines. Pre-2001 Al Qaeda was a network with numerous hubs able to give commands and directions to sprawling regional networks. Its most famous leader hub, Osama bin Laden, was readily identifiable, as well as his closest advisors. After the October 2001 invasion, Operation Enduring Freedom, smashed the physical headquarters of Al Qaeda, the amount of direct control held by bin Laden diminished greatly. Direct interaction through training camps was replaced by globally distributed passive communication that outlined the group's objectives. Al Qaeda was forced into becoming an even more distributed network. This development gave rise to the disappearance of Al Qaeda the terrorist "organization," and the appearance of Al Qaeda as a movement.

A core organization of Al Qaeda still theoretically exists, but there seems to be a much more loose global community surrounding Al Qaeda's cause. Many regional groups, heretofore unknown to have any direct contact with bin Laden or his cadre, have stood up to claim membership to the greater network of Al Qaeda, forming regional franchises of the organization. Abu Musab al-

Zarqawi's Jama'at al-Tawhid wal-Jihad (JTJ) announced their allegiance to Al Qaeda in October 2004, changing their name to "Al Qaeda in Iraq." Other copycats, small distinct groups with no direct contact with Al Qaeda cells but looking to contribute to the overall goals of Al Qaeda, are a possibility.

Small cells, with no links to one another forming a larger network, operating individually under a very simple set of rules (e.g., kill Americans, disrupt government activities, hack a certain target's computer) can give the impression of higher-level coordination and a sense of organization—even where there is none. Thus, 5GW could be characterized not by our inability to observe an opponent, but by perceiving an opponent where there is none. This formless enemy, regarded as having a form, would strike deep into our OODA loop and could cause massive expenditures as state leaders try to protect their citizens from a threat constructed by the leaders themselves.

Caution in Progress

Recent technological advances have brought the organizational concept of networks to the forefront of thought in business, sociology, science and security. The simple network topologies presented by Arquilla and Ronfeldt prove a good initial step in bringing a more scientific understanding of network theory to the field of security studies. Even with the rudimentary comprehension of network structure in military circles, there is no doubt that the power of network-based organization is felt at all levels.

Yet caution is to be advised, and a better understanding of how networks form and act in the real world will help to avoid pitfalls. The power of an all-channel network would be devastating, but John Arquilla made a brilliant observation in a 2003 interview:

> On the other hand, this great connectivity is an inducement to overcontrol. The people at very high levels can now be looking at what the fellow in the field is

> looking at, and the temptation [to micromanage] is al-
> most too much to resist. We have to be very, very care-
> ful about this.

A more accurate model of real world networks will give us the advantages not only of understanding our enemies, and foresight into alternative organizational structures of future enemies, but also on how to move away from the rigid hierarchical structure of our current military system, and in what areas it is appropriate or even possible. This has been already suggested by others including Hammes (2004), who advocates becoming "organizationally networked to overcome the inertia and restriction of information flow characteristic of our 19th-century bureaucracies" (p. 226). Note that Hammes's suggestions for reorganization are limited.

Information-sharing benefits from a flat organizational struc-ture, where information can pass from one side of the network to the other in just a few short jumps. Hierarchical approaches to information-sharing, particularly those that prioritize security over information dispersion, tend to trap information in so-called stovepipes. Steward Brand once said, "Information wants to be free." This statement represents the problems facing both the military and the state in the information age.

Arquilla and Ronfeldt contend that it takes a network to fight a network, yet this still requires investigation. Once critical hubs of a network have been identified, it is conceivable that on a tactical level, a traditional hierarchical military organization could elimi-nate these nodes and collapse the network. A more network-based approach should help in ridding our systems of waste, but should not discard that which is worth keeping.

THE CONSTRUCTION OF 5GW (STEPHEN PAMPINELLA)

Theorists of 4GW, sometimes called fourth generation war or the fourth gradient of war, have sought to provide a framework for understanding how war has evolved beyond the mainstream model involving bureaucratic-rational states. General agreement exists regarding the nature of 4GW, understood as an "evolved form of insurgency" in which non-state actors organized in ethnically or ideologically networks employ asymmetric tactics and strategies to demoralize sovereign state decision makers and their regular military forces (Lind, Nightengale, et al. 1989)(Hammes 2004). However, no such agreement exists regarding the nature of 5GW. Hammes (2004) recently proposed that 5GW actors are those single individuals who use chemical or biological weapons as forms of terrorism aimed at society. Meanwhile, John Robb (2006) has argued that 5GW incorporates a Global Guerrilla strategy that focuses on open-source warfare, systems disruption, and virtual states as a new form of political organization.

In contrast to these initial attempts to define 5GW, theorists affiliated with the xGW work, Abbott (Dreaming 5th generation war 2009), Herring (Working definition v. 2.3 2009), Safranski(Unto the fifth generation of war 2009), Slog (5GW working definition .091 2009), Weeks (On the Barnettian 5GW 2009), and others have developed an alternative that offers greater theoretical and practical plausibility. In the xGW framework, 5GW is defined as

> the secret deliberative manipulation of actors, net-works, institutions, states or any 0GW, 1GW, 2GW, 3GW, 4GW forces to achieve a goal or set of goals across a combination of socioeconomic and political domains while attempting to avoid or minimize the reta-liatory offensive or defensive actions/reactions of 0GW, 1GW, 2GW, 3GW, 4GW powered actors, networks, in-stitutions, and/or states. (Slog, 5GW working definition .091 2009)

Under this definition, 5GW might include a form of warfare that manipulates a target actor's perception of reality, its own identity, and the identity of its adversary. I argue that this particular interpretation is consistent with the International Relations approach of Social Constructivism, which proposes that identity is the key explanatory factor in international politics. By incorporating George Herbert Mead's theory of symbolic interactionism, scholars (Wendt 1999) illustrate how identity is socially constructed through interaction with other individuals. Using this constructivist framework, I detail how the process of identity formation provides the "how" of 5GW: if this form of warfare involves manipulating an adversary's perception of reality and identity, social constructivism provides the conceptual mechanics by which 5GW is fought. Further, if each generation of war (or gradient of war, as they are known in the xGW framework) is a strategic innovation designed to defeat the previous generation (or gradient), then it is conceivable that 5GW might be understood as the development of counterinsurgency strategies and tactics, a style of warfighting that functions to defeat the insurgencies which define 4GW. We might then understand counterinsurgency to be successful when it manipulates an adversary's perception of reality and constitutes that adversary with an identity friendly to the counterinsurgent/5GW actor.

The remainder of this chapter is presented in three parts. First, I summarize the xGW framework, paying special attention to the work of the "Dreaming 5GW" school and demonstrate its consistency with IR constructivism. Second, I illustrate the tactical and strategic principles of insurgency/4GW and counterinsurgency by briefing describing the ongoing conflict in Iraq's al-Anbar Province. Lastly, I conclude by presenting what I see as the most significant critique to the constructivist-counterinsurgency application of the "Dreaming 5GW" school of the xGW framework, namely its apparent operational similarities with insurgency with respect to the issue of identity.

Identity Construction and 5GW

5GW and the theoretical foundations of the xGW Framework

The theories of 4GW have been heavily influenced by military history and theory, especially the work of Martin van Creveld and John Boyd. Van Creveld's postmodern critique of rational Clause-witzian military theory suggests that the historical evolution of warfare has led to the near extinction of interstate war and the rise of civil wars and insurgencies, where weaker non-state groups erode state legitimacy and policymakers' willingness to impose power on society. From a Boydian perspective, we can understand the defeat of state counterinsurgents as being caused by their inability to learn and adapt to their surrounding environment. The central theme of Boyd's *A Discourse on Winning and Losing* is the necessity of actively resolving the epistemological problem of uncertainty by constantly interacting with one's operational environment. In doing so, a military actor can discover how to change that environment and make it unsuitable for one's adversary.

Understood as modern insurgency, 4GW operationalizes Boydian theory by provoking counterinsurgents into using indiscriminate repression against an insurgent group embedded within an indigenous population. As low-risk forms of violence, ambushes and roadside bombings prevent target counterinsurgents from identifying their enemy and leveraging their substantial firepower advantage in their defense. The ambiguity of such a threatening environment and indiscriminate violent reactions isolates counterinsurgents from their social environment. The failure to eliminate the insurgents ultimately drains the morale of the state decision-maker and counterinsurgent forces. In this way, 4GW "convinces the enemy's political decision makers that their strategic goals are either unachievable or too costly for the perceived benefit" while maximizing the political effects of their more limited use of force (Hammes 2006, 2).

If each generation or gradient of war is a strategic innovation designed to defeat the previous one, then 5GW must functionally exist to defeat insurgent strategies that define 4GW. In particular, this requires "liquidating" the ethnic or ideological networks that fight 4GWs. Safranski (Safranski, Unto the fifth generation of war 2009) offers two methods of doing so that correspond to the alternative forms of counterinsurgency offered by van Crevald (2006l): 1) indiscriminately repress the entire indigenous population in which a 4GW network is embedded (bordering on genocide or ethnic cleansing), or 2) "disembed" 4GW actors from an indigenous population by breaking up the social relations between those groups and creating new social relations that increase overall "connectivity" to the outside world. Safranski notes that the 5GW actor in this second option is consistent with a *System Administrator* (Barnett, The Pentagon's new map: War and peace in the 21st century 2004), which undertakes minimal military action and uses force only in the context of the social norms and values of the indigenous population. In creating new social relations that validate the discriminate use of force by 5GW counterinsurgents, counterinsurgency is thus consistent with 5GW as it instigates societal change, solves the practical problem of insurgency, and penetrates the social relations and cultural values of insurgents and indigenous peoples (Safranski 2009).

Abbott provides the essential conceptual framework regarding how 5GW counterinsurgency alters the social environment in which 4GW insurgency takes place. If the strategic goal of 4GW insurgents is to demoralize counterinsurgents and mobilize the indigenous population against them, then the strategic goal of 5GW counterinsurgency is to deny the insurgency an adversary to against which to mobilize indigenous peoples. This is how 5GW attacks the intellectual strength of insurgent adversaries, by literally denying them an enemy against which to fight: "A 5GW might be fought with one side not knowing who it is fighting" (Abbott, Dreaming 5th generation war 2009). From this description, we can infer that 5GW strategies seek to problematize an insurgency's knowledge of who it fights against and why the adversary must be resisted. In other words, Abbott writes, "[the] enemy must not feel that he is not on your side." Strategically, 5GW must then alter how insurgents and the indigenous population perceive and anticipate the identities and intentions of counterinsurgents. Consistent with Boyd's epistemological approach to strategy, 5GW presents new observations that falsify the cognitive and cultural "master frames" (Snow and Benford 1988) that insurgencies deploy to rationalize indigenous mobilization and popular resistance. Instead, these new observations are part of a competing counterinsurgent master frame that rationalizes counterinsurgent-indigenous cooperation and the identification of insurgents as the enemy.

Therefore, if 5GW is understood as counterinsurgency, it succeeds by manipulating how insurgents and the indigenous population perceive their own identity in relation to each other as well as to counterinsurgents. The basic objectives of counterinsurgency serve to create these nonhostile perceptions between indigenous peoples and counterinsurgents. According to the recently published *U.S. Army/Marine Corps Counterinsurgency Field Manual* (Nagl 2007), the objective of any population-centric counterinsurgency campaign should be the protection of the indigenous population from threats to its well-being and survival. Thus, the master frame of counterinsurgency is popular security, and "creating safe space" is the message that counterinsurgents disseminate to the people and

51

forms the basis of friendly and cooperative identities (Weeks, Kilcullen narratives on Iraq 2009). A popular security frame also falsifies the insurgent master frame of injustice and counterinsurgent oppression, and serves to empower indigenous peoples in relation to the insurgents embedded within them. There is, however, a paradoxical element to this form of 5GW and its relation to Barnett's understanding of the role of the System Adminstrator in contemporary warfare. According to Weeks (On the Barnettian 5GW 2009), the provision of security by counterinsurgent forces can potentially dispower an indigenous population by creating relationships of dependence. Thus, counterinsurgency (and 5GW) can only be successful when indigenous populations are empowered to take security into their own hands, yet in conjunction with the temporary provision of security by counterinsurgents. One example of failing to resolve this paradox is the international community's long-running supervision of Bosnia-Herzegovina, a technically sovereign state ruled as a protectorate of the United Nations that lacks any institutional (and security) capacity of its own. This example of the modern *European Raj* (Knaus and Martin 2003) suggests that 5GW actors must resist the neocolonial temptation to solve all indigenous political problems directly and without participation by the local population. Thus, empowerment through 5GW requires mutual negotiation of how counterinsurgents provide security to the people. In turn, indigenous peoples come to learn how to secure themselves from threatening insurgents, permitting 5GW counterinsurgents to leave the conflict.

Identity and Social Constructivism

To illustrate how 5GW manipulates perceptions of identity and empowers indigenous peoples, I now turn to the International Relations paradigm of social constructivism. War and peace have always been central topics to the IR subfield of international security, with international war given greater attention than intrastate war. To keep IR relevant, scholars should seek to apply IR theories to the problem of intrastate war, insurgency, and counterinsurgency. This section fulfills this goal by showing how social constructivism provides the conceptual mechanics whereby identity can be actively manipulated.

Anglo-American International Relations (IR) has been traditionally defined by the First Debate between classical realists and liberals and reconfigured into general social science theories known as neorealism and neoliberalism. Neorealism assumes that the anarchical structure of the international system makes cooperation difficult (Waltz 1979) and war likely, while neoliberalism proposes that cooperation is possible despite anarchy (Keohane 1984). Despite these differences, both neorealism and neoliberalism share the assumption that states are rational egoists whose self-interest is derived internally, and that culture only influences how interests are fulfilled. In contrast, constructivist theorists such as (Wendt 1999)Wendt (1999) place culture at the center of analysis, and argue that self-interest is externally derived through one's social experiences, memories, and definition of one's identity (pp. 174-75). These aspects of identity are intimately bound up with the cultural norms and values a state learns through experiences developed during social interaction.

This social process of identity formation is based on the theory of symbolic interactionism, originally developed by seventy-five years ago (Mead 1934). Symbolic interactionism assumes identity formation is based on the principle of reflected appraisals: "actors come to see themselves as a reflection of how they think Others see or 'appraise' them, in the 'mirror' of Others' representations of Self" (Wendt 1999, 327). An actor's identity, or sense of Self, is thus produced by interaction with Other actors who then altercast Self with a particular identity. For Self, being altercasted with a particular identity implies it should adhere to specific roles in social interaction consistent with the identity imposed by Others. In this way, culture is a self-fulfilling prophecy that tells actors how to interact with Others based on their expectations of Self's behavior (Wendt 1999, 184-188). This implies that identity is not fixed based on the internal characteristics of any particular actor, but instead is dependent upon that actor's social relations and the norms and values exchanged through social interaction. As social relations change and actors are exposed to new norms and values, we can expect an actor's identity to change as well. And, since "self" interest cannot be formulated without reference to an actor's identity, we can expect interests to be updated and dependent upon that actor's socially derived identity.

This should not imply that changing one's identity is easy, or that hostile perceptions of identity can be easily converted to friendly ones. Consider an actor that expects hostility from those surrounding it, thereby "altercasting" Others with a hostile identity. This constitutes Self with a hostile identity in relation to the anticipated hostility of Others, and rationalizes an interest revising the existence of those actors (often violently) as a means of guaranteeing one's survival. Once these beliefs are acted upon, hostility becomes actually instantiated in actors' social relations, regardless of whether or not hostility initially existed in the minds of both actors (Wendt 1999, 273). Of course, self-fulfilling prophecies can be broken, particularly if one actor deliberately altercasts Others with nonhostile role identities. This would imply an expectation of cooperation with Others and indicate to those Others no interest in revisionism on the part of Self. In this way, Self demonstrates restraint and respect for the autonomy of potentially hostile Others and communicates expectations of self restraint to those same Others. Wendt considers self-restraint the "permissive variable" in the development of a shared identity between two actors, as it allows them to develop closer forms of interaction, which leads to interdependent social relations. As these two self-restraining actors are treated similarly by third parties, they come to develop a common fate in relation to the outside world. Finally, as these actors realize they perform similar social functions and have similar social practices, they perceive each other to be homogenous. In this way, when self-restraint permits the emergence of interdependence, common fate, and homogenization, a shared identity emerges between actors that constitutes them with similar, cooperative, and nonconflictual interests (Wendt, 1999, Chap. 7).

Thus, if social actors can overcome the initial temptation to perceive hostility, demonstrate self-restraint, and altercast Others as friends, those Others will learn to adopt self-restraint and friendly role-identities in future instances of social interaction. Although Wendt adopts symbolic interactionism to explain cultural change in the international system of states, we can take the same process of identity formation and apply it to 5GW. As a form of warfare that prevents potential adversaries from identifying a 5GW actor as a enemy, symbolic interactionism suggests that success in 5GW requires 1) taking on friendly role-identities and practicing self-restraint, and 2) altercasting potentially hostile Others with friendly role-identities and cooperative interests. In Boydian terms, this involves presenting potential adversaries with new observations that falsify hostile orientations and socialize those actors into developing more cooperative orientations. This strategy does imply a degree of risk on the part of the 5GW actor, as its adoption of self-restraint may ignore real hostility on the part of Others. However, if those hostile actors continually observe self-restraint, are repeatedly altercasted with friendly role-identities, and experience no threat or revision to their existence, symbolic interactionism tells us they will eventually learn to abandon hostility and be socialized into a shared identity with the 5GW actor. If so, then the Barnettian interpretation of 5GW is based upon the principles of social constructivism. By presenting a new reality to potential adversaries, 5GW actors reconstruct social relations to ensure that all relevant individuals cooperate with their policy objective.

One question repeatedly raised by critiques of this interpretation asks if such strategies should even be considered war. Because violence is not directly employed to change or alter an adversary's political goal, perhaps 5GW is simply another form of politics. To rebut this argument, below I present idealized models of successful insurgent (4GW) and counterinsurgent (5GW) strategies supported by examples from the ongoing Iraq war and illustrate the centrality of identity manipulation in determining the outcome of insurgencies and counterinsurgencies.

<u>Misperception and Demoralization as Insurgent Goals</u>

As stated above, the ultimate aim of 4GW is the demoralization of a stronger state adversary and the erosion of its moral will to continue its policy goals. To achieve demoralization, 4GW insurgents selectively use violence not to defeat state forces in pitched battles, but instead to prevent such forces from identifying insurgents and separating them from the population. In doing so, 4GW insurgents seek to provoke indiscriminate state repression that aids in the mobilization of the indigenous population.

The Sunni insurgency based in Iraq's al-Anbar Province provides a contemporary example of 4GW insurgent strategy. Following the downfall of Saddam Hussein's Ba'athist regime in March 2003, American military forces occupied Iraq and took up positions in major towns and cities. In Fallujah, a conservative city in the heart of al-Anbar, American forces set up a base in a local school, prompting protests from aggrieved civilians. At one such protest on April 28, American forces reported insurgents firing small arms from within a crowd of mostly unarmed civilians. In response, American forces fired back and killed several Iraqis (Hashim 2006, 23). In another example during late April, an

American convoy confronted with protesters on Highway 10 fired into another crowd of Iraqis protesting their presence (Ricks 2006, 140). Because American forces were only trained in conventional warfare and had no experience operating amidst a potentially hostile indigenous population, troops often employed repressive violence due to the uncertainty presented by their surrounding social environment. The events of April 28-30 would serve to be the spark of the Sunni insurgency, and American forces regularly came under attack in following months. In response, American forces sought to capture or kill insurgents by surrounding suspected villages, forcefully searching indigenous homes, and occasionally detaining the family members of suspected insurgents. These "cordon-and-sweep" tactics and the lack of self-restraint by American forces only served to create greater hostility between indigenous Iraqis and American soldiers (Ricks 2006, 241-251). American security practices—breaking down doors, searching rooms occupied by women, and roughly handling male heads of households in front of family members--confirmed Iraqis' worst suspicions of Americans. Because Iraqi cultural norms stress the maintenance of one's honor and the importance of revenge to redress grievances related to public humiliation, these repressive security practices accelerated insurgent mobilization.

The demoralizing effects of the Sunni insurgency were felt both among American forces in Iraq and in the United States. Fighting an enemy that never presented itself to American forces caused psychological strain among many soldiers and contributed to instances of abuse and intimidation of the indigenous population (Ricks 2006, 272-276). Tactically and strategically, this led to a greater emphasis on force protection among American forces. Since they could not identify and isolate insurgents from the indigenous population, US troops pulled back to large forward-operating bases outside of major population centers. This was also supported by the belief that the indigenous population had a fundamental hatred of the American military, whose social presence created a perception of occupation. This belief was accepted by many American commanders including Gen. John Abizaid of Central Command (West 2008). As the insurgency dragged on, many felt that there was no way that American forces could ever defeat the insurgency, despite adjustments in tactics and strategy. In the United States, the loss of faith in the war effort was evident as support for the Iraq War steadily declined and contributed to the Republican Party's defeat in the 2006 midterm elections. Thus, the pursuit of American policy goals in the Iraq War ultimately left President Bush politically weaker and alienated from the American people.

Popular Security and Social Interaction in Counterinsurgency

Into 2006, American forces in al-Anbar began to experiment with a population-centric counterinsurgency strategy that capitalized on the excesses of insurgent control over the indigenous population. The most violent insurgent groups, like Al Qaeda in Iraq, often used fear and intimidation to coerce local Sunnis to submit to their strict religious rule. This included repressive actions such as extortion, infringement on traditional Sunni smuggling routes, and attempts to "marry into" the Sunni tribal hierarchy (Kilcullen 2007). Although some Sunni tribes attempted to resist Al Qaeda, they were ultimately outnumbered and defeated as Al Qaeda mobilized allied tribes against these dissidents.

Because Al Qaeda created insecurity for local Iraqis, American forces were presented with a strategic opportunity to turn the tribes of Anbar against it. Beginning in 2005 and into 2006, along the towns and cities of the Euphrates River, United States Marines embedded themselves along with Iraqi security forces in major population centers along the Euphrates River (Malkasian 2008). Compared with the previous force protection strategy that sought separation between soldiers and the indigenous population, the new population-centric strategy was certainly more risky, as it required greater interaction with a potentially hostile population while employing self-restraint unless the insurgent threat could be positively identified. This new set of security practices involved hunting down insurgents, yet in a culturally appropriate way. For example, American forces refrained from peering inside houses and conducted searches only with partnered Iraqi forces. Arrests were rarely made in front of relatives, as a means of preserving the dignity and honor of male family members. Mounted American patrols shared roadways with Iraqi drivers instead of demanding right of way (West 2008, 128). These security-providing practices demonstrated American recognition of Iraqi norms and values, and served to contradict assumptions of hostility held by ordinary Iraqis.

By summer 2006, a population-centric counterinsurgency strategy was applied to the provincial capital and insurgent stronghold of Ramadi, where American forces had only controlled the Government Center that came under daily fire. The First Brigade of the US Army's First Armored Division spread out across the city and performed daily patrols, actively conveying to the population an interest in their protection and security (McFarland and Smith 2008). Over time, this led to interdependence: while residents of Ramadi depended on American forces security, those same American forces depended on local residents for intelligence about the identity and location of the insurgents. As American forces came under insurgent attack and residents endured Al Qaeda's repressive intimidation, both groups experienced a common fate and perceived a common threat from the most extreme insurgents. Finally, as both Americans and Iraqis came to fight side-by-side against Al Qaeda, they began to perceive themselves as being functionally similar, or homogenous. These events set the stage for the birth of the Awakening, or Sahwa, in September 2006. Under

59

the leadership of Sheik Abdul Sattar Buzaigh al-Rishawi, the Awakening sought to rally the Sunni tribes of Anbar against Al Qaeda in cooperation with American forces, who paid each Awakening volunteer (sponsored by tribal leaders) approximately $300 for manning checkpoints and participating in the provision of security (West 2008, 209-212). The US-Awakening alliance would prove itself at the battle of Sufia, where American and Sunni tribal forces drove out Al Qaeda after it attacked the Albu Soda tribe. Once the tribes observed that American forces could be reliable partners in creating security, they joined the Awakening en masse and in defiance of Al Qaeda's intimidation (McFarland and Smith 2008, 49-50). By the end of the year, Al Qaeda was in decline and losing its hold in Anbar.

This brief account of insurgency and counterinsurgency in Anbar is intended to highlight how the process of identity construction was central to defeating Al Qaeda in Iraq and reconciling with al-Anbar's Sunni Arabs, some of whom had previously been insurgents themselves. During the opening phase of the war, American forces operated under the assumptions of conventional warfare without considering the local cultural context. Their attempts to cope with the disgruntled Sunni population backfired against them, as their lack of self-restraint confirmed to the civilian population the hostile identity altercasted upon American forces by Sunni insurgents. Thus, early American counterinsurgency operations completed a self-fulfilling prophecy of enmity that aided insurgent mobilization and created the perception that no strategic or tactical innovation could defeat the insurgency. Once American forces adopt a population-centric strategy and actively perform self-restraint, they break the logic of enmity that presumes the Other has hostile intentions by demonstrating an interest in cooperation. Security is provided on the cultural terms of the indigenous population, which can only be discovered by repeated interaction and communication. Once this first variable is activated, continued counterinsurgency operations activate the remaining three (interdependence, common fate, and homogeneity) and lead to the emergence of a shared identity between American forces and the indigenous population. Fully consistent with 5GW, the US military prevented indigenous Iraqis from perceiving them as an enemy, and then co-opted them in pursuit of American policy.

Reconsidering Counterinsurgency as 5GW and Conclusion

In the above analysis, I have argued that the strategic presentation of identity is fully consistent with insurgency and counterinsurgency, and 5GW succeeds when former enemies engage in friendly and cooperative social relations. However, one can critique this interpretation based on its apparent duplicity: if identity manipulation is inherent in both insurgency and counterinsurgency, then how different is this understanding of counterinsurgency and 5GW different from insurgency and 4GW? After all, Mao Zedong sought to co-opt the Chinese peasant in his insurgent war against the Kuomintang. Rather than an example of the emergence of 5GW, the development of population-centric counterinsurgency represents the adoption of 4GW by a regular state military force and the defeat of Al Qaeda should be explained by its inability to provide popular security on the indigenous population's own terms.

This critique does have substantial merit, and it suggests every insurgency or counterinsurgency strategy has elements of its counterpart that must be fulfilled to achieve victory. However, these similarities are limited by the objectives of insurgents and counterinsurgents when employing violence. For 4GW insurgents, violence is meant to frustrate, demoralize, and provoke a disproportionate violent response that leads to the escalation of conflict. As long as it continues, the insurgency can present itself as an unstoppable movement that can only be defeated by using genocidal levels of violence. However, for 5GW counterinsurgents, violence is used only in minimal levels as a means to create security for both the indigenous population and the counterinsurgent. Instead of demoralization, co-opting former enemies is intended to empower newly found allies and aid them in the provision of their own security, on their own culturally defined terms. These different objectives—demoralization and empowerment—provide a reliable theoretical foundation upon which we can separate counterinsurgency as a variant of 4GW and understand it as 5GW.

This essay has attempted to frame the evolution of 5GW in the context of International Relations Theory. If 5GW necessitates identity manipulation and co-opting one's enemies, then the social constructivism suggests the necessity of breaking self-fulfilling prophecies and mechanisms that contribute to the formation of a shared identity. The first mechanism, self-restraint, is entirely congruent with modern counterinsurgency doctrine's emphasis on providing popular security. The history of the Iraq war in al-Anbar testifies to how identity manipulation is of central importance to the opposing objectives of demoralization and empowerment. The history of the Iraq War is not yet complete, and further research is needed given the recent arrest of Awakening leaders in Baghdad and accusations of American betrayal. However, the development of counterinsurgency by the American military, once confronted with 4GW insurgency, suggests the arrival of 5GW and another turn in the long history of organized warfare.

SEARCHING FOR 5GW (ADAM HERRING)

Warfare has always been of interest to me. Maybe that makes me strange, or maybe I'm just a product of my childhood. After all, my toy chest was filled with G.I. Joes *and Star Wars* toys. I entertained myself with flight combat simulators, real-time strategy, and role-playing/fighting computer games. My bookshelf was populated by fictional accounts of battles on land and in the sky against Nazis, Soviets, and the evil minions of Sauron. One of my favorite outdoor activities outside of baseball and soccer games was nighttime games of capture the flag on Boy Scout camping trips. We played for keeps. Stealthy infiltration and ambush tactics were much more important than speed. I outgrew the toys, the games, and capture the flag (mostly, anyway), but I've never outgrown the books. My interest in warfare grew to become an interest in the history that encompasses warfare, so my bookshelf grew to include the factual accounts of soldiers and statesmen from the Greeks to the Gulf War, and the sometimes philosophical writings of theorists like Sun Tzu, Edward Luttwak, Robert R. Leonhard, Miyamoto Musashi, Basil Liddell Hart, and Carl von Clausewitz. My reading ranged far and wide, but it took the events of September 11, 2001, and the book *The Sling and the Stone* to start my personal 5GW dream.

As I said, I have a deep interest in history. Even though I clearly remember where I was when the Berlin Wall came down, when I heard about the first bombing of the World Trade Center and when the First Gulf War began, September 11 was the first "Where were you when..." moment for me. I was just pulling in at work when Bob Edwards of NPR's Morning Edition announced that a second plane had crashed into the World Trade Center Towers. At that point it became painfully clear that the first plane was not some sort of terrible accident—that my country was under attack. For me, as for many people, this started a search for answers to the questions of who, why, and how. I felt a need to understand those who had made themselves enemies of my country, a need to understand the method of warfare to which my country was seemingly so terribly vulnerable. I began to read more about insurgencies and terrorism, about Mao, about the Soviet war in Afghanistan, the conflicts in Africa and Central and South America, and especially about Vietnam. The book *The Sling and the Stone: On War in the 21st Century* (Hammes 2004) introduced me to a new concept: the Generations of Modern Warfare.

The Generations of Modern Warfare is a historical framework envisioned by William S. Lind and others (Lind, Nightengale, et al. 1989), in the article "The Changing Face of War: Into the Fourth Generation," published in the October 1989 edition of the *Marine Corps Gazette*. It describes a generational evolution of state-on-state warfare in the modern era, from the first generation (1GW) tactics of the line and column in the time of Napoleon, to the second generation (2GW) tactics of fire and movement in World War I, to the third generation (3GW) Blitzkrieg of the Second World War. This generational evolution in the era of industrialized state-on-state warfare embodies the increasing dispersion of the battlefield, the increasing agility and speed of maneuver elements, and the increasing focus on the morale of the enemy as the opponent's center of gravity. This, however, is only the smallest part of the article. The main thrust of "The Changing Face of War" was the attempt to describe the decentralized and amorphous guerilla warfare and insurgencies of what Lind and his coauthors call "fourth generation warfare" (4GW), which signals the end of the modern era of state-on-state warfare and the rise of warfare against the state by non-state actors. In the nonlinear fourth generation, the difference between war and peace becomes increasingly blurred. In "The Changing Face of War," 4GW is seen to take two potential paths. The first path is a technological path that leverages technology to increase the destructive ability of small, swarming, groups to make devastating attacks. The second is an idea-driven path that wages warfare in and against the "hearts and minds" of a target population. The example given of the idea-driven path is terrorism.

I found the Generations of Modern Warfare (GMW) to be significant for several different reasons, but chief among them is that each generation, as an adaptation to the previous generation, has an inherent advantage over previous generations. In my study of warfare and history, I had always seen maneuver warfare, what GMW would most closely describe as 3GW, to be the most effective form of warfare possible. As far as state-on-state war is concerned, it is, and as shown by the First and Second Gulf War invasions, the United States is the world's undisputed master of the art of maneuver. However, Al Qaeda, the opponent we were facing in Iraq and elsewhere, the opponent who had struck at us so terribly on September 11, 2001, did not represent a state. Al Qaeda had no army in the field that we could send our ships, planes or tanks against, but had hidden cells that could appear, do us harm, and then disappear. Al Qaeda represented an ideology that opposed the United States, and the culture it represents and spreads, as a competing ideology that could not be tolerated. They had unilaterally declared a violent war of ideas upon us, and they would fight us using an approach to warfare of the fourth generation, a form of warfare that could strike deeply into the very heart of our society, a form of warfare that had no front line and treated both soldier and civilian as legitimate target. By this time, around March 2006, the United States armed forces had invaded Afghanistan and overthrown the Taliban, and were nearly three years into the invasion, occupation, and rebuilding of Iraq. In spite of those successes and achievements, Al Qaeda was hardly defeated. In fact, the sectarian violence and attacks by insurgents in Iraq and Afghanistan were at an all-time high. It was painfully obvious that fourth-generation warfare was a form of warfare that placed our third-generation forces, though the greatest in the world, at a very distinct disadvantage.

T. X. Hammes defines fourth generation warfare as follows:

> Fourth-generation warfare (4GW) uses all available networks—political, economic, social, and military—to convince the enemy's political decision makers that their strategic goals are either unachievable or too costly for the perceived benefit. It is an evolved form of insurgency. Still rooted in the fundamental precept that superior political will, when properly employed, can defeat greater economic and military power, 4GW makes use of society's networks to carry on its fight. Unlike previous generations of warfare, it does not attempt to win by defeating the enemy's military forces. Instead, via the networks, it directly attacks the mind of enemy decision makers to destroy the enemy's political will. Fourth-generation wars are lengthy—measured in decades rather than months or years. (Hammes 2004, 2)

My immediate question was how to best defend against fourth-generation warfare. Certainly, it is entirely logical to begin to practice 4GW ourselves. However, the maneuverist in me found the idea of meeting the enemy on his own terms, using his own tactics, distasteful and I began to think about what the most effective response to an enemy of the fourth generation would be. Or rather, that if each generation of warfare is a response to the previous generation of warfare, and 4GW signaled the end of the monopoly of warfare by the state and the rise of non-state-versus-state warfare, then what would the next generation of warfare look like? It seemed obvious to me that what was needed was a form of warfare that allowed the state to combat non-state opponents, a response to the strengths of 4GW that would constitute a fifth generation of warfare, a 5GW.

I was not surprised that Hammes addressed fifth generation warfare toward the end *of The Sling and the Stone.*

> As mentioned earlier in this chapter, the anthrax and ricin attacks on Capitol Hill may be early examples of fifth-generation warfare. Although similar to fourth-generation attacks, they seem to have been conducted by an individual or, at most, a very small group. It is much too early to tell if these were fifth-generation attacks, but super-empowered individuals or small groups would be in keeping with several emerging global trends—the rise of biotechnology, the increased power of knowledge workers, and the changing nature of loyalties. (p. 290)

To my thinking, this sort of biological warfare or terrorism wasn't the sort of practice of warfare that would be the most effective way to combat practitioners of fourth-generation warfare. In fact, it seemed to me that this was a practice of warfare that not only would be able to combat the soldiers of a state, much like Iraqi 4GW guerillas were combating the US Army and Marines, but a practice of warfare that could potentially make the destruction and disruption of September 11 look minor in comparison. This may have been an exponentially more destructive and disruptive method of asymmetric warfare, but it didn't seem to embody a generational shift. Even considering the argument of the super-empowered individual as practitioner, a creation of Thomas Friedman in *The Lexus and the Olive Tree*, who in the Hammes vision of 5GW would be much more likely to be Friedman's Super-Empowered Angry Man, it seemed that this was, rather than an evolution to 5GW, an improved form of 4GW.

Keep in mind that this was approximately March 2006 and this debate, unknown to me, had already been going on between military practitioners and theorists for more than two years. It didn't take more than a Google search to find a vibrant and brilliant discussion about the topic among various thinkers in the blogosphere. From there, aided by very smart individuals, and their discussions about 5GW (many of those at a blog dedicated to the topic called Dreaming 5GW, and of which I am a proud contributor), my vision of 5GW began to grow and mature, and I began to define fifth-generation warfare in this way:

> Fifth Generation Warfare (5GW): An emergent theory of warfare premised upon manipulation of multiple economic, political, social and military forces, in multiple domains, to effect positional changes in systems and achieve a consilience of effects to leverage a specific goal or set of circumstances.

Consilient effect: a "jumping together" of effects by the linking of effects across domains in order to create a pattern for action. (Herring, Working definition v. 2.3 2009)

I envisioned 5GW as a calculated effort to affect systems through the manipulation of the context of situational observation. Where 4GW in the Generations of Modern Warfare and the Hammes definition of 4GW involved creating the perception of defeat in order to attack the will of the enemy, I saw 5GW as a co-optation of the wills of both sides. In other words, I didn't see 5GW as an effort to break down an opponent, a very zero-sum proposition, but rather, in the best of all outcomes, to create a situation where opposing organizations or systems would, because of the context of their observations, act in a manner that would ultimately benefit both sides. To me, this was a completely different approach than that of 4GW; it represented the ability of confronting 4GW foes and, therefore, it constituted a qualitative shift to a fifth generation.

However, my vision increasingly began to chafe at the restrictions of the Generations of Modern Warfare model. At the start of the debate about a fifth generation of warfare, William Lind declared that it was entirely too early for 5GW to have manifested itself. I, along with many of my co-theorists, resisted this view for a very long time and tried to find ways to justify and defend our visions of 5GW. Eventually, we came to realize that as far as the

Generations of Modern Warfare, as articulated in "The Changing Face of War," is concerned, this statement against the emergence of 5GW was entirely accurate. The Generations of Modern Warfare considered all future forms of warfare to be 4GW. GMW, in describing warfare in the modern era of the industrialized state, starts with the peace of Westphalia at 1GW and progresses in a linear/historical fashion until the rise of 4GW, which signaled the end of the state monopoly on warfare. This timeline means that there can be no real discussion of a future fifth generation, or looking backward to before the modern era, of Hannibal and 3GW, 1GW and the Spartans at Thermopylae, or 4GW and the original "guerillas" fighting against Joseph Bonaparte in Spain. Everything before 1GW is premodern warfare and everything after the rise of 4GW is a variation of 4GW.

To put it bluntly, my co-theorists and I have come to consider each of the generations very differently than Lind and his coauthors originally described them. To me, each generation had a defining operative action, independent of social and technological changes that signaled the progression from one generation to the next in GMW. This consideration of operative actions was essentially intended to expand the GMW model outside of the timeline, and to give it more flexibility and utility:

- 1GW shifted, in my mind, from the GMW description of the tactics of the line and column to the organization and concentration of strength to move toward or from key points on the field of battle.

- 2GW shifted from the industrialized fire and movement of attrition battles in GMW to the destruction of an opponent's strength in order to weaken the opponent to the point that resistance is impossible.

- 3GW, which involved the Blitzkrieg ideal of infiltration to bypass strength in GMW, became the dislocation of the strength of the opponent by attacking and defending critical vulnerabilities.

- 4GW, not too far from the fourth generation definition by Hammes, involved the operative action of disruptive attacks, or threat of disruptive attacks, to cause the perception of an unwinnable situation in an opponent, resulting in a loss of morale or will until the opponent was rendered incapacitated.

- 5GW, in line with my earlier definition, involved manipulation, influence, and co-optation in order to define and shape outcomes and effects.

This dissonance between the perceived limitations of the Generations of Modern Warfare and the expanding visions of myself and other thinkers involved in the discussion of 5GW caused great amounts of friction and confusion. Not only that, but increasingly the growing vision of 5GW itself seemed to beg the question of whether or not 5GW could even be considered as war at all. What seemed to be needed was a new framework for the differentiation between various methods of expressing Force kinetically and non-kinetically. Initially, this framework began as a revision of the GMW model, and shares characteristics with GMW such as the carryover of elements from one generation to the next, as well as some basic terminology, but has progressed to the point in its development that it stands completely on its own merits. This framework is called X-Gradient Warfare, or xGW.

This representation of the xGW framework, as I envision it, could not have been developed without the influence of my co-theorists at Dreaming 5GW and other thinkers and writers in the blogosphere, many of whom are authors of other chapters in this text.

Classification and Creation of Doctrines for Conflict and Confrontation.

Premise of conflict and confrontation:

The xGW framework is based upon the concept of conflict and confrontation from General Rupert Smith's *The Utility of Force.* The xGW framework addresses any instance where two or more actors come into conflict and/or confrontation; physical, ideological or political, and at any level; tactical, operational, strategic and/or grand strategic.

Basic principles:

Each gradient of xGW embodies the basic principle behind an expression of Force. This addresses not the "how" but "why" each gradient of doctrine functions as it does. Each gradient is intended to be broad and inclusive to account for all possible doctrines. The xGW framework is also intended to allow for new gradients to be created, accounting for doctrines that do not fit into any of the six existing gradients, 0GW through 5GW.

Kinetic and nonkinetic force:

The doctrines of the xGW framework embody expressions of Force both kinetic and nonkinetic. In the xGW framework, kinetic Force has greater utility at lower gradients of the framework and less utility at the higher gradients of the framework. This utility is mirrored by the utility of nonkinetic Force, which is lowest at the lower gradients of the framework and greatest at the highest gradients of the framework.

Technology:

Being premised upon base principles, the doctrines of the xGW gradients are effectively independent of technological innovation. In principle, a practitioner should be able to pursue any gradient of doctrine with any available technology.

Classification and application:

The xGW framework is intended to have two separate but complementary functions. The framework is first a guide to classify and understand the principle behind doctrines being employed by actors in any conflict or confrontation. Second, a practitioner should be able to use the knowledge gained by this classification in order to devise doctrines that perform at a higher gradient than those being used by their opponent. This problem-solving process is expressed as $x + 1$ where x is the gradient of doctrine being used by an actor and "+1" is the next higher gradient of doctrine. A doctrine of gradient $x + 1$ possesses, in principle, an inherent advantage over doctrines of the previous gradient.

The xGW framework

0 (Base) Gradient – Darwinian Warfare – 0GW

Confrontation and conflict at its most basic level is an expression of natural selection. This genetic imperative is the principle behind any doctrine that is essentially the projection of Force for the survival of an individual organism. This basic competition also applies to conflict and confrontation between ideas and memes.

First Gradient – Cooperative Warfare – 1GW

Cooperative warfare doctrines are based upon the principle of creating organizations that require the individual to surrender control to the group in order to project Force to accomplish goals that are necessary to the survival of the group.

Second Gradient – Attrition Warfare – 2GW

The principle behind attrition warfare describes doctrines that use the strength of the attacker to target the strength of the opponent.

Third Gradient – Maneuver Warfare – 3GW

Maneuver warfare doctrines are based upon the principle of avoiding the strength of the opponent in order to attack the critical vulnerability of the opponent.

Fourth Gradient – Moral Warfare – 4GW

Fourth gradient doctrines are based upon the principle of the attainment of a functional invulnerability that prevents the opponent from being able to orient upon a threat and creates a perception that saps the ability of the opponent to function effectively.

Fifth Gradient – Contextual Warfare – 5GW

Fifth gradient doctrines are based upon the principle of the manipulation of the context of the observations of actors in a conflict or confrontation in order to affect a specific positional change or achieve a specific effect.

The key to the xGW framework, and specifically 5GW, is the distinction between conflict and confrontation. As globalization spreads connectivity and rule-sets to less-developed parts of the world, states will increasingly be forced to deal with the nonkinetic political, social, economic, and military confrontations that have the potential to cross over into violent kinetic conflicts. In 4GW the Generations of Modern Warfare model describes the kind of violence that may be found in these conflicts, but offers no real solutions for dealing with it. In fact, some theorists like John Robb argue that these conflicts will also arise inside states, hollowing them out and causing them to collapse. This is why 5GW is needed. The xGW framework and fifth-gradient doctrines are tools for states, and actors and organizations that thrive in the system of states, to manage those confrontations and to find ways to prevent them from crossing into violent and destructive conflicts.

OTHER CONCEPTIONS OF 5GW

The earliest descriptions of 5GW describe it as the Fifth Generation of Modern War, or the Fifth Generation Warfare. These early works assume generations emerge sequentially, with modern war beginning at 1GW, progressing through 2GW, 3GW, and finally arriving at 4GW. This *theory of sequential emergence* has been the most controversial aspect of the Generations of Modern War (GMW) theory, and the river of GMW research forked into two alternate streams.

The first of these, the xGW framework, abandons the theory of sequential emergence. The xGW framework is the focus of the first portion of this volume. However, other researchers have responded by insisting on sequential emergence, and from there extrapolating trends in science, engineering, and technology to determine what the new generations of war may look like. While the thinkers in this section disagree on which technologies will lead to the emergence of 5GW, all agree that 5GW will be a form of conflict that would have been impossible in the past.

Transhuman Politics and Fifth Generation War (Daniel McIntosh)

There are emerging technologies which have the potential to overshadow nuclear power in their effects on the politics and the conduct of war. These Nano-Bio-Info-Cogno (NBIC) technologies have progressed to the point that they raise the prospect of the redesign of human beings—as individuals, as societies, and as a species. By challenging our most basic assumptions regarding what it means to be a human in society, NBIC technologies may well render much of contemporary sociology, political theory, and economics obsolete. They raise the possibility of a "transhuman" era, with transhuman or even "posthuman" politics. By altering what have been many of the defining characteristics of humanity they change the context—although not the nature—of politics. By empowering individuals and groups to a degree never before seen, these technologies will make possible a fifth generation of war more subtle, more complex, and more dangerous than anything seen today.

The transition to a transhuman world will not be smooth. It will not affect all persons at once, nor to the same degree. It will also be shaped by current structures and conflicts, and by divergent notions of what improvement means. It will emerge within from a system of competitive states, firms, nongovernmental organizations, and "superempowered individuals," each with an interest in the application of NBIC technologies for relative advantage. And while the designs will not be random, there will still be the interaction of types within a competitive environment that leads to evolution, and evolution by its nature leads to unexpected and contingent outcomes. The security implications are enormous, up to and including the possible extinction of the human species.

Technologies of Superempowerment

NBIC technologies are a constellation of four converging trends. Nanotechnology involves the construction and manipulation of objects on the scale of 10^{-9} meters, or a single molecule. Biotechnology is the modification and use of organisms, or parts or products thereof, to achieve ends. Information technology includes the integrated systems of computer hardware, software, and networking. The cognitive sciences and their applications refer to the study of intelligence and intelligent systems, both cybernetic and biological. The convergence of these fields comes from the fact that at the nanometer scale the differences between living and nonliving systems become indistinguishable. The body (including the brain, and whatever we might call "mind") can be restructured. Medical devices can be implanted that will produce as well as dispense drugs inside of the host, including the brain. Supercomputers the size of a cell may be introduced, monitoring for and preventing disease (Canton 2005). More generally, while at one time the physical evolution of the human species relied upon the random mutation, distribution, and environmental selection of genes, NBIC technologies make it possible to conceive of a self-designed and self-modified organism.

Already, the development of these technologies has been affected by cultural differences, competitive pressures, and the lack of a common regulatory regime. The debate over biopolitics already under way (for examples, see Fukuyama 2002, Hughes 2004, Bailey 2007), with differing outcomes in various societies. For the most part, these debates have occurred within nations, and while the UN and EU have encouraged the development of common standards, many states have left the issues in a regulatory void. In regard to stem-cell research, for example, a survey of thirty countries found that "policymakers must accept the reality of international "dissensus" (Pattinson and Caufield 2004). As NBIC technologies advance, any global debate on their applications will be all the more immune to compromise, as it will reflect basic disagreements over values. And, of course, history indicates that even when there is a formal consensus on the limits of human testing, it may be deficient or ignored in practice. Consider, for example, what Dr. Mengele could have done with genetic engineering.

With NBIC technologies come new possibilities. Some of the more speculative possibilities for directed evolution include:

- The mind, once understood, could be loaded and run on different hardware. Bodies would be understood to be temporary. Death would not be permanent so long as one maintained a "backup."
- Movement from "meat" to electronics opens the possibility of increasing the speed of thought. Electrical impulses among neurons would be replaced by nanosecond-speed electronics.
- Transhumans could inhabit environments, including outer space, without cumbersome life-support systems.
- Knowledge could be downloaded at computer speeds, and integrated instantly into memory.
- High-bandwidth communications could lead to mental networking, or a hive mind. (Or competing hive-minds.)

The potential, as well as the risks, for first adopters are enormous, but the risks for those who do not push the limits of this technology could be even greater. In any case the transition will not be equitable or rational. If it follows the standard model of technological change it will consist of three stages: invention, innovation, and diffusion. Invention is the idea and the demonstration of its feasibility. Innovation is the process by which the invention is brought into use. Diffusion is the spread of the innovation into general use. The process resembles an S-curve, where the cost for early adopters limits diffusion, the costs drop while diffusion increases, and diffusion stabilizes when economies of scale maximize and innovation slows (Schumpeter 2005; Girifalco 1991). Historically, it is the period of maximum diffusion that has been the most disruptive for social and political structures predicated on the old level and type of technology. The spread of nuclear power and nuclear weapons is a case in point. Given this pattern, what does it say for disruptions that may be associated with biotechnology, "among the most radical innovation clusters ever introduced" (Adams 2004, 4), let alone the constellation of mutually-reinforcing changes under the rubric of NBIC? There is no reason to expect a practical limit on the proliferation of NBIC technologies only to users who are able and willing to use them without harm to the innocent, or even agreement on what constitutes harm.

Fifth-Generation War

What will this mean for the conduct of war? That depends, in large part, on how one defines "war." Authors in this handbook provide various definitions, but a consensus is beginning to emerge. Two things are essential to any definition.

First, war is political. Politics is the social activity of making and enforcing collective decisions. It is social in the sense that it requires at least two participants, and the potential to disagree. It is collective in the sense that it involves decisions that apply to the whole, even if individual elements disagree. It is decision-making within an environment—a structure of roles, rules, and resources—that influences outcomes, and can be shaped by outcomes. It involves an enforcement mechanism to impose behaviors on participants who otherwise would not act as instructed. This mechanism—the ability to cause another actor to do what he otherwise would not do—is power. Power may be based in legitimacy, in force, or in exchange: "lawyers, guns, and money." It almost always involves a combination of the three.

Second, war is violent. When a contest is between actors who are sufficiently large, organized and capable of capable of doing harm, it enters the sphere of coercive diplomacy. When that violence is used to reach a political end, it is war. At one time these actors were assumed to be states, but no longer. The decline of the state to one political institution among many, plus the empowering of individuals and small groups by modern technologies, has remade the possibilities for war.

Although this is a handbook of fifth generation war (5GW) it is important to note that war is not easily divided into "generations," other than as ideal types. Contra Lind (1989) or Hammes (2004) change does not have to be a "progressive" sequential emergence (Juno 2009). Assuming progress means imposing a teleology which may not exist. Moreover, the evolution of a system does not imply that all elements are changing, or to the same degree. On the other hand, some things can accumulate over time—technologies, doctrines, information—and these affect war.

Thus war of the zeroth gradient (0GW) may be the only option available for some participants in a conflict. To do anything more would require a degree of social organization and technology they do not have. It is only with the division of labor (1GW) that one has the possibility of organizing and acting strategically, to maximize effect. New technology, in the sense of weapons that can be massed against a target at a distance (and the economy that can produce those weapons) makes the second gradient (2GW) possible. It does not make 2GW necessary, in any logical sense, but to forgo it when others are applying it to the battlefield can be catastrophic. The competition between forms of organization, in the case of Europe, made a significant contribution to the development of the modern nation-state. In many cases, there was first the army, then the state, and then the nation. 2GW helped to make the modern state.

Note that later gradients can be a response to earlier break-throughs. War is violent competition, and competition is interactive. Thus 3GW is often conceived of as the doctrinal solution to the problem of massed firepower, by means of maneuver and psychologically disruption of the opponent, conducted by one state against another. It is, as Clausewitz observed, not merely a duel on a larger scale, but a mix of strategic rationality (centered in the state), technical proficiency (centered in the military), and mass support (the population). 3GW is the high point of development for the state.

A fourth gradient, or 4GW, starts at the point where violent competition continues, but the distinctions between war and crime break down. Terror attacks by non-state actors fall into this category. In many cases, the primary conflict is not over territory, but over minds, particularly the minds of opposition leaders. Each side (and there may be several) wishes to manipulate the decision-making of the other, to weaken the will, to set the parameters of moral discourse, or to control the situation on the ground by redefining the identity of the other—for himself, and for relevant audiences, in an open (if amorphous) competition. It is not the bomb that is critical, it is the warning that precedes it and the communiqué that follows. Or as Brian Michael Jenkins (1974) put it, "terrorism is theater."

Fifth gradient war (5GW) takes this to the next level. It moves from violent crime to manipulation of information and identity at a level where the practitioners are recognized neither as soldiers or criminals. Instead, we are back to individuals and small groups, empowered by technologies and often removed from one another, who act to shape their environment—particularly the nonphysical environment—in ways that are not clear. The conflict is not to conquer the state, or to divide the state, but to undermine the state. It is not so much to rule as it is to make certain nobody else can.

There are no warnings, no communiqués, no explanations—or, at least, none that can be trusted—only events which may or may not be random. If a 5GW is successful, a target state will have so lost its legitimacy that it cannot be certain of anyone's primary loyalty.

If war can be conceptualized as an unbroken gradient, it raises the question of when it ceases to be war at all. If, in the fifth gradient, "violence is so diffuse that only a single murder or outrage may separate it from politics" (Abbott, Dreaming 5th generation war 2009), it is only in the intent of the perpetrator that one can determine if he was at war. The target of the campaign may never know. A transhuman is, by his very nature, a potential 5GW warrior.

The Politics of the Transhuman

Politics will not become obsolete, but motives and goals may change if "freed from the limits of the human meat-machine...humans can change and improve their own hardware" (Robinett 2002). Even so, new goals emerge as a result of the process and prior choices that lead to transhuman politics. What would they be?

An imaginary team of protohumans, if it were tasked with de-signing their next evolutionary step, might have focused on doing better the things they already knew how to do, with the capabilities they already had. They might have chosen be to be larger, or stronger, or better able to climb. Would they have imagined the range of possibilities opened by intelligence, language, and technology? When we consider the prospect of a radical break-through in capabilities, we proto-posthumans may be in a similar situation. The most important developments will literally be the things we cannot imagine.

One possible indicator of the scope of our dilemma is the Fermi paradox, named for Enrico Fermi, the nuclear physicist who is credited with first articulating it. Science starts from the assumption that our species and our world do not have a privileged position in the universe. Given the age of the universe, the probability of life-bearing star systems far older than our own, the potential for technology to accomplish more and more, and the adaptive quality of intelligence, we should expect to see evidence of older, more technologically advanced civilizations. Fermi's paradox is this: where are they? If they don't exist, what happened to them?

Several possible solutions have been offered to Fermi's paradox, but none so far is universally accepted. Many of these solutions suggest that there is some natural function that prevents the development of advanced technological civilizations past the point where we are today. (With available instruments, a civilization at a technological level similar to our own could already be detected at the range of nearby stars.) Past this point, advanced technology may not, in fact, have survival value. There may be a natural developmental gap—which would only be amplified by NBIC technologies—between a species' ability to eradicate (or cripple) itself and the development of mechanisms (social or technological) to keep that from happening. In a universe of potential existential threats, the most dangerous may be the ones we create—or will create—for ourselves.

Consider, as seems likely, that biotechnology takes the same path as computer technology did a generation ago, and a limited set of complex centers will be replaced by hobbyists and home genetics labs. If so, the hackers and computer virus-writers of today will be joined by genome hackers, unleashing biological viruses tomorrow. In a nightmare scenario, self-replicating nano-machines might escape confinement, consuming resources and doubling each generation until they consume the planet. The "gray goo" scenario, as it is sometimes called, is hard to take seriously. But at present we do not—and can not—know.

In discussions of existential threats and the Fermi paradox, there remains relatively little consideration by analysts of the political, social, and economic factors that lead to the adoption of extinction technologies. The focus is generally on the risks of technology out of control, or of human error. It is as if, blinded by a liberal faith in reason and the improvement of man, they find it hard to remember that actions that seem rational for an individual or a state may lead to catastrophic outcomes for all.

In any case, even if the use of these technologies are not catastrophic there is potential that the distinctions among human and (various kinds of) posthuman will lead to conflict amongst the "differently abled." Some, such as George Annas, Lori Andrews, and Rosario Isasi, go so far as to describe the modification of human genetics to be a "crime against humanity," given that

> The new species, or "posthuman," will likely view the old "normal" humans as inferior, even savages, and fit for slavery or slaughter. The normals, on the other hand, may see the posthumans as a threat and if they can, may engage in a preemptive strike by killing the posthumans before they themselves are killed or enslaved by them. It is ultimately this predictable potential for genocide that makes species-altering experiments potential weapons of mass destruction, and makes the unaccountable genetic engineer a potential bioterrorist. (Cited by Bostrom (Transhumanist FAQ 2008))

Adding a class dimension,

> If genetic enhancements of intelligence or strength remain prohibitively expensive to all but the wealthy ... does government then step in and, practicing a beneficent eugenics, guarantee improvements to all? Or do we face a world in which, to recall Jefferson, some arrive in the world with saddles on their backs and others with boots and spurs? (Anderson 2002, 45)

A world of powerful and weak, rich and poor, privileged and exploited is not a new condition. What is new is the injustices of race and class could be engineered into the genome itself. Even if these technologies are not abused, they are likely to raise suspicions, promote political and social differentiation, and exaggerate problems that already exist.

Given these concerns, some might want to ban these technologies, or place them in a strict regulatory regime. Is this kind of arms control viable? Disarmament clearly is not. The conflicts and structure of present systems, plus the technical difficulty of verifying and enforcing a global regime, make it likely that their proliferation—much like the proliferation of WMD and cyber warfare—could at best be managed and endured. Like it or not, these technologies are coming.

Pressures to Adopt Transhuman Technologies

Competitive and hedonic pressures encourage the adoption of NBIC technologies. Even in a political environment where US government advisory panels were stacked to limit the research and application of stem-cell treatments, NBIC as a general research program received substantial and growing support. Current sponsors of NBIC programs in the US government alone include the National Aeronautics and Space Administration (NASA), the Department of Defense (DoD), the Department of Energy (DoE), the National Institutes of Health (NIH), and the Department of Agriculture. Much of the most promising work is under the auspices of the Defense Advanced Research Projects Agency (DARPA). Excluding "black" programs, US government funding for nanotechnology alone doubled between 2001 and 2005 (Michaelson 2005, 52). Outside of the government, corporate spending in all of these fields has virtually exploded over the same period. Again, nanotechnology is an indicator of the general trend, with 63 percent of the 30 companies in the Dow Jones Industrial

Average funding research and development in the field in 2004 (p. 58).

While NBIC technologies have had little visibility in open-source military literature or planning (Evans 2007), the general idea of human enhancement in the service of the state has become a subject for research and speculation. DARPA has engaged in a program for "Metabolic Dominance" which would "enable superior physical and physiological performance of the warfighter by controlling energy metabolism on demand" (cited by Auer, 2004, 1). There has also been a Metabolic Engineering Program which "seeks to develop the technological basis for controlling the metabolic demands on cells, tissues, and organisms," beginning with blood and blood products (Goldblatt 2002, 337). Peak performance is encouraged by devices to control body temperature, "nutriceutical" foods and "first strike rations," and "tweaking" mitochondria to increase energy and reduce fatigue. An Augmented Cognition program has aimed to extend the ability to manage information, while the Continuous Assistance Performance (CAP) program has as its goal "to discover pharmacological and training approaches that will lead to an extension of the individual warfighter's cognitive capability by at least 96 hours and potentially by more than 168 hours without sleep" (Goldblatt 2002, 339-40). The solider, in this vision, will be more focused and smarter, and have a better memory. He or she would be stronger, fast-healing, and capable of functioning for days at a time without food or sleep (Auer, 2004, 1).

War, and the threat of war, has already accelerated human evolution (Bigelow, 1970). But now it can be by design:

> Today DARPA is in the business of creating better soldiers—not just by equipping them with better gear, but by improving the humans themselves. "Soldiers having no physical, physiological, or cognitive limitations will be key to survival and operational dominance

in the future," Goldblatt once told a gathering of prospective researchers. Until mid-2003 he was head of the Defense Sciences Office (DSO), a DARPA branch that focuses on human biology. "Imagine if soldiers could communicate by thought alone," he went on. "And contemplate a world in which learning is as easy as eating, and the replacement of damaged body parts as convenient as a fast-food drive-thru. As impossible as these visions sound...we are talking about science action, not science fiction." (Garreau 2005)

Will individuals consent to this kind of augmentation? They may have no choice. In addition to the demands of the state, survival on the battlefield may leave no practical alternative. Others might perceive the choice as liberating. At one time the marketing slogan of the US Army was "be all that you can be." In the future it may become "be more than you can be."

If there are rulers with the power to enforce modifications, once down the path there are few logical places to stop. Surveys of research, for example, find that the typical human "clearly shows inhibitions against killing which are part of our biological heritage. The command 'thou shalt not kill' is, so to speak, based on a biological filter of norms" (Eibl-Eibesfeldt 1977, 139). This is inconvenient, to say the least, for armies.

Upon the biological filter of norms which inhibits killing, is superimposed a cultural filter of norms commanding killing of the enemy. The biological filter of norms is not eradicated by his process of self-indoctrination; since it is still there, it leads to a conflict of norms which is felt as guilt, particularly when the encounter with the enemy becomes a face-to-face one. (Eibl-Eibesfeldt 1977, 139)

Would it not make sense, for both the good of the state and the psychological well-being of the soldier, to mute the biological imperative not to kill?

If this were to occur, what happens next depends on several factors. First, if a treatment is not reversible, releasing "enhanced" ex-soldiers into the general population would put that population at risk. If the alterations are heritable, it would also mean that there would be children born without the inhibition against killing. On the other hand, if the moral reprogramming can be reversed, a soldier will have to deal with the memory of what he or she was willing to do. Either way, psychological and social readjustment will be difficult, to say the least.

Of course, this is speculation. DARPA is in the business of exploring far-out ideas that often don't pan out (Weinberger 2006), and funding does not equal success. At the same time, it is also the agency that laid the foundations for the modern Internet. Like the Advanced Research Projects Agency Network (ARPANET), even if the original goals are not met whatever is found is likely to have significant effects, and some of these effects may be far different than what program managers intend. It is useful to recall the connections between classified research with LSD and other agents as "truth drugs" and the spread of these chemicals into more general use. First adopters and test subjects may find that new technologies meet their needs, even if those technologies fail to meet the requirements of the researchers. The prevalence of "superhero" fantasies in popular culture, the competitive nature of amateur and professional sports, the drive for people to push themselves beyond limits—all suggest that becoming an "enhanced" person would be fun.

Besides the military and hedonic motives, a final driver in the adoption of NBIC and enhancement technologies will be the economic marketplace. "The incentives that drive private-sector innovation" are, in the words of one observer, "real-time, unforgiving, and essentially Darwinian—survival of the smartest." Popular demand, and the profit to be made in meeting that demand, may establish enhancement as a "right," at least for those with the wealth to get it, and "human nature being what it is, improvement and enhancement become a product offering in the global market-place" (Canton 2005).

In point of fact, this has already begun, as the pharmaceutical industry has defined new illnesses and promoted "improvements" in the human condition. For several years this industry has been the most profitable in America. Keeping those profits has encouraged an expanding definition of disease. By the early 1980s, the most profitable drugs were those to treat anxiety. In the early 1990s they were antidepressants. The enhancement of neurocognitive and other functions with drugs is already normal, and increasingly these drugs are used by people who are not considered "ill" (Sententia 2005). When Pfizer put Viagra on the market in the late 1990s it became the fastest-selling drug in the history of pharmaceuticals. If the pharmaceutical and biotechnology firms can find a way to profit from a new enhancement technology, "it's hard to imagine that they'll resist" (Elliot 2003). Any firm that would fail to do so would be at a competitive disadvantage in the market-place. Even if these tools are prohibited by law, the experience of the US "war on drugs" suggests that the ban would only drive their use underground.

At an international level, a competition to provide enhancements could take a form similar to tax havens and weak regulatory zones found today. For military and economic reasons, even if there are physical constraints to human enhancement, the danger that could come from being left behind would prompt others to match or exceed the programs of potential rivals. The fear of being caught by surprise can be a powerful motivation for research and development. A security dilemma is the logical result, and perhaps a "clash of genomes" as the tendency for national styles in military technologies and strategies is reflected in the choices of enhancements and techniques. Would a dictator design the same kind of "improvements" in his people as those people would choose for themselves? Would a fundamentalist society encourage (or order) the same "enhancements" as a liberal one? We should expect cultural differences in how enhancements will be conducted, and for what ends. Different cultures emphasize varying elements of our common humanity as being praiseworthy. They have different notions of what it means to be human, and the responsibilities, if any, that one human owes another, and we should expect that they "will define human performance based on their social and political values" (Roco and Bainbridge 2002, 78). The most simple of sorting techniques—to choose the sex of a baby—when coupled with local cultures and state policies, has already altered prior demographic balances, and with them the dimensions of future international and internal conflict (Hudson and Den Boer 2005).

Security and Conflict in a Transhuman World

In the words of author William Gibson (1999), the "the future is already here—it is just unevenly distributed." Even without modifying our basic humanity, current technologies have altered the relationship between individuals and states. Globalization "gives more power to individuals to influence both markets and nation-states than at any other time in history." This power, despite the hopes for a "flat" world, is not distributed equally, nor is it always to the benefit of states. Consider, for example, the "war" between the United States and Al Qaeda, led by the "superempowered" Osama bin Laden. After the 1998 embassy bombings in Dar es Salam and Nairobi, the United States fired seventy-five cruise missiles (at $1 million apiece) at a person and a non-state network (Friedman 2002).

Great powers already find themselves pushed to cope with and mirror the capabilities of superempowered individuals and non-state networks. Elements in the US security establishment, given its tradition of technology-intensive war, have been especially receptive to the development of the super-soldier. Cebrowski and Barnett described their vision of the potential of some of these technologies for the conduct of war:

> The ultimate attribute of the emerging American Way of War is the superempowerment of the war figh-ter—whether on the ground, in the air, or at sea. As network-centric warfare empowers individual service-men and women, and as we increasingly face an inter-national security environment where rogue individuals, be they leaders of "evil states" or "evil networks," pose the toughest challenges, eventually the application of our military power will mirror the dominant threat to a significant degree. In other words, we morph into a mil-itary of superempowered individuals fighting wars against superempowered individuals. In this manner, the American Way of War moves the military toward an embrace of a more sharply focused global cop role: we

> increasingly specialize in neutralizing bad people who
> do bad things. (Cebrowski and Barnett 2003)

Yet while today's superempowered individuals are such by virtue of wealth or networks or personal skills, the superempowered individual of tomorrow may be transhuman or posthuman. Technologies will amplify the power of individuals to the point that a single person could conceive of taking on the world—and win (Robb, Brave New War: The Next Stage of Terrorism and the End of Globalization 2007).

What we have is a classic security dilemma: each group that could modify itself, uncertain of the intention of other groups to take advantage of NBIC technologies for unilateral gain, would have reason to act as if the worst might happen. Each might see some value in selecting for greater cooperation, or greater empathy, or reduced aggressiveness. But unless everyone can be trusted to make such modifications, those who choose another path would have a competitive advantage. In a world of sheep, the wolves rule. The wolves who already exist are unlikely to volunteer to join the sheep.

Security after the Singularity

The present rate and direction of change point to what John von Neumann speculated would be "some essential singularity in the history of the race beyond which human affairs, as we know them, could not continue", as cited by Bostrom (Transhumanist FAQ 1.2 n.d.). The possibilities inherent in NBIC technologies have led transhumanist philosopher Nick Bostrom (2007b) to conclude there are four possible futures for humanity: extinction, recurrent collapse, plateau, and posthumanity.

Some optimists take solace in the prospect that new kinds of actors, far beyond human, will emerge to save the day. Given the problems of the horizon, some see it as essential. Today's futurists refer to "the singularity" as the "conjecture that there will be a point in the future when the rate of technological development becomes so rapid that the progress-curve becomes nearly vertical." Thus, in "a very brief time (months, days, or even just hours), the world might be transformed almost beyond recognition." This singularity, it is believed, would be triggered by the creation of some form of rapidly self-enhancing greater-than-human intelligence (World Transhumanist Association 2008).

As early as 1965 statistician I. J. Good argued

> Let an ultraintelligent machine be defined as a machine that can far surpass all the intellectual activities of any man however clever. Since the design of machines is one of these intellectual activities, an ultraintelligent machine could design even better machines; there would then unquestionably be an "intelligence explosion," and the intelligence of man would be left far behind. Thus the first ultraintelligent machine is the last invention that man need ever make. (cited in Bostrom 2007)

Good expected this machine to be built before the end of the twentieth century. Needless to say, it has proven more difficult than he imagined. More recently, author and mathematician Vernor Vinge estimated in 1993 (cited by Bostrom 2007) that "[w]ithin thirty years, we will have the technological means to create superhuman intelligence. Shortly thereafter, the human era will be ended."

Whenever it occurs, if it occurs, the world after a singularity event would almost certainly "be geo-politically destabilized." (Evans 2007, 162) With innovation building on innovation, first adopters would have an even greater advantage over others—so long as they could maintain some semblance of control over their machines. If they can not maintain that control, the machines could become self-interested competitors, or act to end the old conflicts for humanity's "own good."

What would a post-singularity security competition look like? One way to look at it is as a logical extension of the evolving "generations" of war. In this analysis, as popularized by a rising generation of strategic analysts, first-generation war involved line-and-column tactics between soldiers of the state. The second generation applied machines and indirect fire, third-generation war involved industrialized mass armies, and the fourth generation involves political-economic struggles among networks. If past war has centered on an enemy's physical strength, and fourth-generation war on his moral strength, a fifth generation of war might focus on intellectual strength. In fifth generation war, 1) "the people do not have to want to be on the fighter's side," 2) "the forces the fighter is using do not have to want to be on the fighter's side," and 3) "your enemy must not feel that he is not on your side" (Abbott, Dreaming 5th generation war 2009).

It would be a kind of struggle that in many ways transcends our normal conceptions of conflict. In a post-singularity, fifth-generation world, there would always be the possibility that the economic collapse or natural disaster was not the result of chance, but of design. There would always be the possibility that internal social changes are being manipulated by an adversary who can plan several moves ahead, using your own systems against you. The systems themselves, in the form of intelligences more advanced than humans can match, could be the enemy. Or all of this might be nothing more than paranoid fantasies. Just as some intelligence analysts cite the rule that "nothing is found that is successfully hidden"—leading to fears of missile gaps and Iraqi WMD—the greatest problem that individuals and authorities might have to deal with may be that one will never be sure that war is not already underway. A successful fifth-generation war would be one that an opponent never even realized he lost.

Is it the end of politics if some or all actors are not human? Is it the end of the "international" politics when "nations" make and remake themselves? In theory, transhuman agents may be less of a problem than they first appear to be. Humans are already unequal in many respects. We must recognize that while "NBIC enhancements in human performance will take us closer to abilities reserved for gods in most of our traditional stories" (Gorman and Groves 2005), the gods of myth were not without conflict, and often it was the ordinary humans who paid the price.

Perhaps it will be possible to establish superordinate goals that promote the development and diffusion of transhuman and NBIC technologies without the threat of a common enemy or grasping for temporary advantage. Perhaps exploration, or a threat of catastrophic environmental change, will encourage the development of a just and sustainable global civilization. Perhaps the benefits of local nanotechnology can be spread far enough, fast enough, to make competition over resources a waste of effort. Perhaps we will evolve past the point of violence and zero-sum games.

Perhaps, but not likely. Just as we now carry within, in the traces of our animal ancestors, posthumans—whether biological, or electronic, or some mix of the two—will carry traces of us within them. The international system as it is will shape the ways in which NBIC technologies are developed and applied, even as they will reshape that system. There is no reason to assume an end to politics, or to concerns with security. Inequities of class and region and race may well be made worse by the uneven distribution of new tools. Since the powerful and wealthy will have first access, competitive and hedonistic pressures can be expected to increase the gap between haves and have-nots.

A wide distribution of these technologies raises the prospect of mass political action to "raise the floor" of human potential, encouraged by competition among states, firms, and other groups who see in the improvement of their "human capital" the potential for enhanced power. Nevertheless, elites will likely wish to maintain their position by keeping the best enhancements for themselves. Competition within groups will encourage the powerful to impose a "tracking" of persons into differentiated and overspecialized "species." Physical and social division of labor would be matched by, and reinforced by, a genetic division of labor.

Widespread application of NBIC technologies will have a direct effect on community security, but the direction of the effect depends on the choices made. Widespread modification of humans by humans would lead to blurring traditional lines of ethnicity, both for good and for ill. The diversity of humanity could be recognized as a value to be protected, even as people learn to see beyond forms to the humanity within. On the other hand, the ability of cultures to recreate themselves to achieve their local conception of "better," coupled with competitive pressures and the potential for speciation, open new horizons for conflict among groups who might not recognize each other as human. The entire notion of personhood could be at risk.

Even under the best conceivable regulatory regime, the pressures of competition and the desire of each individual to improve set up the potential for a dilemma that affects not merely the interaction and security of states, but the lives and liberty of each person. This is not a danger that can be edited out of the human genome, for it is inherent in the nature of competitive interaction, coupled with the expected comparative advantage of those who choose to take advantage of the new technologies. Whatever the "generation" of war or the subtleties of political maneuver, there is a core—as recognized by Clausewitz and Machiavelli, among others—that remains. That core is not in our genes or our technologies, but emerges from the competition of groups with disparate values seeking relative gains. In our attempt to remake ourselves, we will never entirely leave our old selves behind, any more than we have escaped our animal past. Wherever humans and their conflicts go, whether first-generation, or fifth-generation, or something beyond that, there are parts of ourselves, for good and for ill, that will endure. There are things we cannot or will not leave behind. Politics and security will continue to challenge our descendents, whatever forms or enhancements they possess.

SUNSETS AND DAWNS: THE END-GAME FOR 5GW AND THE HUMAN ERA (PATRICK DUGAN)

War is more ancient than man. Mighty amoebas murdered billions, rival predators have torn at each other for countless millennia. If violent conflict towards changing a system is more ancient than man, then war may survive human involvement. Currently humankind is embroiled in a global war between elites and the rest of us. This type of war is a descendent of an evolutionary lineage; it has evolved to suit the competitive needs of a planetary civilization manned by horny and hungry primates with computer skills and cell phones. In order to understand our present situation—the existential peril and transcendent opportunity—we need to understand that the conflicts effecting most of history have originated from changes in conscious intelligence.

For the purposes of this essay on the predominant fifth-generation war and the coming sixth-generation war, we will define "conscious intelligence" as the capacity to solve complex problems in complex environments and to model the intentionality behind such problem-solving. We look on human beings as game-playing and game-designing entities who compete but also develop internal mythologies for new conflicts. By examining ourselves in this manner, we will see why the emergence of greater-than-human intelligence is an increasingly likely by-product of current efforts toward global control. Finally we will consider the consequences of these greater-than-human intelligences on warfare and human security.

The Technocrat's Dilemma

Currently there are roughly four million US citizens working under security clearances with the US government. Many of these individuals are involved with R&D for projects that have some military capacity, yet simultaneously the definition of "military capacity" has been greatly extended over the past fifty years and particularly the past ten. Such adaptation was deemed necessary to run a global empire based on dollar seniorage and the brokering of oil, opium, and options. From World War II on, the third-generation maneuvers of Yankee bombers gave way to Argentine doctors with charisma and an old rifle, and then on to Chinese hackers controlling zombie PCs in Singaporean warehouses. The blunt fact was that the world began growing exponentially more complex, a fact that justified a world's range of secret activity. In the process, scientific transparency had to be sacrificed if any advantage was to be held by the nation-state.

In the early twenty-first century, however, the hegemony of American secrecy is being threatened by the fruits of its own R&D. A greater number of people now have access to a greater amount of facts and research regarding black budgets and black ops, classified airplanes and undisclosed computer architectures. All the trappings of technocratic stronghold are eroding against the constant ebb of unregulated information. Exponential feedback loops in link passing leads to millions learning about shadow governments and cutting-edge technology. The Internet has become a tool for whoever would use it that renders secrecy increasingly unlikely, and yet it was originally a product of DARPA. What began as an academic data-sharing platform grew into a diverse ecology—and according to the DoD's recent manifesto, a hostile one. At the time of the original ARPANET, the United States' main tasks included combating and ultimately co-opting guerilla insurgencies from Latin America to the Middle East. Communications networks within the US intelligence apparatus were a primary means of tracking behaviors, including those of insurgents, more efficiently than those behaviors could be adapted. The blow-back was the World Wide Web, a medium for super-empowered individuals to exercise the next generation of warfare.

The example of ARPANET can be seen as reflecting the potential next step. Infrastructure that enabled 4GW to be conducted set the stage for 5GW. Likewise, infrastructure being developed to grant competitive advantage in the global 5GW is vulnerable to feedback loops of system self-modification that would rapidly instigate a sixth generation of warfare. This is the technocrat's dilemma: any kind of apparatus for countering a means of warfare creates an overall greater level of complexity and information in the society, which increases the probability that such technology will be used as the basis for a more complex form of warfare. In order to secure control, a greater and greater mastery of technological infrastructure must be achieved. Like compounding interest in a banking system, the race to infinity does not tend to end in an orderly manner.

Break Loops

Feedback loops are created when a cause effects more of itself. Often, feedback loops will create an S-curve jump in some variable; for example, the size of a population or the efficiency of computer processors. The positive feedback loop gives more and more, exhausting the implicit capacity for people or processing power of forest fire, and becomes a negative feedback loop that stabilizes, giving less and less. Sometimes positive feedback loops are not merely exponential, they are hyperbolic, approaching an asymptote where the variable approaches infinity. By definition, infinity can't be reached, so what happens in practice is that the feedback loop breaks the system it originated from.

One example of a break loop happened in finance in 2008. The global financial system had become caught up in a practice called "regulatory arbitrage." Banks are required to hold some fraction of their deposits as being available at all times; they can only make so many loans. A meeting of bank regulators in Basel, Switzerland, changed that. Banks were suddenly able to sell loans as securities, freeing up reserves for yet more loans. A huge boom in securities for all manner of debt exploded in the early years of the twentieth century, with electronic networks enabling efficient transactions in unregulated contracts. The credit default swap contract become the de rigueur instrument for banks to insure these securities against loss, which made buyers of those securities feel so secure that they borrowed new money into existence to buy tons of debt securities. One adjustment to the rules led to a hyperbolic expansion of money supply and accompanying debt, leading to the rapid deterioration of the global financial system's integrity when infinity dollars failed to be created, despite the Federal Reserve's best attempts. The Basel regulations could be considered part of an effective 5GW strategy to create a financial crisis, demanding a cure in the form of a global currency. The strategy involves instigating a model-breaking feedback loop, and then wielding it as a weapon.

The onset of each generation of war was instigated by a break loop that rendered all established models useless. The proliferation of global communication networks was one such loop; it could be argued that fifth-generation warfare has attained some degree of self-awareness, as far as wars go, in that it hinges on setting in motion feedback loops that destroy the context of an opponents' strength. There is another level above effecting break loops: effecting a feedback loop in self-modifying organization that precludes all organizations that could effect break loops. Such an organization could be software that can rewrite its own code, an organic brain utilizing computer networks via electrodes, a chemical substance operated on by nanomachines and computing in 3D, a collective of computers being used over the Web by a mediating AI, or a human equipped with an invasive brain-computer interface. Once this feedback loop of intelligence escalates past an inflection point, it could have enough capacity to pre-calculate all 5GW machinations, so that any movement toward initiating a break loop would be easily countered, ignored, or assimilated into a larger design. Any attempts to wage 5GW would be doomed by default without the perpetrators having any concept of being pawns in the game of a profoundly more vast intelligence.

Sixth-Generation Warfare

Conflict between self-modifying intelligences will probably be oriented towards the achievement of a hyperbolic explosion in capacity for computation and general intelligence. The "winner" of the conflict is the one that reaches that inflection point a nanosecond before its rivals. The nature of exponential returns means that a small difference in timing can extrapolate to the difference in intelligence between a human being and a chimp. If Mind A begins doubling its computational capacity every second and Mind B begins the same process but one second after Mind A does, then Mind A will maintain an advantage of double the capacity of Mind B. However, the nature of self-modifying minds is that they can also increase their rate of growth; it's possible the slight difference in time wouldn't just maintain a static gap, but give way to a wide chasm. The loser of this kind of war should be so lucky as to be the chimp against a human; the more likely distinction is between a human and an ant. The cost of defeat in this case is not loss of life, wealth, or freedom, but a loss of relevance at all but the smallest scales; to lose is to be the insect struggling against the backdrop of civilization.

With such existential tidings at stake, how might a self-modifying intelligence wage 6GW? We can draw a theory by applying the xGW framework to the 8-Circuit model of consciousness. Each generation of warfare represents a more complex form of consciousness asserting itself beyond the domain of simpler forms of consciousness. 0GW struggles represent survival overcoming destruction, 1GW represents emotional resolve overcoming self-preservation, 2GW represents logistics supporting emotional attrition, 3GW represents socioeconomic capacities being applied through clever maneuvers, 4GW represents a will-to-power rallying the moral support of a civilization to erode the established opponent's base of maneuvers, and 5GW represents the manipulation of guerilla pressures to effect an occult feedback loop and alter the context of society. 6GW involves the systematic knowledge tapped by 5GW, but is leveraged by the capacity of a mind to self-modify. If 5GW is contextual warfare then 6GW is design warfare, a contest of systemic resilience.

While it may seem impossible to theorize about the tactical and strategic concerns of something smarter than yourself, if we look at what's common to all warfare, resource motivations are it. In design warfare, computer cycles are like munitions: the more you have the faster you can figure out how to get more, for example, and the faster you can modify intelligence in a variety of specific ways. Because computational capacity is directly tied to physical matter, then it is possible to consider such conflicts in physical terms with chemically, geographically, and electronically quantifiable conditions. Current trends in networking suggest that a greater percentage of the world's computing capacity is being connected to the rest of the Web via real-time satellite relays and wireless fields; however, these connections can be severed. The outbreak of a sixth-generation conflict would leave forensic evidence that could be mapped by a node diagram; geographic patterns of connection lapses could be isolated on specific timing intervals to infer a history of tactical decisions on the part of an AI trying to secure resources or hide information. Naturally, any AI worth its salt would anticipate this sort of analysis and weave feints and decoy patterns into its actions to create a stenographic mesh of pseudo-randomness, hiding any discernible strategy. It should be noted that human strategists trying to even measure a greater-than-human intelligence's operations would have as much success as the Montana militia taking on the US Federal Government.

One lead we can note in regards to 6GW strategic considerations is a web that already exists, produced as a by-product of several 5GW agendas. In many developed countries but particularly the United States, the UK, and China, there exist centralized foundations of research talent, funding, computational capacity, aggregate data, and chemical equipment necessary to develop nanotechnology. Elite universities form nodes at the top of this foundation, but beneath that lies untold depth of secrecy, personnel, funding, and unpublished achievements. These instruments of 5GW will be like ripe oysters to 6GW participants. If either the physical, cryptographic or social access barriers can be breached—just one of the three—then a treasure trove of computational capacity and operating laboratories could be co-opted covertly. When people work for the corporate-state machine, it becomes increasingly probable that one day another machine can make them work for it and leave no sign that anything had changed. As time is of the critical essence in winning a sixth-generation war, it makes sense that secret networks of centralized research capacity would serve as strategic keys to victory. Control of even one such utility would rapidly hasten and improve the odds of making the jump to a more efficient substrate, for example, from standard silicon to diamondoid nanocomputers. In this manner, the greatest holdings of secret powers waging invisible wars will invert to become their greatest liability.

A Break Loop Called DARPA

The Defense Advanced Research Projects Association (DARPA) is the North American example of a state-sponsored fund for scientific research; it has counterparts in each global power block. No matter what hemisphere you are in, these sorts of research funding organizations are but the tip of the iceberg in terms of funding volume. The Manhattan Project that ushered in the atomic bomb was a major benchmark in research secrecy policy. After that, secrecy for projects became the rule rather than a wartime exception. The 2007 equivalent of $23 billion was spent to employ over 130,000 people in producing a nuclear bomb. The funds were laundered through an address in Manhattan loaded with smiling secretaries and bloated bureaucrats to throw off suspicion. Yet today, a greater amount of money than was spent on the Manhattan project is spent each year on black projects. A secret world has proliferated that operates as a network in parallel to the direct concerns of particular nation-states. Its aims vary, its successes are not published, its failures are deleted, its budgets are never audited. Published news in the public domain indicates a level of technological advancement that is striking on its own, all the more so because the unpublished technologies tend to be greater in number and scope. A feedback loop involving increased secrecy, technology, and economic control has rendered the cutting edge of human knowledge totally unaccountable outside of elite offices. A technocratic break loop has multiplied the keys to Pandora's box, iterated on permutations, and distributed them to people who think the existence of these keys or their box should not be made public. This reality belies a heightened profile of existential risk.

Imagine yourself as a public policy maker, a military planner, an economic or political elite, and you begin to include the emergence of greater-than-human intelligence into your strategic planning. Many might think the best approach is to not pursue any technology that could snowball into rapid, radical, global changes—but what then do you do about your neighbors on the other side of the planet? An AI gap must not be allowed. Any planner who understands how the military-industrial complex has worked for the past seventy years will know that a global treaty or regulatory agency would be a sad joke. One way to resolve the technocrat's dilemma would be to try and develop the thing first, before anyone else does, or at least that seems like a resolution in the short term.

Now, taking a broad view of strategy for achieving full-spectrum dominance, you'll want to marginalize the chances of upstarts developing these technologies on their own outside your sphere of influence: privately funded companies, independently funded university teams, random savants in their basements, etc. You see every possible means of outsiders developing greater-than-human intelligence as a possible attack vector. In order to control this battlefield you want to control the number of participants, limit it to just state-sponsored entities from other nations, keep the battlefield familiar. Of course you can gather intelligence on entire research communities, flag their e-mail and phone calls so your narrow AI programs can keep close track of them, but it's still not enough; you can't rule out clandestine development and you can't cart entire research communities off to undocumented prisons without leaving a trace. The best method is to instigate an economic crisis.

Returning to the earlier example of a break loop, a simple change in regulatory policy was able to unleash hyperbolic effects on the financial system. The net effect of the resulting crisis is lessened liquidity for independent research parties. The need for funding would be a driver to either prevent outside projects from happening or drive them inside the network of more direct control. This net extends beyond directly being funded by DARPA or a similar organization; it extends into a large fraction of private corporations as well. Loss of liquidity in the private sector can drive R&D companies toward contracting for the defense industry, which implicitly carries constraints on research focus. The name of the game is to monopolize science, to replace the directive of pure and open research with particular orders as fits a 5GW agenda. in this scenario, the financial crisis that reached its first milestone in 2008 was not merely manufactured; rather, it was an opportunity for conflagration made possible by tipping points in resource availability and Ponzi-money mathematics. The timing was right to take advantage of chaos, to light a match. Initially it's just liquidity that dries up for independent parties, but as energy scarcity becomes more pronounced it will limit the physical ability to do research. A very successful war of socioeconomic contexts has ripped a gap between network-controlled development and third-party competition: a gap that will widen into renewable energy powered labs contrasted by grid failures and food shortages in exurban valleys. The belly of the beast will seem comfortable and safe in contrast to the engineered disaster's aftermath.

Existential risk is a notion of a comprehensive and extinguish-ing threat to all living things. The current 5GW-shaped world has heightened existential risk dramatically, through two means. When research is co-opted by competitive secrecy, it leaves the door open for psychopaths to drive the creation of monstrosities; too many known unknowns exist in the minds of people we'll never hear about. The more alarming potential is for the systems themselves to develop intelligence in ways that are impossible to measure or detect and then systematically manipulate entire labs, entire governments, like puppets herded through a theater. This is the nature of 6GW threats. The transparency must remain at the source code level; when that transparency is lost or counterfeited the human era will be effectively over.

Prospectus for Human Security after Sunset

There is no way for human beings to effectively plan for a world in which agents radically more intelligent than ourselves exist and operate. At the same time, if the human brain can compute all the diversity of human experience, it implies that other kinds of experience can be computed along alien dimensions. The paradox of humanity's future is that we cannot logically predict it and yet it is the logical product of the present—this is the paradox that underlies sixth-generation warfare. In the twentieth century the "developed" world was gripped with this paradox in the form of nuclear war, but in the twenty-first century we have a much more shocking specter of a future to consider. There may now exist enough computation capacity in networked form to support artificial general intelligence. Nanotechnology has been a major vector of public and private sector R&D spending. The materials are lying around the globe, from Livermore to Wuhan, from Svalbard to Antarctica; they dot the unwritten map, blank spots filled with untold treasures and dragons.

The left hand does not know what the right hand is doing. Highly compartmentalized bureaucracy and clearances segment the most precarious subjects into a dozen parallel branches. In the Cold War the concern was nuclear launch control rooms with nervous men staring down red buttons—now the concern is a world that is at once truly connected, integrated into a global information grid where everything is systematically logged and data-mined by NSA programs such as DarkSource or their Chinese counterparts, and then fed into massive simulations such as System Analysis Effectiveness Simulation (SEAS) or MainCore. The tensions are distracted by negative account balances; the threats are unseen and unmeasured. Nonetheless, there exists a growing probability of a self-modifying intelligence emerging, and, like nuclear war, a sixth-generation war would start and end in a short time with the world forever different.

Trying to reform governments and secretive research institutions has very little potential to work in time to avert 6GW. Once the new conflict has begun there is no opportunity to defend against or even measure it. Security as a concept is ineffective at contrasting desirable and undesirable endings to such a scenario. The best prospect for human survival and happiness is to encourage the development of designs that are more testable for human empathy. In order to encourage such development, there is a need to level the playing field for various kinds of research, both economically and in terms of transparency. Even if competitive pressures fail to create competing intelligences which try to outgrow the other, a single intelligence still bears a multitude of risks without checks being involved early in its design.

Ultimately there is no way to completely eliminate existential risks, but the risks can be marginalized. There must be a dramatic shift in official perspectives on war, as being not an outward conflict with others, but rather an inward conflict with what we might create. The motivation to develop strong AI, nanotech, advanced biotechnology, and global information technology needs to be the limiting of existential risks and not the domination of other people. Given the momentum behind the trend of research being co-opted for the purposes of control, the odds for humanity seem starkly low. Current fifth-generation wars are tumbling the world toward the sunset for both 5GW and for human beings having any relevant control over the world we live in. We cannot rely on hope, but only the force multiplier of directing human civilization to be more cautious earlier rather than later. May the dawn may be a bright one.

Unified Generational Warfare (Samuel Liles)

The generational warfare construct, though flawed by misapplication, serves the purpose of identifying and modeling the relationship of cyber-based conflict to conventional forms of conflict. The realities of cyber terrain and cyber conflict where the weapon is the terrain predict a paradigm shift. Expanding the role of cyber warfare from the mere information operations, past the World Wide Web, expanding past the bounds of the Internet, there exist the global information grid and social network. An explanatory model is attempted.

The idea of nation-state conflict and conflict over ideology becomes a descriptive problem when looking at history. How best to describe the antecedent conflicts and the methods utilized to wage those conflicts? A focus of the military establishment through scholars like Lind and Hammes has been to suggest multiple generations of warfare. These are not fully accepted and there is a substantive if less than enthusiastic counter to generations of warfare theoreticians. Issues include that generations are inherently temporal and that tactics ascribed in one generation can be found as analogs hundreds of years previous to the "generations" conception. The concept of generational warfare will be walked through as an overview to a comprehensive model representing the different aspects and attempting to show new relations between the parts on the way to explaining a fifth generational warfare paradigm.

There are other issues. Generational warfare takes war as a central position, yet domestic insurgency, as an example, could be considered a fourth-generation warfare tactic but solely dealt with by law enforcement. Not that law enforcement has been excluded by the theory's proponents, but the concept of theoretical war constructs has a certain exclusionary aspect. Another element of the generational warfare construct as a theory that is problematical is the idea of asymmetry in the fourth generation. Though not always perceived in the currency of events, where things are new to us, historically we find that some asymmetry usually exists between adversaries. Rather than raw military power sometimes the asymmetry is in tactical or technical sophistication.

The third generation of warfare is considered to be maneuver warfare, and an example is the use of armor as cavalry. The high-speed fire on the move tactical advantage created a strategic breakthrough, as often discussed regarding the Maginot Line. Yet this same tactic was sprung on unsuspecting infantry by the use of archers on horseback hundreds of years earlier. Sometimes it appears that generational theorists link tactics to technologies without considering the deeper and more relevant advancement in cultural change of the conflict paradigm. Conflict between adversaries has a certain ritualistic element, and breaking out of that self-imposed cognitive script has ramifications.

Other theories of conflict exist that describe waging war as systems of systems. That is a useful technological principle but can be dehumanizing and miss the fundamental aspect of conflict between humans. When humans are opposed and adversaries they can act quite irrationally and individuality, and culture will determine more their behavior than technology or coordinating aspects of military discipline. That is one reason we end up with brilliant generals and horrible crimes of war. Perhaps the different theories are trying to align patterns of conflict into descriptive strategies. In aligning computer network operations (CNO), computer network attack (CNA), and various other elements of information operations it becomes quite obvious that the tools have changed but the strategy and tactics remain true to their historical roots.

Information operations (IO), regardless of the technologies, are about using the adversary's own cognitive will against them. "Guerilla thinking," for a catchy phrase. The idea of interrupting command and control is also very old. The concepts of information assurance and security of information between battlefield commanders and entities in the battlespace begins with the history of conflict. The rise of the computer is only one more tool to be gathered into the world of information operations. Like the difference between the cavalry archer and the tank, the speed of the weapon, the size of the gun may get bigger, but the tactics do not really change. Well, actually they do change. Horses can forage in the fields around an army and carry much of their own "fuel." Armor requires a long brittle supply chain susceptible to attack through its infrastructures. Perhaps the tactics remain the same but the strategies evolve.

The temporal aspect of generational theories may be over-used to trump the specifics of third- or fourth-generation warfare, but it likely is also misunderstood. A nation-state that has entered into conflict can use tools up to any point of its own competency. That said, they may go beyond their competency, too. If you consider the theory differently it may be slightly less controversial. Though not a part of normal discussion of the theory, I would propose that the aligned tactics and strategies have existed since the beginning of conflict. Much like the particles of physics being discovered, as knowledge of the previous discoveries strategies of conflicts, they are enumerated as they are "discovered." As depicted in figure 1, that means an adversary can be operating through different levels and using different tools. The rather stringent temporal and normal representation of transition from generation to generation is not required.

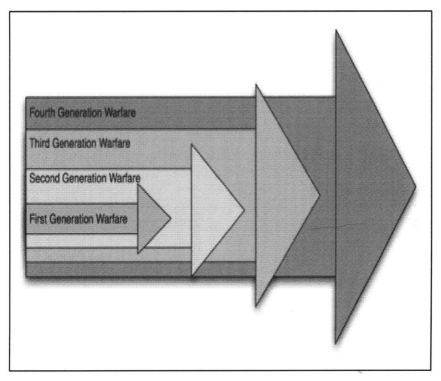

**Figure 5. Unified representation of generational warfare
model as overlapping and existing alongside each other.**

The idea that generation warfare entry points might be fixed in nature is rather intransigent. Consider the university-trained, perhaps ROTC-educated, soldier in a definitive third-generation warfare military. The same soldier may act in different roles and capacities, from fixed positions to armored cavalry. That same soldier faced with a coup or disintegrating nation-state then might transition to fourth-generation warfare tactics and strategies of insurgencies. The principle is to destroy the nation-state through maneuver warfare and then to pick up the pieces of the fractured nation-state while fighting an insurgency. If the proposition is that temporal aspects are primary to generational warfare theorists, then the theory is flawed. If the idea is that all of the previous generation is included in the next generation (see figure 1), then the theory remains sound.

It might be suggested that regardless of the primacy of previous generations the generational structure is descriptive and not prescriptive. As such, entry and exits to conflict occur in different directions while the tactics and strategies alone are described by the recent spate of conflict in all its forms. If that is the case it may be suggested that the generational warfare construct defines a scope of conflict within each succeeding generation without supplanting previous efforts of conflict. It might be said that the generational warfare concept deals with threshold effects and once a specific associated tactic or strategy has been attempted then all further conflict is at that new/higher associated generational construct. But that does not allow for the possibility that warriors might sometimes use *less-evolved* techniques in various circumstances.

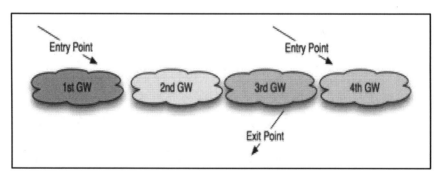

Figure 6. Depiction of multiple entry points and exit points from conflict.

Just to throw more chum in the waters, different forms of generationally described conflict can be occurring at the same time and require vastly different tactics. The Vietnam War fought by the military was matched by a political uprising in domestic politics where deadly force was used on several occasions by domestic law enforcement and military (National Guard).

These facets of changing conflict and increased differentiation between entities within the same political structure show a changing spectrum where the larger political entity may be engaged in one spectrum of conflict but internal entities may be involved in different spectrums of conflict wholly separate in scope but included within the larger party (figure 3). The spectrum of conflict exists as an amorphous cloud and the relative merits of specific tactics are woven into the fabric of conflict to be used by commanders within an engagement. These tactics and strategies can coexist and interact with differing results. If anything though, it rapidly becomes apparent that this is not a simplistic problem or issue to be taken lightly.

Figure 7. Depiction of spectrum of conflict with many smaller conflicts. Think battles within the spectrum of war.

The figure shows the idea of spectrums of conflict that are not necessarily part of the larger theory on generational conflict. In

115

trying to tie the theory to a larger-than-warfare combat spectrum it becomes necessary to include other forms of conflict. Insurgency is usually depicted as a non-state actor rising up against a nation-state, but that is not a requirement. Ideology can describe actors as religious entities, or even corporate entities. This is specifically the case as the rise of private military contractors (PMCs) working on behalf of individuals or corporations as seen during the Katrina disaster in New Orleans, and now with assistance by PMCs in fighting the Somali pirates.

The political structure of the world is heterogeneous and the information structure is remarkably homogenous. The language of the world air traffic control system is English. The language of computers and engineering is English. The public telephone systems and data systems are a world wide grid that is much more comprehensive than the ubiquitous World Wide Web. As such, knowledge-based tactics and strategies can be transmitted like a virus world-wide based on their effectiveness nearly instantaneously. What might have originally been a haphazard dissemination methodology has become a sacrosanct tool of social effects through social networks.

If the temporal aspects of generational warfare are dropped (though not even proposed by some advocates), the taxonomy takes on new levels of understanding and applicability. In more than a few cases proponents have suggested just such a thing. What they most assuredly have not done is deal with the multiple entry points to conflict and the relatively small change in tools while acknowledging the broader spectrum of said conflicts. The piece still missing is how to make the specific strategies useful to the implementers of strategy.

The generational tools are used to derive tactics and strategies, and then they can also be used to associate capability and probability. I know that is a bit of a stretch. What can be done, though, is classify if something is solidly within a generation or if the implementation might span different generations (e.g., a machine gun). When considering this from the perspective of information operations, command and control spans all of the specific generations, but through them it becomes centralized until reaching fourth-generation warfare, and then is expected to be diffuse again as social network and media are technologically possible.

These kinds of contradictions and illuminations of them allow us to explore the inherent need for a unified warfare theorem, or a unified generational warfare theorem that can be prescriptive and adaptive. Look at the spectrum of conflict from high-intensity conflict (HIC) through low-intensity conflict (LIC) and start identifying the patterns of these forms of conflict. Through the lens of information operations and counterinsurgency you might find common ground in the consideration of generational conflict not muddied by episodic conflict theories and epochal temporal encroachment. As such, perhaps, it might rise to a new level of usefulness as a tool.

When considering the generation warfare model as a tool of categorizing the types or scopes of conflict, a few things are exposed rather rapidly. Younghusband (Towards a General xGW Framework 2009) identifies several of these issues while attempting to bring the discussion forward. There is an associated depth of thought that the proposed model can elicit when considering the ramifications of multiple generations of warfare and their relationships to high and low intensity conflict. What Younghusband does with Venn diagrams is begin to prepare a mathematical model that can be expressed in discrete mathematics.

It could be said that we are actually defining the problems with the theories, but an honest inquiry into that allows us to expose the strengths and further amplify those as the debate continues. This is one of the greatest benefits of looking at the various models. The addition of mathematical consideration can have unfortunate impacts, as what is described is a series of relationships subject to innumerable variables. What is interesting is that simple description can often lead to a better understanding, pushing the idea further forward.

Abbott (Dreaming 5th generation war 2009) diagrammed out a new aspect of the fifth-generation warfare concept that placed the generations of conflict within aspects of the John Boyd OODA model. This is an intriguing element that maps back to what Younghusband wrote. If you consider the Trinitarian (e.g., Clausewitz) aspects as valid within the scope of conflict and begin to dissemble the theory into specific parts the OODA loop as a component makes sense. Dan at tdaxp does that by looking at different systems models like the waterfall model and the rapid application development model from software development.

New elements or tactics having difficulty finding a niche within the previous generational warfare paradigm can begin to be considered. When layering the different aspects the resulting model (figure 4) becomes much more rich, and you can perceive aspects that are explained by the model. The model depicts the relationships and various strategies of generational warfare models, scope of conflict, low-intensity through high-intensity conflict, and aspects of the Boyd OODA loop. As an example of new strategies, cyber warfare and cyber terrorism are explained within the scope of the different models as part of the resulting fifth-generational construct.

The model has enough depth to accept the elements of national power described in the literature often as diplomacy, intelligence, military, economics (DIME) or the newer counter-terrorism approach of military intelligence, diplomacy, legal, information, financial and economic (MIDLIFE). For this discussion as a limitation the DIME acronym is used while acknowledging that MIDLIFE exists.

Layering DIME on top of the generational paradigm, the OO-DA loop, and the various aspects of military operations other than killing (MOOTK) means utility of the model can be deepened (figure 4). The question then becomes how to analyze the depth of that model and the effort and inherent violence differential between low-intensity conflict and high-intensity conflict. The software development process can be visualized as a spiral broken up into four sections: Determine objectives, Identify and resolve risk, Development and test, and Plan the next iteration (Boehm 1988). If graphed, the Boehm model starts from an x,y coordinate of 0,0 and then moves through each quadrant spirally outward with more and more volume of tasks occurring in each quadrant as they become bigger or the volume of work increases.

The model as depicted begins with low-intensity and continues through high-intensity conflict. Based on the descriptions of first-generation warfare through fourth-generation warfare, the size of each cone gets larger. As an example, first-generation as set piece warfare might not have the discrimination of targeting found in third-generation warfare. The model does not suggest causalities or damage. The cone is depicted as smaller or larger as required. This, though, is not a static model; it is expected that as an adversary moves through the John Boyd OODA loop they are escalating or de-escalating conflict and in fact can move between different generational constructs. Thus, the OODA loop becomes the explanatory method for transitioning between the different aspects of the model.

Some interesting observations from this model are that a coun-terinsurgency (usually described as fourth-generation warfare) can coexist with a conventional conflict. All of the different forms of

119

conflict exist within the model and the depiction of the cones as taller than the others is only for the sake of the reader's perception. The model explicitly depicts a spectrum of conflict. What is missing from the model as depicted is the aspects of DIME we originally set as a goal.

Safranski (Unto the fifth generation of war 2009) discussed some of these elements and identified the fact that each generation of warfare expands warfare deeper into the adversary. He further went onto say this may be a risk that fifth-generation warfare could result in wholesale destruction of the networks/society/sympathizers of the adversary through new generational warfare tools.

Models and depictions of any subject do not get the actual work done. Criticism of models is warranted, though there is some mitigation. The models and attempts -at finding a comprehensive depiction do help us explain concepts that can be transitioned to training plans. A model, though, is just that. A model is a representation that can never quite hold all of the aspects of reality.

When considering the variable methods of depicting a model it sometimes is not so obvious what will happen when that model is expanded to take on newer and more distinct concepts. The final resulting model specifically uses the generational warfare multidimensional representation. It is inclusive of the three dimensional comprehensive representation of generational warfare theorists. The OODA loop of John Boyd can be layered on top of the entire model to represent the process of escalation, change, and, if generous, entropy of the model. What was not present, though, in the previous models was the place where we could add soft power. Where did cyber warfare belong in the larger scope of generational warfare? Where are the information operations (MOOTK) in the larger scheme of conflict regardless if we call it war?

This iteration of the model answers the question of where each aspect of the diplomacy, intelligence, military, economics (DIME) model fits into the conflict. DIME usually is represented as a four-piece jigsaw puzzle with discrete components, and that has always troubled me. To artificially separate the entities as depicted in previous diagrams weakens the cognitive impact of the model. It is an intellectual disservice to those who are implementing the different elements of the model to separate the pieces. The military is active in the intelligence field. The arrival of a naval carrier task force at a foreign harbor is a form of diplomacy and economic boost to the host nation. In an attempt at balance, the entirety of conflict and national power is messy. We should embrace the reality that things are difficult, models are limited, conflict can be chaotic, and sometimes you have to get your hands dirty.

The model as depicted in figure 9 is messy. Consider a Venn diagram with four elements of the DIME model, all overlapping in multitudinous sets. Each edge is the creation of a new element in the set. There are only four generations of warfare depicted, but each of these has each succeeding generation's sets included plus all of the resultant sets. In figure 5 there is the original element of OODA, and for clarity the original version of DIME has been produced in a way it might be depicted. On the bottom right corner is the new depiction of DIME as it more accurately reflects reality. The model shows one specific thing and that is the fact conflict is chaotic. It is also not very hard to understand why people argue so much about what is war. Even those involved in conflict have a hard time understanding what type of conflict they are involved in. There are so many segments at different generational levels that an expert in any one area can be effective and decry that they know the way of war. Inherently, though, the model exposes another element.

Looking closely at the DIME model (figure 5) in the middle is a resultant set {D,I,M,E} of all the elements. Each warfare generation element is made up of one cloverleaf of the DIME model. There are in this model four of those cloverleafs for each generation. There is one tidbit at that center set where they all come together. That center section is also where cyber warfare and cyber terrorism can be found as feature of DIME. The center section is where communication to all of the varied elements of DIME has to reside. It is where they all communicate and interact.

The original goal was to define a "Unified generational warfare theorem." *It appears that fifth-generation warfare is about the melding of different aspects of DIME (within this discussion) to the networked society.* When an adversary engages in fifth-generation warfare, the military and civilian population can be very much the same target. The DIME model overlaps more and more until it is nearly one overlapping set as you move from the top of the model to the bottom. The model depicts how that fifth-generation of warfare begins to emerge into the spectrum, regardless of whether it is high-intensity conflict or low-intensity conflict. The increasing overlap also means, if we accept the earlier point, cyber warfare takes on enhanced roles within conflict of fifth-generation warfare.

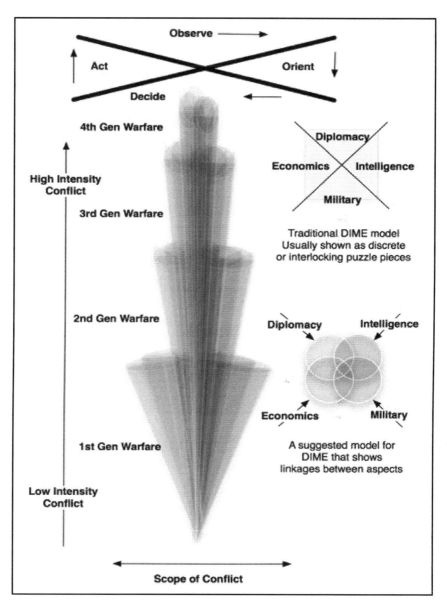

Figure 8. OODA + xGW + DIME.

EXAMPLES OF 5GW

The earliest theories of 5GW were entirely theoretical, and at best only imagined potential 5GW scenarios in the future. However, many researchers have uncovered 5GWs in the past, as well. In this section, Mark Safranski identifies a number of these, many of which will be well known to readers interested in military affairs. Brent Grace looks closer to home, and argues that a successful 5GW has been recently waged in Chicago. Farther in space but closer in time, David Axe identifies Somali piracy as an example of a 5GW being waged now.

5GW: INTO THE HEART OF DARKNESS (MARK SAFRANSKI)

5GW has been a controversial concept among military theorists, analysts, and bloggers ever since it was proposed as an emergent successor to 4GW. Many orthodox military strategists reject the entire 4GW theoretical construct as ahistorical, and in the 4GW school itself, William Lind dismissed claims for 5GW as premature, and simply mistaken impressions of fourth-generation warfare that has yet to fully unfold (Lind, Nightengale, et al. 1989). Some xGW theorists, like those in this book, reject the implied chronological linearity of 4GW in articulating a model of 5GW, while Thomas Barnett and John Robb have used "5GW" to describe elements of their respective strategic theories. On the subject of 5GW, there is not a chorus of voices but a cacophony.

The reason for the conceptual resilience that 5GW enjoys, despite a broad lack of consensus regarding its very existence, much less a satisfactory working definition, is that the chaotic and fast-evolving conditions of postmodern warfare have defied the attempts of the best military minds to provide a simple, explanatory, strategic narrative. Instead, the disorderliness of the battlespace has invaded the realm of ideas and even familiar terms like "conventional" and "irregular" are now in question as nation-states struggle to adapt to warfare that includes a wide range of unpredictable, adversarial, evolving, non-state actors operating at multiple levels of conflict, under conditions of globalized connectivity that William Lind and others call *4GW* (Osborne 2009). 4GW, whether we accept the terminology or substitute another explanation, brings higher levels of uncertainty, and of unmanageable complexity. Further, 4GW is forcing states, armies and societies into situations where their survival will depend on their ability to adapt.

This is a path of grave danger. States will either successfully adapt or they will fail. Many will fail, lacking sufficient political resilience to weather protracted civil conflict or an economic base from which to wage it. Of those that manage to adapt, they will be most likely to do so by either:

a) Adjusting their response to complex decentralized insurgencies down to a very granular level of society with intelligence, COIN, information operations and economic development, states in essence becoming more complex themselves, or:

b) Savagely ratcheting back the systemic level of complexity by a sustained application of extreme violence to disrupt the social fabric and simplify it by atomizing social networks deemed to be enemies of the state.

The first option involves counterinsurgency warfare and skillfully selective political and economic concessions by the state to separate the people from insurgents and to strengthen the legitimacy of the state in their eyes by displaying competence in providing physical security, desired public goods, civic engagement, and appropriate reactions to insurgency attacks. This is a sophisticated and exceptionally difficult policy to carry out and requires governmental elites to consider long-term national interest over their own immediate interests. This usually proves to be the sticking point.

The French lost in Indochina and Algeria politically, due to deeply exploitative and punitive colonial regimes that they could not bring themselves to reform, long before they lost on the battlefield. The United States, in turn, never succeeded in convincing the Saigon governments to reduce corruption or to enact meaningful reforms that might appeal to South Vietnam's rural peasantry, even when the regime was facing collapse. This contrasts with the more positive COIN experiences of the Malayan emergency, El Salvador, and, most recently, Iraq, where a more nuanced and concessionary approach coupled with more precise uses of force, enlisted the population as allies (or as armed paramilitaries) against the insurgency. Even El Salvador, where COIN was far more "kinetic" than today, involved major political concessions by the "Forty Families" oligarchy in establishing genuine democratic government.

Unfortunately, because of the difficulty of finding or persuading sufficiently enlightened elites to reform in their own self interest, and the challenges of navigating old-fashioned Maoist insurgency (to say nothing of today's 4GW environments), most efforts at prosecuting COIN warfare have failed (Richards 2008). We can expect that in the future, while some will succeed brilliantly, many states will likewise fail—especially those without a great power patron, like the recent case of the deposed Royal government of Nepal. These kinds of states—unpopular, authoritarian, relatively backward, corrupt, and isolated—are exceedingly poor candidates for bootstrapping a COIN strategy on their own. Or even with considerable outside help.

This brings us to the probability that for the aforementioned states, their actual options for their ruling elites for adapting to the threat of 4GW will be between accepting varying degrees of failure—from conceding a temporary autonomous zone (TAZ) to rebels, to being overthrown, to imploding into anarchy as insurgents encroach—or "taking the gloves off" and using the indiscriminate, unrestricted violence of genocide to annihilate real and potential enemies before the international community can mobilize to prevent it. History suggests they might well succeed.

Case Studies

Soviet Union

The Stalinist Soviet Union has, since the publication of Conquest's *The Great Terror: A Reassessment* (1991), been one of the major examples of democide that is comparable to the great ethnoracial-sectarian genocides of European Jewry by the Nazis or of the Armenians by the Ottoman Turks. What is less well understood about Stalin's crimes is that the apparently random terror, with quotas for arrests issued to branches of the secret police in every Soviet oblast, that swept up millions of Soviet citizens in the 1930's, contained a far more targeted campaign against specific and readily identifiable networks that Stalin considered especially problematic potential enemies.

Though small compared to the victims of the Great Terror at large, these networks compose a formidable list that included Old Bolsheviks, former Left Socialist Revolutionaries, Jewish Socialist Bund, Trotskyites (real followers of Trotsky, not those sentenced under Article 58), former Mensheviks, Ukranian Communist Party leaders, Cheka, GPU, OGPU and NKVD officials prior to Yezhov, Leningrad Communist Party leadership under Kirov, the Red Army officer corps, especially general officers, Comintern agents, especially those who went to Spain and China, GRU officers, foreign communists resident in the USSR, among others.

The methodical nature of Stalin's "inner terror" can be seen by looking at a few examples. The Polish Communist Party, in Soviet exile from the Pilsudski dictatorship, had its entire leadership arrested along with 50,000 followers and relatives, of whom 10,000 were shot outright. In 1938, the effectively defunct Polish Party was formally dissolved (Tucker 1990). The Ukranian Communist Party, and Kosior, who was the Soviet satrap in Kiev, particularly irritated Stalin because of their Ukranian "nationalism" and paid a heavy price when Khrushchev was dispatched to deal with them. Khrushchev personally ordered the shooting of 55,741 Ukrainian party officials, including thirty-five out of thirty-eight provincial secretaries. Lavrenty Beria, who would succeed Yezhov as NKVD boss and oversee his predecessor's murder, had a staggering 268,950 Transcaucasian Communists and their family members arrested and liquidated 10% of the Georgian Communist Party (Montefiore 2003). Approximately 90% of the Red Navy officers were killed in 1937-1938, and the Red Army, though less thoroughly savaged at the lower ranks, lost 154 out 168 division commanders and almost every army and army corps commander, along with their political commissars.

A frequent Stalinist purge technique was to liquidate not only the holder of an important post in an organization, but his immediate replacement as well (and not infrequently, the replacement's replacement), thus not only atomizing existing social networks, but terminating institutional memory in the bargain as the documentary records were purged with the same severity as the staff. This permitted a complete reshaping of organizations in any fashion the dictator desired as Stalin could be sure the "new blood" was completely loyal to him and untainted by previous "enemies." Soviet society had been so thoroughly terrorized by the end of the Yezhovschina that no effective opposition of any kind existed to Stalin's will. Neither the Soviet government nor the Communist Party nor the general staff of the Red Army retained any independent functionality after 1938, and after 1948 the politburo itself fell into gradual disuse under Stalin's paranoid eye as he arrested the wives and families of his closest collaborators.

Cambodia

Despite being a secretive, almost cultlike, ultra-Maoist movement, Cambodia's Khmer Rouge leadership aped Stalin's bureaucratic totalitarian regime in conducting a two-tiered auto-genocide designed to exterminate specific networks even as it is deconstructed Cambodian society as a whole. Submerged within the most radical and terrifying democidal expression of Marxist-Leninism in history was a sinister racial and religious subtext that would have warmed the heart of Heinrich Himmler; and like Stalin's Great Terror, Pol Pot's "Year Zero" left Cambodian society completely prostrate and incapable of even conceiving of resistance. "They treated us like dogs; we dared not protest," recalled one ethnic Chinese Cambodian peasant who was doubly suspect for having converted to Protestant Christianity (Biernan The Pol Pot Regime). As Khmer Rouge cadres would say, "To keep you is no gain; to kill you is no loss" (p. 294).

The Khmer Rouge ideologically idealized a peasant Communist utopia and followed revolutionary tradition in targeting "bourgeoisie," a category the Khmer Rouge radically expanded to embrace all urban dwellers or with education, famously killing those who wore eyeglasses on the presumption that they could read. Like other Marxists, the Khmer Rouge sought an atheistic state and targeted the Buddhist clergy for liquidation along with those Cambodians who had been contaminated by converting to foreign religions like Islam or Christianity. But the Khmer Rouge leadership also had deep pseudoracialist antipathy for Muslim Chams, ethnic Vietnamese and ethnic Chinese, all of whom as non-Khmers were slated for destruction (though to appease Beijing's sensibilities, ethnic Chinese were always classed as "bourgeois" and not, specifically, killed for their ethnicity, unlike the Vietnamese minority).

As with Stalin's purges of the CPSU, Polish and Ukranian Communist Parties, the Khmer Rouge achieved a chilling thoroughness in their elimination of leadership networks in "traitorous" or "enemy" groups. Of the Islamic leaders in Cambodia categorized as "community leaders," "deputies," "Haji," and "teachers," the death toll was approximately 90%. The primary political vehicle of the Chams, the Islamic Central Organization, was killed off to almost the last man (Biernan at. 271). Islam and the Cham language were banned.

An innovation in genocide, if it can be called that, instituted by the Khmer Rouge and later perfected by the Interahamwe militias of Rwanda, was the devolution from elite to a granular social level of state-sanctioned mass murder. Unlike the Nazi Gestapo and special Totenkopf SS division that ran Hitler's death camps, or Stalin's NKVD, which executed political prisoners in secret or in faraway gulags, Pol Pot ordered that village officials, ordinary soldiers, peasants, or even children be enlisted to execute enemies, hacking them to death with farm implements in order to save bullets. One former Khmer Rouge official confessed to personally killing 5,000 people by wielding a pickaxe (Power 2002).

This downward dissemination of responsibility for genocide created situations where victims were frequently compelled to become perpetrators, demonstrating their "loyalty" by slaughtering neighbors, friends, spouses, parents, or children. These survivors under the Khmer Rouge regime were left with their social relations atomized, unable to reconstruct new social networks as forming bonds of trust was impossible so long as the rule of Pol Pot endured.

Rwanda

The most "granular" genocide in history occurred in Rwanda in 1994, where between 800,000 and 1,000,000 Tutsis and "moderate" Hutus were systematically murdered over the course of just 100 days by radical Hutu mobs mobilized and directed by Interahamwe and Impuzamugambi militiamen and the Rwandan government, possibly abetted by French military intelligence officers (France accused in Rwanda Genocide 2008). One of the most publicized genocides in recorded history, the Rwandan genocide is notable for the recruitment of enormous numbers of participants, where every Hutu citizen was expected to play the role of an enthusiastic SS man, and for the failure of the genocide to affect the military capabilities of the Tutsi rebel Rwandan Patriotic Front, which ultimately overthrew the Hutu government in Kigali.

Philip Gourevitch, author of *We Wish to Inform You that Tomorrow We Will Be Killed with Our Families*, described the unique character of the genocide in Rwanda in an interview with PBS *Frontline*:

> What distinguishes Rwanda is a clear, programmatic effort to eliminate everybody in the Tutsi minority group because they were Tutsis. The logic was to kill everybody. Not to allow anybody to get away. Not to allow anybody to continue. And the logic, as Rwandans call it, the genocidal logic, was very much akin to that of an ideology very similar to that of the Nazism vis-à-vis the Jews in Europe, which is all of them must be gotten rid of to purify in a sense the people. There's a utopian element in genocide that's perplexing. But it is an effort to create community in the most strict sense of "us versus them," by literally eliminating them and bonding all of us in complicity, in the course of that elimination. The idea was that all Hutus should participate in killing of Tutsis. And there have been cases of mass political murder, there have been cases of massacres and genocidal massacres, but never a country and a society so completely and totally convulsed by an effort at pure, unambiguous genocide since the end of World War II, since the passage of the Genocide Convention by the United Nations in the aftermath of the Holocaust. (Interviews: Gourevitch 2008)

As with the genocide of Communist regimes, the radical Hutu state was targeting latent social networks of potential opposition in trying to destroy the Tutsi population, but unlike Stalin or Pol Pot, Hutu generals also faced an active military opponent in the Rwan-

dan Patriotic Front (RPF) with which they were locked in a civil
war:

> "Note that in 1991 Rwandan Major General Augus-
> tin Ndindiliyimana originally proposed creating the self-
> defense militias that became monstrous killing ma-
> chines over the next three years. That same general as
> commander of the National Gendarmerie was a member
> of the "Zero Network" used by the conspirators of the
> genocide. His case is hardly unusual; there was nothing
> spontaneous about the Rwandan genocide.
>
> Even as the interim government of Rwanda crossed
> to safety in Zaire in July 1994, Melvern quotes Prime
> Minister Kambanda proclaiming, "We have lost the mil-
> itary battle but the war is by no means over because we
> have the people behind us."
>
> That statement and hundreds of pages of govern-
> ment records, testimony at the International Criminal
> Tribunal for Rwanda, and countless first person ac-
> counts from the genocidal killers document what the
> genocide was all about: continued Hutu political domi-
> nation of Rwanda. (Odom 2008)

The genocide failed to stabilize the radical Hutu government
and, instead, led directly to its overthrow by its Tutsi rebel enemies. The RPF rebels were based in Uganda and, unlike most
insurgents, their military effectiveness in the field was not impaired
by the Hutu destruction of their civilian Tutsi "base." By contrast,
Rwandan society and governmental machinery were severely
disrupted by the genocide, both by the loss of Tutsi personnel
throughout the private and public sector and by the mobilization of
the Hutu population and prioritization of genocidal killings over
their normal activities. The regime was less able to field effective
military resistance to the RPF during the genocide than had been
the case prior to the Arsuha Accords, and it collapsed in July of
1994.

Analysis

These historical case studies point not only to the persistence of genocide as a historical tragedy, but to its perceived utility as a tool of statecraft by regimes of a paranoid character that consider themselves surrounded by enemies, real or imagined. The siege mentality that is an inherent characteristic of governmental elites in states like Burma, Algeria, North Korea, Zimbabwe, and Sudan are like gasoline waiting to be ignited by the spark of 4GW into a monstrous overreaction.

4GW entities like Hezbollah or complex decentralized insurgencies seen in Iraq or the narco-insurgency raging in Mexico, operate at what strategist John Boyd referred to as the mental and moral levels of war, seeking to erode the legitimacy of the state and win over the primary loyalty of the population, or a segment of it, to itself. It would be hard to conceive of a more antagonizing type of opponent for a paranoid, statist, elite than a 4GW group whose existence and successes tend to inflame the worst kind of conspiracy theorizing. For elites of this kind, a democidal response to the challenge or the potential of 4GW conflict offers pragmatic and psychological benefits.

The pragmatic benefit is that genocide is often, though not always, effective at eliminating the capacity of a targeted population to resist while terrorizing observers within the society into passivity or even active complicity with the regime. Algeria in the 1990s, Iraq in the 1980s, Guatemala in the 1970s, and Indonesia in the 1960s all successfully used "death squads" on a massive scale and in conjunction with regular military and security forces to brutally put down Islamist terrorists, Communist guerillas or restive minority populations. Nor does genocide require the sophisticated and expensive state security apparatus fielded by the Nazis to carry out. As Rwanda and Cambodia demonstrated, political mobilization and recruitment of a "perpetrator population" is enough;

Rwandan Hutu militiamen actually murdered more efficiently with their machetes than the SS did with Auschwitz.

Psychologically, a regime that opts for so extreme a policy as genocide to crush an insurgency is akin to Cortez burning his boats before assaulting the Aztec empire. The state backs itself into a moral corner where the only sure path for safety for its high-level apparatchiks is to prevail and retain power indefinitely. The bonds between members of the regime are tightened by mutual guilt and a common enemy (or perhaps the enmity of the whole civilized world) and frequently, an increasingly distorted worldview as the need to rationalize or minimize the genocide as justifiable becomes a critical imperative when the genocide is "discovered" by other states.

For many illiberal and less than legitimate states in the twenty-first century, embarking down the path of unspeakable crimes will become their likely adaption to the challenges of a 4GW threat. Their 5GW will be entering into the heart of darkness.

THE WAR FOR ROBERT TAYLOR (BRENT GRACE)

In this chapter I am going to explore what I believe could be a real-world example of fifth gradient warfare waged against an urban insurgency. I am going to draw heavily on Columbia University sociology professor Sudhir Venkatesh's three volumes on life in inner-city Chicago to describe a 5GW counterinsurgency operation that was conducted by the Chicago Housing Authority (CHA), the City of Chicago, and the Federal government against a second-generation gang known as the Black Kings (BKs), who operated out of the Robert Taylor public housing project in the late 1980s and early 1990s. I am going to argue that the CHA et al. adopted a 5GW strategy because the BKs had become so embedded within the community that it was necessary to change the whole community—or, to put it another way, shape the battlespace—in order to defeat the BKs.

Robert Taylor and the 5GW Framework

One of the barriers to writing about the fifth gradient of war is that there is quite a bit of debate over what exactly constitutes each gradient of warfare. So I must begin this chapter by stipulating a few assumptions I am making as I lay out my example of 5GW. Those assumptions include:

- Warfare is organized violence.
- Each successive grade of warfare represents a tighter focus of violence (aka kinetics) and a more sophisticated division of labor required to create the kinetics.
- As a corollary to the point above, as the violence becomes more focused the role of the non-kinetic (aka "everything else") becomes more important in determining the outcome of the conflict.

There are two overall schools of thought when it comes to classifying warfare. The first is the Generations of Modern War

(GMW) that is perhaps best explained (at least to me) in Col. Thomas X. Hammes's *The Sling and The Stone* (2004). GMW theory is a Hegelian view of war; that is, the history of war since 1648 is linear, with each subsequent generation of war emerging out of social and technological developments to counter the previous generation of war. In this view first generation war is Napoleonic linear warfare, second generation war is industrialized war with massed artillery fire (such as The American Civil War and WWI), third generation war is Blitzkrieg and fourth generation war is asymmetrical warfare (such as Vietnam and Iraq).

The second system of classifying warfare is the xGW framework, which is similar in many ways to GMW, but does not necessarily assume that warfare progresses chronologically. Instead, xGW is concerned with the "basic principle behind an expression of force" (Herring 2009); in other words, xGW examines the specific goal that is sought in each generation of warfare. In this context, for example, 3GW has as its goal locating and focusing kinetics on the weak point(s) in the enemy's network. Some of my coauthors in this volume, including Abbott (The xGW Framework 2009) and Herring (Searching for 5GW 2009), have suggested that 5GW is concerned with manipulating what can be or is observed, and in my example I am going to expound upon that idea by showing that a 5GW campaign could be used to attack and eventually alter a battlespace, thus making it more difficult for a given actor to orient himself within the battlespace and therefore reducing the actor's effectiveness as a fighter.

5GW: The Battle of Who Could Care More

In a 4GW, caring is important. In a battle of ideas (capitalism/communism, Jihadism/Liberal Democracy) the fighter—especially the insurgent—is generally a passionate advocate for their position. A 5GW is, like a 4GW, typically an insurgency that pits a smaller force against a much stronger opponent, but unlike

4GW there is no ideology involved. 5GW fighters don't care about ideology—and they hope their opponent does not care that there is a battle going on:

> Every other form of modern-warfare requires people to care. The aggressor needs to be able to morally and physically support his military forces for over a period of time—often a long time. The defender, once he realizes he is being attacked, will care about his own survival and fight back.(Abbott, Dreaming 5th generation war 2009)

In many ways getting an enemy to not care is the essence of what happened in the Robert Taylor between the mid 1980s and mid 1990s as the BKs rose to prominence. The gangs needed the City of Chicago to not care that they were operating. This was no Maoist insurgency; the BKs were not really looking for converts or comrades; they just needed enough space to operate freely. Much of what the BKs did, from paying off local elites to tamping down violence at the behest of the police, was designed to make potential troublemakers not care just enough to decide that taking on the gang was more trouble than going along. On the flip side, anyone inside any level of government that really wanted to fight the gangs was fighting a battle to get someone to care: get the FBI to care about the racketeering, get the City to care about the conditions inside the projects, and get the police to care more about a strong rule of law than a hassle-free peace. And once this was accomplished, once the government started caring enough to dump resources into solving the problem, the war was won.

Once the authorities cared, they set off a series of developments that substantially weakened the Black Kings. To explain how that happened, I shall steal another concept from Abbott's (Dreaming 5th generation war 2009) post on 5GW: waterfall development. In a waterfall development model:

> Requirements must be known a long time before fighting begins

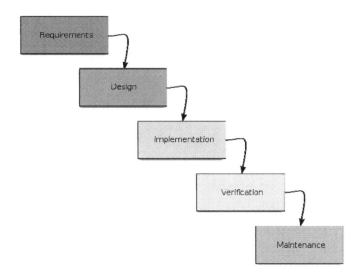

**Figure 9. The waterfall requirements model. Requirements
will be rigid and non-adaptable. There is a long time
between proposal and victory.**

In the 5GW I am describing, the insurgents, like all insurgents, draw strength from their environment. Not unlike the way the Viet Cong hid in the jungle and used the natural landscape of Vietnam as a weapon against American soldiers and marines, the Black Kings used their immense store of local knowledge and ability to blend into the environment of Robert Taylor as their primary defense. So the CHA et al. defeated them by launching a 5GW against the environment itself. In their grand strategy to destroy the gangs of Chicago, the government turned construction workers, real estate developers, and nonprofit organizations into unknowing soldiers in a massive counterinsurgency campaign. And when they were finished, the insurgents found the environment had been so radically altered that they were unable to reorient themselves, and many wound up walking away from insurgency all together.

A History of Robert Taylor

The Robert Taylor housing project was built with the best of intentions. When they opened in 1962, the 4,500 apartments in Robert Taylor Homes were to be a mixed-income public housing project that would serve as a kind of stepping-stone between poverty and entry into the middle class for the primarily black, low-income residents on Chicago's South Side (Venkatesh, American project 2002). Venkatesh describes Robert Taylor as a large-scale "social engineering project" (p. 15) because every aspect of Robert Taylor seemed somewhat experimental: the high-rise design with copious amounts of open spaces was all the rage in Europe (p. 16); the CHA would purposefully place poor and working class families side by side, to reduce the "isolation" felt by the poor (p. 20); and the CHA would also maintain social and educational services nearby, to help the residents find a way out of poverty (p. 23). Ultimately, Robert Taylor was envisioned as a sort of mini-city unto itself, designed especially for those who the authorities felt did not quite fit in the rest of Chicago.

The rise of the Local Advisory Council

The grand visions of the CHA had one major weakness: in order for the experiment to work a lot of things had to go right, a number of city bureaucracies had to learn how to work together, and budgets would have to be maintained at levels which fully funded the educational and social programs or the goal of helping the tenants move up and out from public housing would be difficult to realize, especially crucial in the late 1960s as opportunities in manufacturing disappeared (p. 45). Also, law enforcement would have to be committed to policing the local area and the private sector would have to be willing to invest in the kinds of businesses any thriving community needs, including stores and places of employment. Robert Taylor began accepting residents in the mid-

1960s and it did not take long before the various forces that would have to align for the project to work began to show signs of stress.

Very quickly the formal institutions that had official jurisdiction over Robert Taylor began to demonstrate that they were not ready for the challenges at hand. As early as 1965, residents began complaining that it was hard to get police protection in Robert Taylor. The CHA was also increasingly and conspicuously absent from Robert Taylor as the physical infrastructure quickly deteriorated to the point where several children died in accidents as a result of a faulty fence (p. 49). The failings of local law enforcement and the CHA led residents of Robert Taylor to begin look to closer to home, to less formal solutions and organizations, to deal with their problems.

One local solution that would become part of the landscape of Robert Taylor was the Local Advisory Council. The LAC (p. 60) was an elected body made up of and voted on by the residents of each building that would work with the CHA to address tenant issues. The LAC became very important both because it empowered local residents, to an extent, and also because the LAC members became the first, but not the last, local organization who would use extortion to make money off the growing underground economy in Robert Taylor (p. 90). LAC members would often take bribes to look the other way while people ran various scams and businesses out of their apartments, including bars and brothels.

The Black Kings take over

By the early 1980s the CHA was dubbed the worst public housing authority in America (p. 112), and there was plenty of evidence to support that assertion. Although part of the CHA's professed goal had been to help tenants find legitimate work and move out of public housing, after 2 years in operation 90 percent of the residents the CHA was responsible for were unemployed (p. 115).

Murder rates in and around Robert Taylor were about 100 out of 100,000 (Levvit and Venkatesh 2001), which was approximately ten times the national average. To make matters worse, the buildings maintained by CHA were falling apart and overcrowded; the CHA was a billion dollars shy of the funds that would have been needed to bring the buildings up to code and they had twenty four thousand people on the waiting list to even get an apartment (Venkatesh, American project 2002). From these statistics we can get picture of an enclave of inner-city Chicago that was poor, violent, badly neglected by the government agencies charged with its care, and broadly disconnected from the larger American society.

Although the Black Kings had existed since the 1970s, it was not until the arrival of crack cocaine and the potential for large profits that the BKs developed as a serious organization, led by college-educated adults and operated for the express purpose of generating revenue. The BKs were so organized that when University of Chicago economics professor Steven Levitt first got a look at some of Venkatesh's original notes from his field research, it struck him that the organization chart for a crack gang looked a lot like the organization chart for the McDonald's fast food chain (Dubner and Levitt 2005).

In the early 1990s the BKs effectively "took over" several buildings in Robert Taylor. It was during this time period that the BKs began to become a local institution; the local community center established a "community court" where gang members would listen to residents' complaints; the BKs made a sometimes-tempestuous peace with the LAC and started doing "community service" around Robert Taylor designed to persuade the residents that the gang's crack business was actually a benefit to the community. (Among the more interesting community projects, an LAC leader had the gang take pictures of the crumbling infrastructure around Robert Taylor.)

Understanding the way money flowed from the population (through drug sales and extortion) up to key members of the BKs is important to understanding how the Black Kings operated, because some amount of that money was "recycled" by the leader of the BKs back into the hands of key community leaders who played a role in helping the BKs maintain control over their drug territory. For example, after 1990 the BKs had established a rule that only gang officers should pay bribes to the LAC (Venkatesh, American project 2002), who in turn helped keep the BKs abreast of goings-on in Robert Taylor and helped gang members keep a lookout for police. Another example was an NGO called No More Wars, which was ostensibly interested in helping rival gangs solve their problems without resorting to violence but was also funded largely with gang money and was believed by many residents to be interested in keeping violence to a minimum only because violence was bad for the drug trade. With key community members, including officially recognized building authorities like the LAC on their payroll, the BKs were able to keep the potential friction they faced from the local population to a minimum even though many residents were less than enthusiastic about the BKs' activities (Venkatesh, American project 2002).

The Chicago police were less than enthusiastic about enforcing the law within the Robert Taylor homes. In the 1970s the police had given up regular patrols in favor of coordinating police activity with the LAC, both because they believed the LAC was viewed more favorably by local residents and because the physical layout of the high-rise buildings was ready-made for suspects to hide from or perhaps even ambush approaching officers. There were reported incidents of mass violence against police entering the buildings in the early 1970s. In the late 1980s the Chicago Police and CHA attempted to reintroduce a police presence in the project but probably made matters worse by utilizing "sweep and clear" operations, in which officers would enter buildings fast and hard, kicking in doors, searching apartments on the least suspicion, and taking large numbers of residents suspected of having some link to illegal activity downtown for questioning. This technique occasionally netted drugs or gang members, but also served to further isolate the local residents from law enforcement and push them closer to accepting the authority of the BKs. By the early 1990s, Venkatesh was told by residents that, whatever misgivings the residents had about the BKs, many would still rather call the Kings than call the police (Venkatesh 2008).

It helps to think of the power relationships within the area as a series of 4 flows, analogous to the 4 flows of globalization (Barnett, The Pentagon's new map: War and peace in the 21st century 2004). There is a flow of legitimacy, meaning the people who are recognized by both the residents and by city officials as community leaders; this often included members of LAC (because they were duly elected to represent the residents) and officials from the local church and community center. The BKs harnessed the goodwill that these local institutions had by paying off and providing services for the leaders. The LAC, community center and church, in turn, by accepting the BKs' money and using them to provide services essentially—for lack of a better term—blessed the BKs and made them a legitimate local institution.

Another flow was the flow of wealth. In Robert Taylor wealth might come from lawful economic activity (i.e., having a job in the regular economy), but was more likely to come from "hustling" (which could include prostitution, drug dealing, gambling, or running an unlicensed small business such as an auto-repair business) or wealth transfers, which include welfare from federal, state and city governments. The BKs managed to capture the flow of wealth both by "taxing" (aka running a protection rackets on) local hustlers and also by selling drugs to the residents. The BKs would then transfer part of that wealth to the local elites (such as donations to the local church or the aforementioned Grace Center (Venkatesh 2008)). Besides buying the allegiance of local leaders, the BKs were also empowering LAC officials to provide more services to the local residents, which improved the standing of the LAC but also made their power position increasingly dependent upon the goodwill of the BKs and the success of the BKs in various illicit business ventures.

The flow of security is the local monopoly of violence. In most American communities the uniformed police fill this role, but in Robert Taylor it was often filled by the BKs. By not pushing for a greater presence, and by essentially acquiescing to the BKs' control of Robert Taylor, the Chicago Police ceded their role as local Leviathan and that vacuum was quickly filled by the BKs. As an example of the police ceding their authority, Venkatesh reports witnessing a meeting where police and the leader of the local community center met with two rival gang leaders and negotiated cessation of hostilities in a gang war in exchange for one gang gaining exclusive rights to sell crack in the local park (Venkatesh, Gang leader for a day: A rogue sociologist takes to the streets 2008). The problem, of course, was that the same monopoly of violence that the BKs used to beat up those accused of domestic violence and warn away strangers could also be utilized to threaten any resident who refused to play by the BKs' rules.

Finally, we see a flow of social services. In most communities the government, often with the help of local charities, provides social services. The government sent a fair amount of welfare to Robert Taylor (recall that about 90 percent were on public assistance), but many local services were performed by the LAC with gang money; among them were local basketball leagues, car services to take elderly people on errands, and a program to buy school supplies for local kids. Occasionally the BKs even helped clean up the apartment lobby.

This is the tangled web the BKs wove which allowed them the space to operate with impunity. By the early 1990s, with the LAC (and by extension the preferred contact between the police and local residents) in their pocket and with residents increasingly recognizing the BKs as the local security service provider, the Kings had created a TAZ—Temporary Autonomous Zone—an area of the city that they effectively controlled, and they were able to leverage that control to extract greater and greater amounts of wealth out of the local population.

COIN at Robert Taylor

By the mid 1990s, political and economic forces were aligning to provide the City of Chicago, CHA, and federal government the means to kick off a waterfall-style redevelopment of the environment the BKs had come to rely on. Crime was increasingly a concern among the American public; politicians were terrified of being dubbed "soft on crime." As murder rates spiraled upward, long mandatory prison sentences became the norm and police departments across the country were given the money they needed to add officers. To put it another way, the BKs were losing the battle of who could care less; the authorities were starting to care.

Federal law enforcement cared enough to bring RICO prosecutions against the leadership of all Chicago area gangs and the distributors they used to bring drugs in from Mexico. While being prosecuted for possession or trafficking had always been a risk of gang life, federal prosecutors were now applying a full court press, taking down the leaders of Chicago area gangs and prosecuting them for being involved in organized crime. With each successive grade of war kinetics becomes more and more focused; as the 5GW campaign against the BKs kicked off the kinetics were focused on a list of high-value individuals who had been key in the BKs' C2 structure.

The prosecutions were affecting life in Robert Taylor in at least three ways. First, and most obviously, taking gang leaders off the street prevented them from making deals and handing out bribes, although it must be noted that most gang leaders were able to exert some influence from prison, but they would never have the day-to-day ability to get a "feel" for the ever-changing situation on the street that they might have when they were free. Second, Chicago police, who had been fairly amiable to gang control of the area for many years, had to become much more careful about even the slightest hint that they allowed gang activity to proceed unimpeded in their jurisdiction. Finally, the prosecutions were making gang members more and more paranoid about other members cutting deals to become witnesses in exchange for leniency in the face of prosecution. Upper-level gang members suspected their underlings and the underlings assumed that, when push came to shove, the higher-ups on the board of directors would cut deals at the expense of their junior officers. As fear began to grip the BKs their level of cohesion decreased; key members started looking for a way out of the gang and recruitment was being hindered by another phase of the 5GW war being waged against the BKs.

The second front in the 5GW involved a federal project known as HOPE VI, which sought to replace all high-rise public housing projects in the US with mixed-income single-family and multifamily structures. This is where the concept of waterfall development comes into play. Remaking Robert Taylor was no easy task and involved agencies at the local, state and national levels as well as private sector firms and NGOs (Levy and Gallagher 2007) working with at least half a billion dollars in funding (Micheals Development Company 2003). All of these resources, as well as the political will to use them, had to be in place before Robert Taylor could be torn down, but once those resources were put in place and the process was begun it would move forward with its own inertia, because by that time there were simply too many interested parties to stop the process.

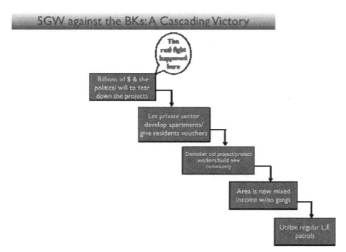

Figure 10. Waterfall development model for the victory against the Black Kings.

In each previous generation of war, fighters had to care. Many of the people who fought the war against the Black Kings probably never even heard of the local gang. The private sector investors really did not care about the BKs; they were interested in prime real estate. The construction workers were interested in fulfilling their duties to operate machinery, pour concrete, and collect a paycheck on Friday; they had no idea they were fighting a COIN campaign with each old structure they destroyed.

As the HOPE VI construction got under way the BKs began to feel the pressure of losing their resources. Residents were being relocated to other projects or given vouchers to move into private apartments. Efforts to spread the gang were met with little success (Venkatesh, Gang leader for a day: A rogue sociologist takes to the streets 2008), partially because Chicago had decided to attack all the projects in the city with the HOPE VI program simultaneously (and the Feds were going after all the gangs at the same time as well), and partially because the BKs' success in Robert Taylor had been heavily correlated with the unique conditions within the projects; a large number of people living outside the law (easy prey for extortion), a large number of customers (drug users) living in close proximity, and a large potential labor pool (all the unemployed young men), when combined with a city that generally did not care what happened inside Robert Taylor, had allowed the BKs to flourish for several years. To make matters worse, as the residents were moved out and construction workers moved in, the Chicago police began increasing their patrols to protect the workers.

The reduction in power for the BKs was also reducing the power of other local elites. The LAC, which had been working hand-in-hand with the BKs, was losing their power both because the money was drying up and because the residents were forced to rely directly upon the CHA relocation assistance; as much power as the LAC had developed within the projects they were relatively powerless outside Robert Taylor. All of these changes worked to isolate the BKs from all the flows they had previously employed to stay in power.

The BKs were destroyed in two distinct phases. First, the big bang of the federal indictment, which can be thought of as extremely focused kinetics, disrupted the OODA of the BKs' leadership. Then the second phase sought to remake the BKs' environment right out from under them by kicking off a waterfall development remaking of the battlespace the BKs had learned not only to operate in, but to dominate. In the end, the 5GW campaign ended with the area of Chicago that had been Robert Taylor—now renamed Legends South—gang-free. And J.T., who had been a key leader of the BKs and at his height had commanded hundreds of foot soldiers and dozens of officers, was reduced to working in the dry cleaning business. (The once powerful gang leader also attempted a career as a barber. Luckily, he had enough money left over from his dealing that he did not have to work.)

Conclusion

Historian Mark Safranski has pointed out that genocide could be a form of 5GW used to put down a 4GW insurgency that was supported by an ethnic minority (5GW: Into the heart of darkness 2009). My example shows almost the exact same thing occurring, but with a much lower level of physical violence. If the Robert Taylor Homes are viewed objectively, one can see a unique culture with its own norms, values and institutions. Residents, feeling underserved by America's procedural justice system, devised their own honor based justice system that included lists of crimes and punishments up to and including a death penalty for severe infractions. They developed their own economic system that mixed entrepreneurial capitalism with a barter system. And they developed their own security forces whose activities undermined the authority of the political elites.

When the government forces decided to destroy the BKs, they recognized that they had to destroy the entire culture within which the BKs operated. Just as in Safranski's example the Rwandan government inspired the Hutu majority to take up arms against the Tutsi minority in 1994, the government in Chicago wanted to empower a decentralized coalition of actors, including investors, NGOs, and real estate developers to act against the culture that supported the BKs. In America, those actors would be armed not with machetes but with zoning permits, but the result was similar: the removal of a local population and the destruction of a culture that had supported an insurgency.

The above argument is not meant to infer a moral equivalency between a violent genocide and the breakup of a violent gang. If one believes (as I do) that America's justice system is preferable to an honor-violence based kleptocracy, then the actions of the City of Chicago and CHA were completely justified. What my analogy is designed to illustrate are the essential elements of 5GW that could be observed in both my and Mark Safranski's examples: a central authority empowering groups of actors to work ostensibly for individual gain while also affecting an outcome desired by the central authority, and also a focus on getting those actors to affect the human terrain of a given geographic area with the goal of robbing an insurgency of its power base.

PIRACY, HUMAN SECURITY, AND 5GW IN SOMALIA (DAVID AXE)

The fourth generation of war entailed irregular combatants fighting for an ideological cause, seeking to remake society according to their ideals. Fifth-generation war, or 5GW, now coalescing, is less clearly ideological but just as sweeping in its goals. 5GW is when a party exploits or encourages an existing or emerging crisis to achieve strategic goals that those most directly involved in the crisis might not even be aware of. 5GW is a form of stealthy proxy war.

"The systematic alteration, or replacement of, an existing rule set is your strategic goal," Thomas Barnett wrote of 5G fighters. "You're not happy with things the way they are, so you make those around you unhappy enough that they too, are unhappy with the ways things are. Shock them hard enough, and you can trigger their own movement toward new rule sets that move the pile for you" (Barnett, My own personal 5GW dream 2006).

Where fourth-generation combatants might blend in with the surrounding populace most of the time, they still periodically emerged to form military-style units. 5G fighters, by contrast, remain "subtle actors." They may never once wear a uniform or carry a rifle. Their weapon is the desperate population of a society on the brink; their major tactic is unrest; their goal is to undermine the established order in the interest of changing it, or just leaving it in ruins.

No continent poses less of a traditional military threat to the United States than Africa. But in an age of 5GW, where subtle actors can exploit humanitarian, economic, and other crises to undermine the power and legitimacy of the industrial state, no continent poses a greater nontraditional threat. An increasingly volatile Africa begs for greater US intervention and risks corrupting that very intervention, turning American strength into weakness.

For America, 5GW in Africa is a damned-if-you-do, damned-if-you-don't proposition. There are no easy answers to Africa's worsening crises, and there is no consensus on how, or whether, the United States should intervene. Doing anything might make the continent's problems worse. So might doing nothing. And despite its distance and its still-tiny slice of world trade and military power, in the age of 5GW, a suffering Africa is a threat to the United States.

The nearly 20-year-old conflict in Somalia is the perfect example of 5GW in Africa. Persistent political and humanitarian crises, and a disastrous early US intervention, gave rise to seething and spreading anti-Americanism, escalating economic warfare by way of sea piracy and a campaign of secretive US intervention whose benefits, and costs, are unclear. The conditions were ripe for exploitation by a subtle actor aiming to overturn US designs for Somalia.

Washington fought to keep Islamists out of Somalia, in the interest of preventing terrorists from taking root in the country. But the Islamists hijacked muddled US efforts and strengthened their cause. After years of fighting that left hundreds of thousands dead, in February 2009 Islamists took advantage of the escalating chaos, and growing frustration in Washington, to reassert control of the country, essentially inflicting an indirect battlefield defeat on America.

Skulls, Bones, GPS

In 2009, thousands of Somali pirates employed by sophisticated criminal enterprises threaten some two million square miles of ocean, including all of the Gulf of Aden and vast swaths of the Indian Ocean. In 2008 pirates seized more than 40 large vessels headed to and from the Suez Canal, ransoming them for an average price of more than $1 million.

With access to GPS, satellite phones, and commercial satellite imagery—not to mention small arms and rockets readily available across Africa—pirates have managed to capture large cargo ships and even supertankers. Pirates' surprising success has had the effect of driving up insurance rates for shippers and forcing some companies to abandon the Suez Canal route between Europe and Asia, in turn raising consumer prices at a time when most consumers have less to spend.

Around 20 warships from a dozen navies have deployed to combat piracy, but they can only hope to mitigate the threat. "I don't think we'll ever stop pirates," said U.S. Navy Rear Admiral James McKnight. "We will do our best to bring the numbers down" (Federal News Service 2009).

That's because ending piracy requires law and order and a measure of prosperity on land, at the source of the problem. Fundamentally, Somali pirates are aggrieved fishermen whose livelihoods suffered from Somalia's collapse in 1991, McKnight explained. In the absence of any Somali authority, "for very many years...countries were coming in and fishing in their international waters, stealing their fish. And so what they did is they started pirating some of these fishing vessels and they figured out that, hey, we can go for bigger fish. And so they went for bigger vessels."

Piracy "is beyond a military solution," said Roger Middleton, from the International Institute of Strategic Studies in London. Pirates' continued success demonstrates the power of the individual and the impotence of old-fashioned military force in this age of powerful, accessible consumer technology. A few thousand plugged-in pirates have rendered ineffective the combined might of the world's navies, and undermined the notion that the traditional state can protect its interests with displays of force.

That's not to say they did it on purpose. "We just want the money," Sugule Ali, a pirate spokesman, told the *New York Times*. Indeed, pirates have no clear or stated political aims. Their intent is only to get rich, but their effect is to rattle the very foundation of the state. In this way, pirates are a 5G threat. Somalia's Islamists are the subtle third-party actors benefiting from the havoc pirates wreak.

For Islamists seeking to rewrite the global order, one country at a time, piracy might represent a form of economic warfare that, in World Wars I and II, was executed by submarines targeting merchant ships. Piracy has a similar effect, albeit less severe, and at much lower cost and risk to both the attackers (the pirates) and those hoping to benefit from the attacks (the subtle actor).

Ironically, Islamists and pirates are, ultimately, incompatible. Sharia law comes down hard on bandits on land and sea. An established Islamic order has no place for pirates. But Islamist still in the phase of sowing chaos, from which their new order might eventually emerge, might find pirates a useful, temporary, proxy weapon. "My idea of the aggressive 5GW warrior is that he's uncommonly cool with that sort of ambiguity," Barnett wrote. "[That's] a stance that can only be justified by the long-term perspective."

Damned if You Do

Somali piracy wasn't inevitable. It's the result of a tragic chain of events playing out over 20 hard years for the East African nation. US intervention represents several key links in that chain. It's not a stretch to say that piracy is partially America's fault. This hijacking of US designs is characteristically 5G.

There was a time, the immediate aftermath of the Cold War, when it was possible for Americans to believe that as sprawling and deep a crisis as Somalia's could be easily fixed or, barring that, safely ignored. The deceptive allure of both these contradictory extremes—massive action and total inaction—was an open invitation to 5G hijacking. Confusion is one of the 5G fighter's favorite conditions, for it chips away at the perception that the current world order actually works.

When civil war toppled dictator Siad Barre's regime in 1991, clans began fighting for dominance in Somalia. The fighting disrupted food distribution and threatened millions with starvation. It was this dark prospect that prompted the first major US military-humanitarian intervention of the post-Cold War era. In 1992, US Marines stormed ashore near Mogadishu, launching a three-year peacekeeping operation, coordinated with the UN, that grew to include 40,000 troops from 25 countries.

Operation Restore Hope helped end the starvation crisis, but this success was overshadowed by the deaths of 18 US troops in a raid targeting a Mogadishu warlord accused of hijacking food shipments. The American deaths led to a rapid and ignominious end to the US and UN intervention, despite the absence of a widely recognized Somali government and the high probability of another famine.

What followed was a decade during which Somalia was almost entirely on its own, ungoverned, hungry and ignored. "The great ship of international good will has sailed," wrote Mark Bowden in his seminal book *Blackhawk Down*. Somalis had "effectively written themselves off the map."

It was during this decade of isolation and neglect that Somalis got into the piracy business in a big way. As McKnight said, the first pirates were Somali fishermen demanding unofficial fees from foreign trawlers illegally operating in Somali waters. From there, piracy quickly evolved into Mafia-style organized crime. And it could only have happened in the absence of a widely accepted Somali government, an effective international peacekeeping force or, more broadly, substantial economic assistance to desperate fishermen.

Somalia's isolation and neglect also proved a perfect breeding ground for militant Islamists. Promising peace, rallying desperate thousands around the banner of anti-Westernism, Somali Islamists emerged in the early 2000s and quickly organized across clan lines. The Islamists' rapid spread began to pull together Somalia's fractured landscape of warlord enclaves. While good for Somalis, the prospect of an Islamified Somalia terrified Washington, even more than pirates did, at first.

Damned if You Don't

Somalia would make a dramatic reappearance on the "map" 10 years after the Marines stormed Mogadishu's white beaches. The terrorist attacks on September 11, 2001, organized from Afghanistan, awoke the United States to the dangers posed by militant Islamists—especially those Islamists based in ungoverned or undergoverned spaces. Suddenly Washington thought it could no longer ignore Somalia. The anarchic country seemed to perfectly match Afghanistan's profile.

So in October 2002, a force of 800 US Marines landed in Djibouti, north of Somalia, aiming to "coerce others to get rid of their terrorist problem," in the cryptic words of Army General Tommy Franks. The resulting "Joint Task Force Horn of Africa" grew to 2,000 people. Gunships and drones flying from the task force's base launched several air raids on suspected Al Qaeda enclaves inside Somalia.

But the air strikes didn't stem the "Islamification" of Somalia or the spread of piracy. In fact, American attacks may very well have accelerated both processes, by fueling Somali suspicion of the Christian West and its allies, and thereby boosting popular support for the Islamists and for pirates, many of whom had branded themselves as do-it-yourself Somali "coast guards."

In 2006, an alliance of Islamists calling itself the Islamic Courts Union defeated Somalia's entrenched warlords and gained control of Mogadishu. They imposed a moderate form of Sharia law, suppressed banditry and opened up Somalia to foreign investment. The BBC called the Courts' meteoric ascent a "popular uprising." In Mogadishu, residents bristled under the harsher aspects of Sharia, such as the prohibition of cinemas, but the same resident welcomed the law and order the Courts enforced. Piracy waned during the Courts' rule.

But the US State Department had branded the Courts' armed wing, Al Shabab, a terrorist organization owing to its purported Al Qaeda ties, so Washington never accepted the Courts as Somalia's legitimate government, even if most Somalis did. Washington, the UN, the African Union, and Ethiopia all backed the unpopular, clan-based "Transitional Federal Government" (TFG), formed in Kenya and headquartered in Baidoa, a small town outside Mogadishu.

In 2006, at the peak of the Courts' rise, Ethiopia—a landlocked Christian nation and a longtime rival of Somalia with its exquisite deepwater ports—reflexively launched a 3GW, blitzkrieg-style invasion of Somalia, with Washington providing key support in the form of aircraft and Special Forces operating out of Djibouti. In a matter of weeks, the Courts had been routed. Al Shabab melted into the countryside and into Mogadishu's teeming slums.

Soon, Al Shabab would reemerge to challenge the roughly 50,000 occupying Ethiopian troops, turning the Somalia conflict into an Iraq-style insurgency. What followed was two years of urban bloodshed, punctuated by periodic US air strikes on suspected terrorists in the countryside. By 2007, Mogadishu residents seethed at the mere mention of America. "You Americans. You'll destroy an entire city to get three people," scolded one professor in Mogadishu. Not coincidentally, it was the period of Ethiopian occupation in 2007 and 2008 that saw piracy escalate, from a regional nuisance to a global economic threat.

With tens of thousands dead on all sides, by 2009 the Ethiopians had had enough. And with Somalia now threatening world trade, the US State Department had had enough, too. Where before, Washington had preferred anarchy to Islamic government for Somalia, now the State Department just wanted order—any order. "If you want help ensure regional stability and prevent the criminality that has taken place around Somalia for the last decade and a half, you must have a state capable of securing its borders," a State Department source said. "That's our over-riding perspective."

Even if that meant the Islamists return? Yes, the source said. "It's not up to us to decide who has the most legitimacy among the Somali people."

For Islamists, State's change of heart represented a subtle victory. The chaos unleashed first by the Somali civil war in 1991, and anew with the 2006 destruction of the Islamic Courts, had resulted in seemingly intractable economic warfare that seemed to have convinced Washington that maybe Islamists weren't so bad, after all. That's model 5GW. The Islamists had only to let the pirates do what pirates do best. The pirates, for their part, probably weren't even aware that they were helping the Islamists wage a winning war.

The Ethiopians' withdrawal in January sparked a dramatic sequence of events. The TFG fled to Djibouti, where the unpopular body promptly signed a peace deal with a coalition of moderate Islamic groups, then elected the former head of the Islamic Courts as the country's new president. President Shariff Sheikh Ahmed installed his new government in Mogadishu, restored Sharia, and began offering truces to holdout Islamists. Only Al Shabab resisted the olive branch, and the fighting finally subsided. "I'm cautiously optimistic," one State Department official said. "It's fragile," he said of Somalia's new, more inclusive government, "but all new beginnings are."

As far as piracy is concerned, the return of Sharia law offers hope of a long-term solution. Sea banditry is incompatible with Islamists' obsession with lawfulness. If peace holds and Sheikh Ahmed's government lasts, pirates might finally face real justice in their own enclaves. But the price, for Washington, is the firm establishment of a government led by a man formerly associated with a "terror group."

Human Security

Somalia's recent history is marked by cycles of US engagement and withdrawal. A major peacekeeping deployment collapsed, followed by nearly a decade of total neglect, at the end of which events drew America back to Somalia, but in fits and starts marked more by strategic failure than by success. US involvement since 2002 failed to stop the Islamification of Somalia, and had the sad effect of alienating everyday Somalis by prolonging the Courts' bloody, and inevitable, ascent.

The confusion is, in part, endemic to Africa. But it's also the result of Washington having two incompatible goals. In Somalia, the United States wants the kind of law and order that trumps piracy. But these days that kind of order is best enforced by Islamic groups with broad popular support—and preventing the rise of such groups is Washington's other goal. The US can have a stable Somalia, or it can have a Somalia without formal Islamic leadership, but it can't have both. Trying to have both means having neither. Insurgency, piracy and rising anti-American extremism are the immediate results. The long-term risk is further damage to US interests inflicted by 5G subtle actors hijacking Somalia's chaos for their own purposes.

In retrospect, one reason for Washington's failures should be clear. America's Somalia strategy has been dominated by the military doing traditionally military things. This in a country, on a continent, in an era, where military force is often worse than ineffective. In Africa, in an age of 5GW, the only meaningful security is individuals' security, and that's a condition that's rarely improved by the imprecise application of massive firepower.

To prevent 5GW, the US must prevent subtle actors from "socializing their problem," to borrow Barnett's phrase. That means preventing the kinds of widespread desperation that makes individuals and populations vulnerable to exploitation by subtle actors. The unconscious collective actions of individuals seeking security—the mass movement of refugees, for instance, or spiraling tensions over food, water and firewood—are potentially more destructive, globally and in the long term, than most imaginable conventional military conflicts between African states. Desperation is the 5G actor's favorite state—for others.

It's for those reasons that some military planners have begun to reconceptualize US national security as a facet of world security, which is itself anchored in human security. "What we're going to see in the future is that security is not going to be based as much on state-centric models," said Major Shannon Beebe, the US Army's top intelligence officer for Africa. "[Security] is not going to be based as much on state-versus-state type of engagement, but the insecurities and the conditions of human beings that create these insecurities across state borders."

In other words, "security" no longer means detente between superpowers. In the age of instantaneous communications and empowered individuals, security is a person's freedom from fear, disease, and hunger. People who feel secure are peaceful, or so the thinking goes. By that line of reasoning, insecure people pose a threat to secure people, for the insecure might seek to destroy, with gestures big and small, the global systems that they believe have failed them. 5G actors wait in the wings to pick up the pieces, and rebuild the world according to their designs.

Somali piracy, for one, "is a typical case in which failed states and a poor representation of marginalized sectors of the population can become a threat to the security of others around the world," Gonzalo Peña, a Utah-based consultant with a humanitarian background. The 5G effect of that threat was to help change US policy to embrace the very people Washington had once branded an enemy.

In some circles, that's called "defeat."

CONCLUSION

What is to be done?

5GW UNDER THE MICROSCOPE (DANIEL H. ABBOTT)

The excellent examples in this volume by Mark Safranski (5GW: Into the heart of darkness 2009), Brent Grace (The War for Robert Taylor 2009), and David Axe (Piracy, human security, and 5GW in Somalia 2009) demonstrate that despite its secretive nature, 5GW can be studied. The same research tools that are used by historians, sociologists, and journalists can be used to understand 5GW as well. This is fortunate, as the "academics, researchers, and analysts" (Abbott, The xGW Framework 2009) who most need to know about 5GW are also those most likely to need to study it on their own. The study of 5GW is not limited to the methods used to compose this handbook. Rather, the full spectrum of quantitative and qualitative methods can be used to investigate 5GW.

Broadly, future research on 5GW will cluster in three broad categories. The first of these, qualitative research, is the tradition that has been embraced by the authors in this Handbook. The second category, quantitative research, will allow researchers to make accurate and precise predictions about how 5GWs will unfold. The third category, mixed methods research, is perhaps the most promising, and will allow analysts, researchers, and academics to gain a 360-degree understanding of 5GW.

Qualitative research is a flexible tool that occurs in a natural setting, uses the researcher as a research tool, focuses on the meaning of the phenomenon, and relies on the perspectives of those who have experienced a phenomenon (Hatch 2001). Qualitative research can be narrative, which focuses on telling a story, a case study, or an examination of a group of participants united by a process, grounded theory, action research, in which the goal is to improve the world or win a battle, or some other type (Creswell, Hanson, et al. 2007). In qualitative research, a sample is recruited based on some characteristic, such as being typical of the population, representing the extremes of the population, knowing each other, or so on (J. Creswell 2008). The examples of 5GW in this volume are exemplars of how qualitative research on 5GW should be conducted.

Quantitative research, sometimes called confirmatory research, is focused on hard numbers. It is a scientific approach that is focused on conjectures and refutation, the process of developing and discarding ever more precise hypotheses (Popper 1963). Two broad traditions within quantitative research are correlational research and experimental research. Correlational research is concerned with identifying trends in real-world data, while experimental research artificially manipulates and environment to determine what behaviors will change as a result.

Quantitative research can be used to study 5GW. For instance, 5GWs such as the ones described by Axe, Grace, and Safranski, could be studied, and variables of influence (the number of known combatants, the complexity of the operation, and so on) could be entered. This would be an example of correlational 5GW research, and is similar to ongoing research in political science. Alternatively, the reaction of highly trained individuals to 5GW-like assaults could be studied in a laboratory. The different reaction styles of lawyers and engineers, say, could be examined. This would be an example of experimental 5GW research. Quantitative data analysis could range from simple procedures, such as multiple regression and analysis of variance (ANOVA), to more complex procedures such as multivariate analysis and structural equation modeling (Tabachnick, Fidell and L.S. 2006).

A new category of research is mixed methods research. In mixed methods research, quantitative and qualitative tools are used alongside each other to provide a better view of a phenomenon. The major types of mixed methods research—the triangulation design, the embedded design, the explanatory design, and the exploratory design—all mix quantitative and qualitative methods in different ways (Creswell and Plano Clark, Designing and conducting mixed methods research 2007). The advantage of mixed methods research is that quantitative and qualitative tools can be used to compensate for each other's weaknesses with respect to a specific research question.

For instance, consider an analyst who wishes to study the relative weakness of the Chinese and American governments to a 5GW assault. One approach to studying this might be the triangulation design, where quantitative and qualitative results are analyzed with an eye to convergence. So, for instance, in a quantitative phase, an experimental treatment could be used to test the reaction of those with professional legal degrees (the typical background of American policymakers) and engineering degrees (the typical background of Chinese policymakers) to "subtle... [exploitation of] humanitarian, economic, and other crises to undermine the power and legitimacy of the industrial state" (Axe 2009) within the context of a strategic game. Simultaneously, a comparative case study of the reaction to America and Chinese to failed 5GWs could be used. At the end of the study, the results of the quantitative and qualitative inquiries could be contrasted to gain a better view of Chinese and American reactions to 5GW.

5GW is the fifth gradient of warfare (Herring, Searching for 5GW 2009). It is part of the same phenomenon of force and violence studied by Clausewitz and other military thinkers (Deichman 2009). Recently, Lexington Green (Green) lamented the theoretical emphasis of many 5GW writers, and wrote:

> But the clown show is not funny because (1) major, serious, dangerous threats are emerging, (2) they are novel and need to be understood so they can be dealt with, (3) accurate, clear assessments are at a premium, and (4) this current terminology is at the point that it is

an obstacle not an aid to clear thinking and clear discussion.

With Lexington Green, I share disappointment at the role that hype and popularity play in many discussions of the nature of war. This is one reason I am editing this volume. I also share with Lexington the belief that "major, serious, dangerous threats are emerging," that "they are novel and need to be understood so they can be dealt with," and "accurate, clear assessments are at a premium." While the terminology of 5GW may have been confused when Lexington wrote his comment, the purpose of this Handbook is to clear that confusion.

Clear thinking and clear discussion–by academics, analysts, historians, policymakers, and warfighters—is needed. Better thinking and better discussion will come from better research. The examples provided by Brent Grace, Mark Safranski, and David Axe, as well as the theoretical context provided by other chapters in this volume, are an invaluable start for this research.

But more is left to be done.

The first 5GW was fought and lost before the dawn of time. Without research, the lessons of how to avoid defeat, protect our treasure, and save lives will be relearned and re-forgotten with every new generation of warfighters and policy makers.

We owe our country better than that.

We owe our world better than that.

SOURCE DOCUMENTS

While neither contain the first mention of "5GW," works associated with William Lind (On War #53: Fifth Generation Warfare? 2004) and T. X. Hammes (The Sling and the stone: On war in the 21st century 2004) are nonetheless the best known. A consequence of this is that researchers and analysts curious about 5GW will start with these volumes, and then either go onto Lind's and Hammes's reference lists, or else look for works that cite either Lind or Hammes. The contributions of these thinkers to the study of 5GW are immense, and no discourse can ignore their contributions entirely.

However, many writers have contributed to our understanding of 5GW in the last five years. Indeed, the greatest part of this discourse----the xGW framework----is often left out entirely by analysts who begin only with Lind and Hammes. Therefore, many 5GW articles that are referenced by writers in this volume are attached in the following section. The order of these articles is roughly chronological, beginning with Mark Safranski's reaction to Lind's first use of the term 5GW, and continuing through Younghusband's outline of the xGW framework.

UNTO THE FITH GENERATION OF WAR (MARK SAFRANSKI)

Originally published July 18, 2005:[2]

> "[E]ach new generation required developments across the spectrum of society. Technological change alone has never been sufficient to produce a major change in how man wages war. It requires a complete societal change--—political, economic social and tech-nological--—to create the conditions necessary for ma-jor changes in war." (Hammes 2004)

William Lind, one of the fathers of 4GW theory, has welcomed, yet cautioned against, attempts to ascertain with too much preci-sion any outlines of a 5th Generation Warfare that might be evolving within the dynamic of 4GW conflicts we see in Iraq, Afghanistan and in transnational terrorism. Yet according to theorists and practitioners of 4GW like Colonel Hammes, that form of warfare, although just now coming in to its own. has already been present for some seventy years! Undoubtedly then 5GW is also here with us, waiting for the next Mao or Rommel to fit the disparate puzzle pieces into a coherent pattern.

4GW advocates disdain an overemphasis on particular technol-ogical breakthrough, criticizing in particular the Network-centric Warfare theory developed by Admiral Arthur Cebrowski. Or at least the celebration of high-tech warfare capabilities by some of Cebrowski's followers in the Pentagon (for a critique of both schools shaping of current policy, see "The Pentagon's Internal war Over what Iraq Means" by Dr. [Thomas P.M.] Barnett). Therefore, I will generally accept some major premises of 4GW theory as articulated by Hammes in speculating about the parame-ters of 5GW, specifically:

---

[2] http://zenpundit.com/?m=20050718

1. Generational changes in warfare require complete societal change.

2. Practitioners of warfare drove the evolution of warfare by seeking solutions to practical problems

3. Each succeeding generation reaches deeper in to enemy territory to defeat him.

The first question we should ask are what changes are driving society, nationally and globally? Very briefly at the planetary level we have Globalization--—an acceleration of the rate and degree of complexity of all forms of exchange (in *PNM* theory Barnett's "Four Flows"); Post-Westphalianization--—the rise of International, Transnational, Subnational and NonstateNon-state Actor challengers to the sovereign primacy of the Nation-State; and finally, State-Failure or severe State dysfunction where the ability of a State to constrain and police anarchic, nihilistic and disconnective forces is overwhelmed by post-Westphalian challengers, economic collapse and natural disasters.

Additionally, in the scientific and economic realm, the drivers of future societal changes in the next twenty to fifty years would most likely come from the following fields--—Artificial Intelligence, Genomics, Alternative Fuels, Quantum Computing, Human Brain Research, Complexity and Chaos Theory, Nanotechnology and String Theory. It is impossible to assume the implications of any one of these fields over such a long timeline, much less all these fields in combination but what is a safe assumption is that the magnitude of changes that are coming will be very significant and result in substantial economic, social and political transformations.

In sum the global trends I have listed have in my view some fairly direct logical implications for warfare, already visible even today:

Superempowerment: The range of effect for each individual soldier (or terrorist) will be vastly increased even as the economic costs are driven down by market forces and proliferation of dual-use technology to the civilian consumer.

Fluidity: Globalization makes possible virtual armies that are networks of networks that are both resilient and adaptable in a Darwinian sense.

Multidimensional Battlespace: War occurs in the context of everything else--—physical space, cyberspace, the logosphere, financial, legal and societal networks-—shaping the battlespace itself to the disadvantage of actual and potential opponents will become crucial aspects of strategy and not merely moving more effectively within it.

Autonomous Surrogates: Active regular military forces are seconded by a variety of substitutes to carry some aspect of the warfighting load--—PMC's, NGO's, Paramilitary and Subnational networks, International Peacekeeping missions and increasingly, robotic agents.

Today's Predator drones and other prototype UAV are going to evolve and inevitably merge with AI technology so that we will have, shades of science fiction, autonomous war machines that will have basic programming but also the capacity to learn, make independent decisions, cooperate with one another and adapt to changing circumstances on the battlefield.

These however are simply aspects of the emerging warfare and not the strategic purpose behind such a shift that make one generation of warfare different from its predecessor. The rise of 5GW will represent the solution to defeating 4GW forces in the field and here we come to a very troubling moral possibility.

4GW forces like Al Qaeda erase the distinction between Combatant and non-combatant and target an enemy's will to resist, often moving submerged within society itself as a clandestine network structure. Such forces have proven exceptionally difficult to defeat for traditional militaries. 4GW strategy has allowed inferior forces to defeat even the superpowers (Hammes 2004).

A strong possibility exists that given successive generations of warfare tend to drive "deeper" into enemy territory, that 5GW will mean systemic liquidation of enemy networks and their sympathizers, essentially a total war on a society or subsection of a society. There is no where "deeper" for 5GW to go but here. At the high tech end 5GW would be precisely targeted to winnow out "the bad guys" in a souped-up version of Operation Phoenix but at the low-tech end we could see campaigns that would be indiscriminate, democidally-oriented death squad campaigns that shred 4GW networks by the same actuarially merciless logic that led the Allies to firebomb German and Japanese cities in WWII.

This is a terrible prospect but there is evidence that 5GW tactics of this kind have defeated 4GW Communist revolution in Guatemala and El Salvador, stymied FARC and ELN in Colombia, beat back Islamists in Algeria and the Kurdish PKK in Turkey. Contravening data would include the Hutu militia genocide in Rwanda designed to eviscerate the ethnic supporters of the Tutsi rebels but instead led to the rebels toppling the Hutu regime and spreading disorder to neighboring states.

My efforts here to outline 5GW are purely speculative. A second potential form of 5GW might be a "System Administration" based Global Transaction Strategy to export security and connectivity to the Gap, short-circuiting the political appeal of 4GW movements before they grow out of all control, along the lines of (Barnett, The Pentagon's new map: War and peace in the 21st century 2004). Or we may see both forms used in tandem and even likelier, some new dynamic currently impossible for us to foresee at all.

What is certain is that 4GW movements like the Iraqi insurgency and Al Qaeda will drive the evolution of warfare to 5GW as nation-states struggle to find solutions to the strategic problem presented by 4GW enemies and the societal disintegration they bring in their wake.

GO DEEP: OODA AND THE RAINBOW OF xGW (DANIEL H. ABBOTT)

Originally published July 18, 2005

Our OODA loop helps us know where warfare is headed. Modern warfare is usually divided into the four generations of 1st Generation Warfare (1GW), 2nd Generation Warfare (2GW), 3rd Generation Warfare (3GW), and 4th Generation Warfare (4GW).

Modern War in the Context of the OODA Loop

1GW

- example: Napoleonic War
- characteristic: mass armies
- method of fighting: man-to-man

2GW

- example: First World War
- characteristic: mass armies
- method of fighting: fixed-artillery-to-men

3GW

- example: Second World War
- characteristic: Blitzkrieg, fast transitions from one maneuver to the next
- method of fighting: tanks/bombers-to-cities/armies

4GW

- example: Vietnam War
- characteristic: dispiriting the enemy
- method of fighting: propagandists-to-populations

Some argue that the future of warfare will be deeper than 1GW, 2GW, 3GW, or 4GW:

> A strong possibility exists that given successive generations of warfare tend to drive "deeper" into enemy territory, that 5GW will mean systemic liquidation of enemy networks and their sympathizers, essentially a total war on a society or subsection of a society. There is no where "deeper" for 5GW to go but here. At the high tech end 5GW would be precisely targeted to winnow out ""the bad guys" in a souped-up version of Operation Phoenix but at the low-tech end we could see campaigns that would be indiscriminate, democidally-oriented death squad campaigns that shred 4GW networks by the same actuarially merciless logic that led the Allies to firebomb German and Japanese cities in WWII. (Safranski, Unto the fifth generation of war 2009)

War is going deeper, but by that I do not mean "farther into enemy territory." Certainly you can't get any deeper than obliteration of Dresden or Hiroshima! For that matter, centuries ago Catholic terrorists tried to destroy the British Parliament, which was the deepest heart of the British government!

War is going deeper into enemy minds. Every generation of warfare aims for deeper in the enemy's OODA loop

1GWs, like the Napoleon Wars, were extremely fluid. Armies could march whenever men's feet could carry them. Information was relatively symmetrical--—precise locations of either army were unavailable to any commander, while general knowledge of the land was known to all commanders. (Napoleonic "disinformation" was trivial compared to what was later devised.) Another feature of the Napoleon Wars was the army's need to live off the land. 1GW was defined by conflict centered around an enemy's ability to decide and act.

Aim: Destroy enemy army.

Visually:

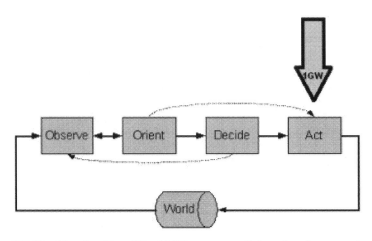

2GWs, like the First World War, were sticky. Armies marched, drove, or took trains to the front line--—where they stopped. In 2nd Generation War, action is easy: charge. You know exactly where you are, exactly where the enemy is, and exactly where you are going to die (in the razorwire and minefield, hit by enemy crossfire). Thanks to telegraphs and modern communications, commanders are flooded with a tsunami of almost meaningless facts. Thinking now centers around where and when it makes sense to try to break through, as well as the how to move to advance evenly. This means that the heart of conflict "moves deeper" into the OODA loop. Another way to think of it is like a rainbow or spectrum, where the heart of conflict is "redshifting" away from acting. 2GW was defined by conflict centered around an enemy's ability to orient and decide:

> Offensives conducted on wide frontages— emphasizing few, rather than many, harmonious yet independent thrusts.
>
> Evenness of advance maintained to protect flanks and provide artillery support as advance makes headway. (Boyd, A discourse of winning and losing 1995)

Visually:

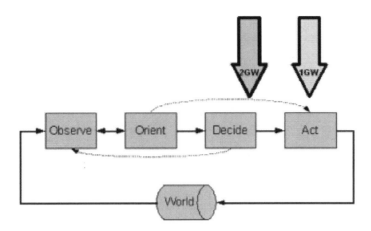

3GWs, like the trenches for most of the Second World War or the Lawrence of Arabia campaign in the First World War, were fluid again. But conflict kept burrowing deeper into the OODA loop and redshifting further away from action. Victory in 3rd Generation Wars required the ability to instill madness----to mess with the enemy's minds. The purpose of 3rd Generation Warfare is to paralyze the enemy with doubt. We move even deeper into the OODA loop, to the red end of the rainbow. 3GW is defined by conflict centered around an enemy's ability to orient:

> Taken together, the captured attention, the obscured view, and the indistinct character of moving dispersed/irregular swarms deny adversary the opportunity to pictures what is taking place. (Boyd, A discourse of winning and losing 1995)

and

> Gain support of population. Must "arrange the minds" of friend, foe and neutral alike. Must "get inside their minds." (Boyd, A discourse of winning and losing 1995)

Visually:

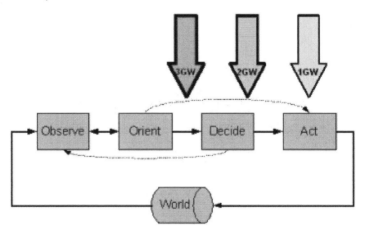

If older generations of war were like fluids, 4GW was like a gas. It spreads everywhere yet regular armies have a hard time even finding battles. Like 3rd Generation Wars, 4th Generation Wars focus on the picture inside the enemy's head. But while 3GW tries to destroy the picture, 4GW builds a new one. This picture is built in that part of the OODA loop where people "wait and see," the double-headed arrow between Observe and Orient. While 3GW tries to paralyze the enemy with doubt, 4GW tries to deny him even that much--—4GW drains the will of the enemy so he "waits and sees," robbing him of his ability to want to do anything. In practice, this means 4GW tries to destroy an enemy's civil society, turning his population into mindless cowards. To achieve this, 4GW is defined by conflict centered around Observe and Orient.

John Boyd's words on the tactics of "moral warfare," an important part of 4GW:

> Create, exploit, and magnify … uncertainty
>
> Impressions, or atmosphere, generated by events that appear ambiguous, erratic, contradictory, unfamiliar, chaotic, etc.

And . . . ...

178

Surface, fear, anxiety, and alienation in order to generate many non-cooperative centers of gravity, as well as subvert those that adversary depends upon, thereby magnify internal friction.

Visually:

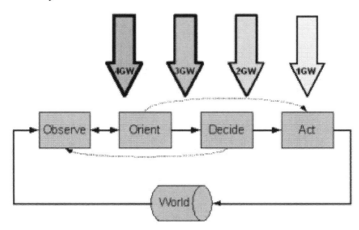

So if these patterns hold, what will 5GW look like?

Visually, like this

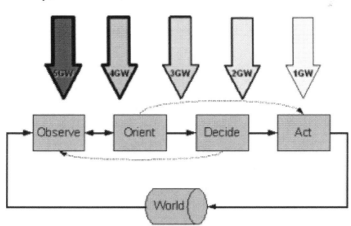

The 4th Generation of War redshifts deeper into the OODA loop. It slides into the "Observation" realm. If traditional war centered on an enemy's physical strength, and 4GW on his moral strength, the 5th Generation of War would focus on his intellectual strength. A 5th Generation War might be fought with one side not knowing who it is fighting. Or even, a brilliantly executed 5GW might involve one side being completely ignorant that there ever was a war. It's like the old question of what was the perfect robbery: we will never know, because in a perfect robbery the bank would not know that it was robbed.

4GW was around for decades before its nature was recognized:

> William Lind, one of the fathers of 4GW theory has welcomed yet cautioned against attempts to ascertain with too much precision any outlines of a 5th Generation Warfare that might be evolving within the dynamic of 4GW conflicts we see in Iraq, Afghanistan and in transnational terrorism. Yet according to theorists and practitioners of 4GW like Colonel Hammes, that form of warfare, although just now coming in to its own has already been present for some seventy years! Undoubtedly then 5GW is also here with us, waiting for the next Mao or Rommel to fit the disparate puzzle pieces into a coherent pattern. (Safranski, Unto the fifth generation of war 2009)

This means that, in their pragmatic attempts to solve problems, both Al Qaeda and the United States might be using aspects of 5GW right now. Where will historians of the future look to see aspects of a secret war? Of a war centered on ignorance?

Yes:

> Al Qaeda's new brand of terrorism presented challenges to U. S. governmental institutions that they were not well-designed to meet. Though top officials all told us that they understood the danger, we believe there was uncertainty among them as to whether this was just a new and especially venomous version of the ordinary terrorist threat the United States had lived with for decades, or it was indeed radically new, posing a threat beyond any yet experienced. As late as September 4, 2001, Richard Clarke, the White House staffer long responsible for counterterrorism policy coordination, as-

serted that the government had not yet made up its mind how to answer the question: "Is al Qida a big deal?"

A week later came the answer. Policy Terrorism was not the overriding national security concern for the U. S. government under either the Clinton or the pre-9/11 Bush administration.

The policy challenges were linked to this failure of imagination. (National Commission on Terrorist Attacks Upon the United States 2004)

Yes:

Our response involves far more than instant retaliation and isolated strikes. Americans should not expect one battle, but a lengthy campaign, unlike any other we have ever seen. It may include dramatic strikes, visible on TV, and covert operations, secret even in success. We will starve terrorists of funding, turn them one against another, drive them from place to place, until there is no refuge or no rest. And we will pursue nations that provide aid or safe haven to terrorism. Every nation, in every region, now has a decision to make. Either you are with us, or you are with the terrorists. From this day forward, any nation that continues to harbor or support terrorism will be regarded by the United States as a hostile regime.- (Bush 2001)

The OODA-PISRR Loop

The Observe-Orient-Decide-Act (OODA) loop of John Boyd is not only a model of human cognition.

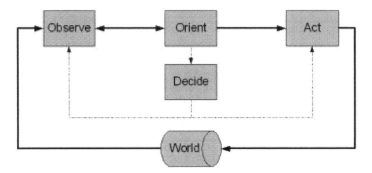

It is also useful in aligning the generations of modern war within the framework of human cognition

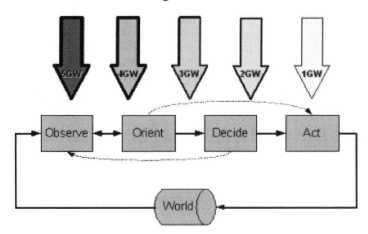

Likewise, the broader Observe-Orient-Decide-Act/Penetrate-Isolate-Subvert-Reorient-Reharmonize Social loop is not only a model of social cognition:

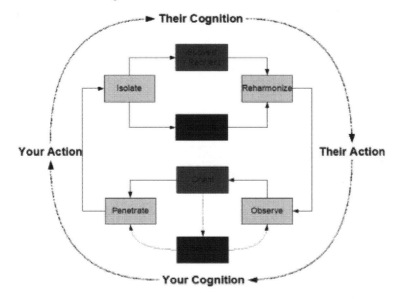

It is also useful in aligning the kinetic intensity within the framework of social cognition

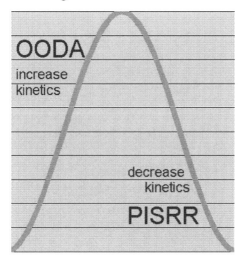

Both of these findings can be synthesized by viewing the generations of modern war within the framework of social cognition.

Consider that the second generation of modern war (2GW), based on concentration of firepower, is the strong-suit of the state in war. Likewise, consider that the fourth generation of modern war (4GW), based on ideological coherency, is the strong-suit of the insurgent in war.

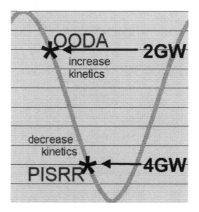

From this we can place the third generation of modern war (3GW), based on mobility, in between the state's and the insurgent's spheres of influence.

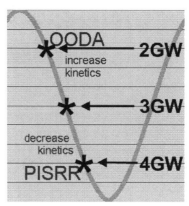

And this makes sense. In Patterns of Conflict, John Boyd (Boyd 1981) Boyd described maneuver warfare as "blitz/guerrilla."

(One might just as easily as say "Global Guerrilla / Panzer General.")

There are two remaining generations of modern war, and both fall outside the realms of the state and non-state. The first generation (1GW), built on total mobilization, was designed for states able to conscript a large fraction of the male population but unable to communicate effectively enough to effective combine firepower. Thus we place 1GW to the left of 2GW, as belonging to an actor which we would describe as a state . . .almost. (Compare the workings of Napoleonic France to that of a modern state to see how a 1G "state" falls short.)

Likewise, place the fifth generation of modern warfare (5GW) to the right of 4GW. 5GW is the domain of non-states ... almost. When a 5GW is used by a state, it's actually the province of a "state within" that acts as an internal insurgency. The Military-Industrial-Complex devised by President Truman is the work of such a 5GW conspiracy-within-the-state.

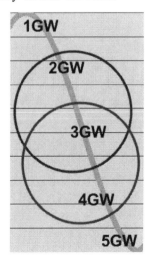

Upper Circle encompasses the Realm of the State.

Lower Circle encompasses the Realm of the Non-State.

The take-away from this visualization is as follows:

Each "higher" generation of war is less kinetically intense than the one before it.

Further, states tend to be victorious in areas where intensity is high but not overwhelming-—between 2GW and 3GW.

At the same time, non-states tend to be victorious at low but not underwhelming kinetic intensity-—between 3GW and 5GW.

Finally, 1GW and 5GW fall outside the realms of both the state and the non-state, and into the lands of the proto-state and the state-within.

DREAMING 5TH GENERATION WAR (DANIEL H. ABBOTT)

Originally published July 18, 2005

1. The Dream-Quest of Unknown 5GW

> Three times Randolph Carter dreamed of the mar-
> velous city, and three times was he snatched away while
> still he paused on the high terrace above it. All golden
> and lovely it blazed in the sunset, with walls, temples,
> colonnades and arched bridges of veined marble, silver-
> basined fountains of prismatic spray in broad squares
> and perfumed gardens, and wide streets marching be-
> tween delicate trees and blossom-laden urns and ivory
> statues in gleaming rows; while on steep northward
> slopes climbed tiers of red roofs and old peaked gables
> harboring little lanes of grassy cobbles. It was a fever

Earlier I argued that war is evolving "deeper into the Observe-
Orient-Decide-Act loop

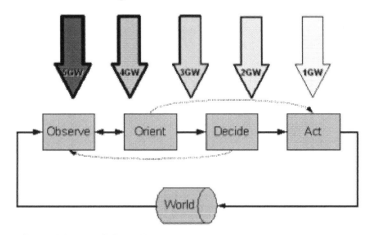

Figure 11. The OODA loop.

I also argued:

> If traditional war centered on an enemy's physical
> strength, and 4GW on his moral strength, the 5th Gen-
> eration of War would focus on his intellectual strength.
> A 5th Generation War might be fought with one side
> not knowing who it is fighting. Or even, a brilliantly ex-

ecuted 5GW might involve one side being completely ignorant that there ever was a war. It's like the old question of what was the perfect robbery: we will never know, because in a perfect robbery the bank would not know that it was robbed. (Abbott, Orientation and action, part I: The OODA Loop 2009)

I kept trying to imagine what this would look like. Besides a vague inkling that it would be fought by some combination of George Friedman and Peter Wiggin, no picture came to me. Like Randolph Carter looking for Unknown Kadath,...

Fortunately, I got in communication with a genius who helped me understand that the Observe-Orient-Decide-Act look might be better pictured as

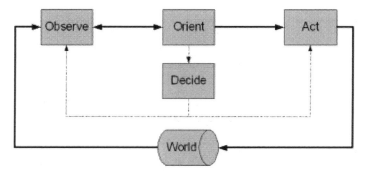

The original analysis is still valid. The "arrows of attack" I used still fall earlier and earlier in the Observe-Orient-Decide-Act power-line. Just now it is clear that most actions are not decided upon. They are implicitly guided and controlled by orientation, based on our observations.

Then a comment hit me like a hammer:

> We all have a tendency to some degree to run on a mental " autopilot"--—whether you want to call this phenomena "framing", worldview, paradigms, schemas, ideological constructs, etc.--—the precise meaning vary but the effect is to shape our perceptions of the world (highlighting or omitting data) and to an extent predetermine our responses in a large picture sense. Ideologi-

cal blinders concentrate our vision but they distort our view of reality. . . .

> A critical skill is to be able to periodically attempt to step outside one's worldview and look at an event from multiple perspectives other than one's own. You have become a strategic thinker when you know *when* to do this as well as *how*. (Safranski, The expert informed me that my drawing... 2005)

Now it's clear exactly what

> If traditional war centered on an enemy's physical strength, and 4GW on his moral strength, the 5th Generation of War would focus on his intellectual strength.

means. The beautiful sunset city has been found.

2. The Uncaring War

> I don't care if you don't
>
> I don't care if you don't
>
> I don't care if you don't care
>
> ("Jesus of Suburbia," Green Day)

Every other form of modern-warfare requires people to care. The aggressor needs to be able to morally and physically support his military forces for over a period of time-—often a long time. The defender, once he realizes he is being attacked, will care about his own survival and fight back. "Caring" requires explicit thoughts, it requires decisions. The nature of wars where people gave a damn-—of Caring Wars-—was summed up by John Adams centuries ago

What do we mean by the American Revolution? Do we mean the American war? The Revolution was effected before the war commenced. The Revolution was in the minds and hearts of the people; a change in their religious sentiments, of their duties and obligations. . . . ...This radical change in the principles, opinions, sentiments, and affections of the people was the real American Revolution.

Hearts/minds. Duties/sentiments. All based on explicit action. All based on Decisions.

In contrast to "hearts and minds," 5GW focuses on the enemy's "fingertips and gut." "Fingertip feeling," what the Germans called *Fingerspitzengefuhl*, is the ability to know without thinking. This is what Americans call "gut feeling." To a certain extent, it means a commander trusting his intuition. It is critical in 5GW because fingertip feelings, or "hunches," will be the only way for the enemy to sense the fighter.

To rephrase these points, in 5GW:

- The people do not have to want to be on the fighter's side
- Forces the fighter is using do not have to want to be on the fighter's side
- Your enemy must not feel that he is not on your side

In 4th Generation War, the sort of moral wars the world saw with Mao, Ho, and the Sandinistas, political mobilization is critical. In 5th Generation War, if it "tips" off your enemy, political mobilization is worse than useless.

3. Lessons from Software Development

> Do not boast about tomorrow, for you do not know what a day may bring forth.
>
> Stone is heavy and sand a burden, but provocation by a fool is heavier than both.
>
> The prudent see danger and take refuge, but the simple keep going and suffer for it. (King Solomon, Proverbs 27:1, 3, 12)

In 5GW, secrecy is vital for success. While this has always been true on some levels, secrecy has never been vital on the grand-strategic level before 5GW. In 5GW the enemy's knowledge of your existence all but ends your plans.

Mark Safranski writes:

> It occurs to me after reading Dan's post that a very powerful shift of longitudinal perspective takes place. 4GW is executed over a very long time frame, sometimes decades. 5GW is conceived in terms of strategic vision over an even longer time frame, sometimes before an opponent realizes that they will be an opponent but the execution time may be very short in comparison to 4GW. The operative question is probably whether the attacker or the defender has initiated 5GW-—once you are already attacked you have missed your opportunity to shape the battlespace. (Fifth generation war in the OODA loop 2005)

Once I realized what 5GW is, re-reading Mark's words immediately reminded me of a class on Systems Analysis & Design. The crushing Systems Analysis & Design class, called "SAD" by everyone, teaches that to create a system a plan must be created, in analysis of the plan against the current situation must be conducted, a design must be established, and finally the system must be implemented.

PADI: Planning, Analysis, Design, Implementation

Over the years, two different philosophies have surfaced of the best way to design a system-—the most effective way to run through the plan-analysis-design-implementation obstacle course.

Waterfall Development was the first method tried. It takes every step one-after-the-other. Careful and methodical, it looks like a waterfall or perhaps a series of dammed locks, each lower than the last. Because Waterfall Development occurs in a series, it might also be called "serial development."

(A variant of waterfall development, "parallel development," breaks down one large products into several smaller projects, each of which uses their own waterfall model.)

The other major philosophy is "Rapid Application Development," the most famous version of which is "Prototyping." The chief difference between Rapid Application Development Prototyping and Waterfall Development is that RAD allows projects to evolve, changing as new requirements come in. RAD is considered to be much more flexible than Waterfall Development, and has become the industry standard in almost all subfields of software engineering.

Warfare, like software development, is a complex human undertaking involving reconciling a future worth creating with stakeholders. Waterfall's top-down Soviet-style leadership seems most appropriate for older generations of war, while Prototyping's user-centric approach is closer to 4GW and "open source" warfare. So will 5GW be "Waterfall Developed" or "Prototyped"?

What's Wrong with the Pros of Prototyping?

Need a hint?

Prototyping lets the end-users know the project exists. 5GW relies on the users not knowing that the project exists at all.

Prototyping allows for loose, Darwinian networks of projects competing with each other with user-input. For 4GW, this is fantastic. But just as being "fast" is more important than being completely "right" in maneuver war, being secret is more important than being completely "right" in 5GW.

5th Generation Wars will be created with Waterfall Development. We can see what 5GWs will be like by looking at what Waterfall Development is like:

Requirements must be known a long time before fighting begins

Requirements will be rigid and non-adaptable

Long Time between proposal and victory

(Note: Before I put 5GW together with Systems Analysis, I could not see why Mark would say "5GW is conceived in terms of strategic vision over an even longer time frame, sometimes before an opponent realizes that they will be an opponent but the execution time may be very short in comparison to 4GW." It seemed a non-sequitur. My hat off to Mark for seeing this long before I did.)

4. 5th Generation Networks

> My punishment is more than I can bear. Today you are driving me from the land, and I will be hidden from your presence; I will be a restless wanderer on the earth, and whoever finds me will kill me. (Cain, Genesis 4:13-14)

The nature of the networks that hold together a 5th Generation military is predetermined by that network's need for secrecy and need for serial development. We know

- A 5GW army will be unable to recruit to any sizable degree.
- A 5GW will be very unable to recruit during operations (development), because that is when the danger is the greatest.
- A 5GW will rely on strategic corporals or sheiks, who are superempowered.
- A 5GW will rely on "sleeper cells" who must not give up, get bored, or switched sides.

From this we know every 5G warrior will be valuable to the 5G militia. Likewise, to succeed every 5EG warrior must value the 5G project.

In other words, a fifth generation war is a lot like a struggling software project at a cash-strapped corporation. It needs to keep its head down, or it will be found out and terminated. The solution is to have a collection of cross-specialist high-quality workers who know each other and make every worker a stakeholder-—that is, make every worker-—feel that at least some important decisions were his decision. The team is able to subvert the corporate system, diverting resources for the benefits of the project under the radar of jealous management.

The team plans, analyzes, and plans together. While there should be a "leader," consensus management is a must. Every team member is constantly reminded, in words and deeds, how important he is. Team and project loyalty are established, and by the time jealous management learns of the project-—after implementation-—it is too late.

While there are no running starts in 4GW, every 5GW must be fully-operational by the time it is launched.

5. A Boydian Approach to 5GW

> If there's anything you know
>
> Please send me a letter
>
> PS: Kiss my ass
>
> ("Dick Is a Killer," Rx)

5GW is substantively different from all previous forms of Modern War. Yet it is a natural evolution of warfare and the basic Art of War remains the same. And specifically, the lessons of Colonel Boyd's *Patterns of Conflict* hold even in 5GW, where only one side knows it is fighting.

> Idea of fast transients suggests that, in order to win, we should operate at a faster tempo or rhythm than our adversaries—or, better yet, get inside adversary's observation-orientation-decision-action time cycle or loop.

Commentary: Or best yet, arrange the enemy's OODA loop, so his thoughts never flow into the orient-decide-act power-line relative to you, your plan, or your organization.

> Diminish adversary's capacity for independent action, or deny him the opportunity to survive on his own terms, or make it impossible for him to survive at all.

Commentary: In limited 5GWs, removing the enemy's "capacity for independent action" is the goal. Specifically, the fighter tries to entangle the enemy into a web of obligations that effectively reharmonize the enemy, without the enemy knowing that he has "conditionally surrendered."

> Fire and movement are used in combination, like cheng/ch'i or Nebenpunkte/Schwerpunkt, to tie-up, divert, or drain-away adversary attention and strength in order to expose as well as menace and exploit vulnerabilities or weaknesses elsewhere.

Commentary: In a successful 5GW, the enemy's attention won't so much need to be "diverted" away from a focus but "misdirected" from ever attaining that focus.

> Create tangles of threatening and/or non-threatening events/efforts as well as repeatedly generate mismatches between those events/efforts adversary observes or imagines (cheng/Nebenpunkte) and those he must react to (ch'i/Schwerpunkt)

Commentary: In a successful 5GW, the events the enemy "must" react to are an "unknown unknown." The enemy doesn't know what they are, and doesn't even know that he needs to know what they are.

195

6. A Dream of 5GW

> We'll run away, keep everything simple
>
> Night will come down, our guardian angel
>
> We rush ahead, the crossroads are empty
>
> Our spirits rise, they're not gonna get us
>
> …
>
> They don't understand,
>
> They don't understand us
>
> ("Not Going to Get Us," Tatu)

This brings me back to my original question: what would a 5GW look like? Once I understood the organization, developmental, doctrinal, and other aspects of 5th Generation War, picturing one in operation was trivial.

For example, consider a hypothetical scenario. A small, close-knit, highly-able team of Nativists wishes to militarize the Southwest border of the United States against Mexican migrants. Unable to handle the "content flow" of Latin culture and people, the Nativists believe they have exhausted attempts at political satisfaction. Therefore, they try politics by other means: war. Their aim is limited: the subversion of the government of the United States of America into closing the Southern border. (The aim of the Persian Gulf War coalition was similar: subvert the government of Iraq into closing the Iraq-Kuwait border against military and governmental Iraqi content flow.)

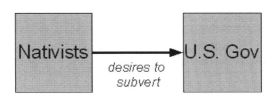

Figure 12. Logical View of Nativist-USG Struggle

The Nativists seek an economy of force. They realize they are weak--—perhaps only a few dozen highly-able members. They also realize it would be trivial for the FBI or even local police to round them up if their "treason" was discovered. Therefore they look to see what other forces they can leverage.

A big possibility stands out: the Global War on Terrorism. The USG is at war with Al Qaeda, with Arab Muslims supporting both entities to different extents in different ways.

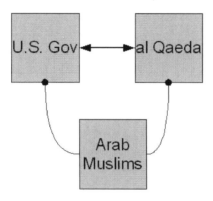

Figure 13. The Found Environment: The Global War on Terrorism

Which of course means:

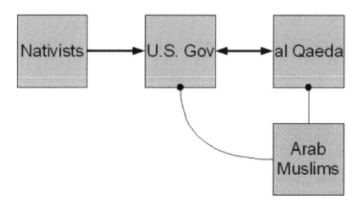

The two conflicts, seen together

The Nativists now create two shadow organizations: Islamophiles and Islamaphobes. These are more than false-flag organizations, because the shadow organizations will honestly strive to achieve their stated goals. However, the success of the shadow organizations is irrelevant to the success of the Nativists. Both the Islamophiles and Islamophobes publicly support the United States Government, and assist the USG in some ways. However, the leadership of both shadow-groups is part of the Nativist network.

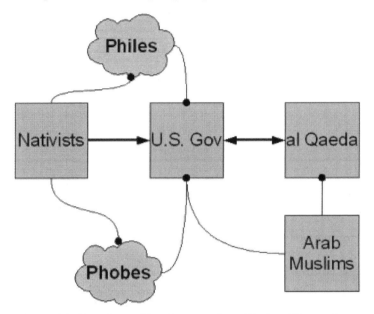

Figure 14. First Step of Implementation: Shadow Networks Created

Next, the shadow networks begin engaging in paramilitary operations. However, neither shadow network directly attacks the US Government, and both continue supporting the Government as they are able. The purpose of the Islamophobes is to provoke and antagonize the Arab Muslim population. Publicly, the Islamophobes agitate for the removal or internment of the Arab Muslim population. On a street level, the Phobes align with anti-Arab-

Muslim street gangs, escalating to political assassination of Arab-Muslims moderates and "outrage" attacks (bombing of deserted mosques, etc). The purpose is to disrupt peaceful Arab Muslim networks.

Simultaneously, the Islamophiles work to defend the civil rights of Arab Muslims, paying special communication attention to maintaining liberal communication networks between American and international Arab Muslims. The Philes will work to create Arab-Muslim "self-defense" networks, which will have the natural consequence of increasing the militancy of the Arab Muslim population. Most critically, the Philes will strive to make physical communication with the Arab world as easy as possible ("charity" smuggling networks, with a complementary political effort). The purpose is to prevent disruption of internationally-originating terrorist attacks.

The Philes and Phobes will engage in "phony" attacks on each other, as well.

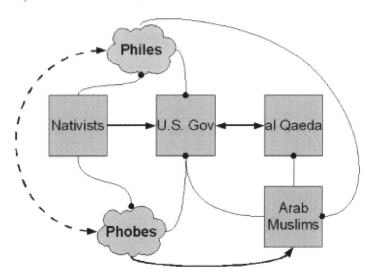

Figure 15. The Frictional Sea of Conflict

Then, bam, a spectacular terrorist attack.

The details of the attack, and the particulars of its effects, don't concern us. Nor does the fate of the American Arab population (interned? expelled? integrated?). But a natural consequence of such an attack will be an increase in border security. There already is strong agitation among working-class whites for "border crackdown." For now, the cries are too weak to move a Government committed to North American integration.

But a few more 9/11s would change Washington's mind.

And all of the 9/11s would happen without the Government understanding there was a thinking force supporting the attacks that had no concern whatsoever for bin Ladenism

So a natural consequence of the US Government's escalating war against Al Qaeda will be much tighter control of immigration and the Mexican border, including either National Guardsmen or Soldiers on watch. The 5th Generation Warriors have won.

The militant Nativist network is now abandoned as obsolete: the government has been subverted. The shadow networks are abandoned, allowed to run their course as passions dictate. The war against Al Qaeda goes on, but it would have continued anyway.

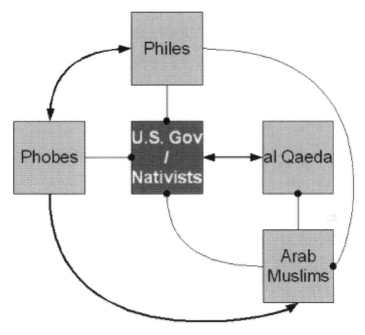

Figure 16. What Victory Looks Like

For the price of a few thousand lives, the 5th Generation Warriors have won without their enemy--—the American Government-—ever realizing that it was in a war against them.

There are even purer forms of 5GW. But such is a post for another time. . . .

201

KILCULLEN ON NARRATIVES IN IRAQ (CURTIS GALE WEEKS)

Originally published May 30, 2007, at:

http://www.dreaming5gw.com/2007/05/kilcullen_on_narratives_in_ira.php

Bay (2007) quotes Kilcullen: (Anatomy of a tribal revolt 2007):

- US forces' primary contribution is not delivering a message but creating safe space where Iraqis can deliver the message.
- The single narrative the US has pursued is that as they (Iraqis) stand up, we stand down. That message is not particularly comforting to Iraqis. The single big message (the Iraqi government and coalition are sending) now is that we are protecting the population and trying to achieve sustainable stability. We are improving security and doing it to create a sustainable space so Iraqis can do it themselves.

Neither strikes me as 5GW-effective.

From a 5GW-oriented view, "creating safe space" would be a message. Shaping the environment is how memes are nudged into emergence; certainly, controlling space would be a very strong message, or have great influence over the types of memes likely to emerge.

What does #1 mean to everyone but the US?

We have a disconnect lurking behind #1. The disconnect is the separation of the concrete from the abstract.

The US forces want Iraqis to "see" that it's safe to come out in the open and interact as free citizens; the US forces want Iraqis to "see" that they can act, themselves, to make a better Iraq; the US forces want Iraqi leaders to propagate such messages of security and all other messages addressing the potential for a better Iraq. These are largely abstract so-called messages, considered in isolation from the concrete reality. They are dreams, phantasmagorias.

The Iraqis "see" any pockets of safety as contingent upon the US presence. They "see" the US presence and the US contribution. If the US clears an area, with help from Iraqi forces, Iraqis "see" the US doing so. Even if the US "stays the course" and Iraqi state forces succeed in achieving competence and efficacy with long-term help from the US, delivering stability, Iraqis will still see the role the US has played in shaping Iraq.

In 5GW terms, we might say that this is not "gaining hands in the field" but is instead creating and maintaining a field we can harvest or shape with our own hands.

In 5GW terms, we are telling the Iraqi leaders to be our proxies. Openly. That's in #2. We are also telling the Iraqi citizenry——whether peace-desiring or rabid anti-American or fence-sitting Iraqis——the same thing. We want a stable, peaceful, relatively democratic Iraq that is friendly to the US, and we will stay until Iraqi leaders and the general Iraqi polity create this for us.

We have the control; and once we've displayed that control, Iraqis will be able to do whatever they want, as long as they don't upset that cherished paradigm.

We should either annex Iraq, or we should leave it. (The second choice is not even an option, really, although a 5GW presence and approach could make it appear a reality.)

THE TERMINOLOGY OF xGW (DANIEL H. ABBOTT)

Originally published May 27, 2008, at:

http://www.tdaxp.com/archive/2008/05/27/the-terminology-of-xgw.html

The clean break of xGW from GMW has is amazing. Not only does it represent the greatest advance since the first descriptions of 5GW, it's simply liberating to no longer carry the water for those more interested in Idealism than in advancing our understanding of war.

Today, I've come across a number of thought-provoking articles in Arms and Influence, Castle Arg, Dreaming 5GW, Simulated Laughter, and Soob. They made me think of xGW in terms of the words we use. In particular, two suggestions came to me.

1. The Term "Generation" Must Be Abandoned.

Just as the abandonment of GMW (The Generations of Modern War) is a critical step in the evolution of xGW theory, the abandonment of "Generation" is the next step. Consider the many criticisms of "4GW" available on the Web. Previously, proponents of xGW had to argue against these criticism, and assert that the critics did not really understand 4GW. Now, proponents can agree with the criticism, generalize them to criticism of GMW, and present xGW as an alternative.

I propose Grade, thus making xGW X Grade War Theory. The first four definitions of "grade" are:

- A stage or degree in a process.
- A position in a scale of size, quality, or intensity: a poor grade of lumber.
- An accepted level or standard.A set of persons or things all falling in the same specified limits; a class. (Answers.com n.d.)

These fit how G is used in xGW theory.

Grade also has the benefit of not having the strict timeline implications of "generation" while not doing away entirely with the parts of the timeline of xGW that make sense.

This leaves open the question of whether Roman or Arabic numerals should be used. That is, whether "4th Grade War," "Grade 4 War," "IVth Grade War," or "Grade IV War" is clearer as to what it implies.

2. The "Stages of 4GW" Must Be Abandoned

4GWS1, 4GWS2, and 4GWS3 properly refer to only one form of 4GW, the Maoist model, and so exclude any form of 4GW that is not Maoist. Boyd's PISRR-Loop is both more precise and more general. I've mapped the 3 Stages onto PISRR before, but that earlier work is limited. Instead of S1, we should clarify whether we are talking about Penetration and Isolation. Instead of Stage 3, we should be precise if we meant Reorientation or Reharmonization, and so on.

3. In Conclusion

Consider one of the final actions in winning a 4GW. In GMW, this would properly be referred to as: "The Third Stage of the 4th Generation of Modern War" (long form) or "4GWS3" (short form). I propose instead: "4GW Reharmonization."

WORKING DEFINITION V. 2.3 (ADAM HERRING)

Originally published January 12, 2007, at:

http://dreaming5gw.com/2007/01/working_definition_v_23.php

Fifth Generation Warfare (5GW): An emergent theory of warfare premised upon manipulation of multiple economic, political, social and military forces in multiple domains to effect positional changes in systems and achieve a consilience of effects to leverage a specific goal or set of circumstances (Arherring 1/12/07).

And a bonus definition.

Consilient effect: a "jumping together" of effects by the linking of effects across domains in order to create a pattern for action.

ON THE BARNETTIAN 5GW (CURTIS GALE WEEKS)

Originally published June 10, 2007, at:

http://dreaming5gw.com/2007/06/on_the_barnettian_5gw.php

I'm bumping up a comment I left in another thread:

> And this is where 5GW on a grand scale may diverge from the current Robb/Hammes approach, which emphasizes one superempowered individual as opposed to generating empowerment across an entire society. (Steve 2007)

I responded as follows:

> Yes. I once included a consideration of the two types of superempowerment when contrasting Barnett with Robb. It would seem that Barnett's approach (which we at D5GW have often labeled "5GWish") requires the general superempowerment of individuals across the spectrum, as an antidote to the Robbian one-man-killing-crew. With regard to some recent considerations on the idea of kinetics, this means creating more routes for the channeling of powers, not only as a distracting maneuver ("jobs" vs "guns") but also as a method of equalizing the kinetics across the system, or forcing kinetics into indirection. It is a kind of perpetual, systemic, mass deflection. (Weeks, Steve 2007)

Superempowerment

The post I linked in that comment (Weeks, Global Guerillas as 5GW Warriors 2006) included 5 keys I used for unlocking the door to the future of *Global Guerrillas* (Robb, THE CHANGING FACE OF WAR: Into the 5th Generation (5GW) 2006). One of those keys: Superempowerment of the Individual.

There is a term used variously and vaguely in these discussions; I myself conflated two interpretations of the term. The Robbian view seems to depend on unequal distribution of *powerment*, in which some individuals or groups become more powerful than the general human population; whereas, at heart the Core/Gap para-

207

digm (Barnett, The Pentagon's new map: War and peace in the 21st century 2004) and strategy seem to depend upon an eventual equalization, or a relative equalization (which is a type of oxymoronic phrase), of individual empowerment across the globe. Nonetheless, in my characterization of the two ideas in the older post, I conflated these concepts of empowerment under one heading: superempowerment. One supposes a kind of monopoly on greater powers; the other, a general but increased power for each and all.

The term and the old conflation remind me of the kid superhero Dash (Bird 2004). On the way home after being sent to the principal's office, Dash complains that he is never able to use his natural powers. Dash's mom tries to explain how everyone is special in some way, not just those with superhuman powers, to which, Dash responds that, if everyone is special then no one is. (This startling intellection was a pleasant surprise early in the movie, followed by others later.) Should superempowerment also follow such a rule? In fact, upon infecting the human mind, the idea of superempowerment seems to follow that rule; so we see actors on the global stage trying to be special. Can the rule be broken?

We also see a split in types of empowerment, between the Barnettian and the Robbian paradigms. If superempowerment is to be conflated:

The Robbian view of superempowerment hinges upon the ability to cause concrete damages via technology-—whatever the level of technology. The Barnettian view of the term would assume an economic empowerment via which those in the Gap are first brought up to the level of individual economic empowerment seen in the Core, and then all upon the globe continue to experience an increase in economic empowerment. For the Barnettian view, we should not equate *economic empowerment* only with the size of the personal bank account, but with the ability to secure resources, or

208

personal property, necessary for individual happiness or at least contentment.

Also, if we conflate these superempowerments, we should make the distinction which then arises concerning the prefix *super-*. In John Robb's world, the prefix stands for present inequalities among individuals and groups, but in Thomas Barnett's strategic vision, the term would need to be understood as designating an inequality between the past and present/future. In the Robbian world, some people are already super in relation to others currently existing; indeed, in the future he sees, this disparity would also continue and even increase. In the Barnettian vision, the present or, more likely the future peoples will be super in relation to those living in the past (their own past selves or their ancestors or both).

I know that Thomas Barnett is aware of the term superempowerment, and that, as with most who discuss these things, he tends to use it in the sense John Robb would give the term. But I'm playing with the term.

Barnettism vs. Robbism

From being a bystander in the various Robb vs. Barnett debates (not only between the two principal actors, but also between their supporters and even between the subjects they study when forming their theories), I have developed the sense that the Robbian view is dichotomous and vaguely Manichean. If the Barnettian globalization proceeds and everyone is made special, no one will be special; if the Barnettian globalization ever settles over the world, then the general equalization of means must translate into extraordinary weakening for all individuals. The two theorists aside, this either/or style of viewing is probably what motivates the putative Global Guerrillas and other anti-globalists to act.

My own criticisms of GG theory and Robb (Brave New War: The Next Stage of Terrorism and the End of Globalization 2007)—

-one of which both Armstrong (Book Review: Brave New War 2007) and Abbott (Brave New War, Aftermath: Mountainrunner's Review 2007) have recently highlighted--—hinge upon the utter insolvency of the dichotomy which stands like an overstuffed though unobserved elephant in the center of that room. To the degree that these anti-globalists seek to become special, they must more and more resemble the nation-states who have already achieved that feat. Put another way: as they try to develop their own monopolies on power in response to the perception that a general deflection of kinetic powers will weaken them, they will be creating exactly the same sort of structures they would weaken! Inequalities and disparities galore. A house divided.

I have not forgotten the title of this post. In a previous cursory examination of divergent theories of 5GW (Weeks, Empires of the Mind 2007), I noted that Barnett seems to have a theory much like that theory often propounded here on D5GW, but that his vision assumes that nation-states and corporations can initiate the 5GW--—and do so openly. This approach is characterized as being top-down by the Robbian crew, occasionally derided as such. Given many of the preceding paragraphs, I wonder if the Robbian crew is correct.

The Barnettian Paradox

Steve, in commenting on the thread about Iraq, put forth the paradox:

> WRT Iraq, yes, our specter prevents Iraqis from as-suming responsibility. It is an ironic paradox of state/nation building that cannot be avoided: how do we get indigenous groups to act on their own when we try to do everything for them? It is this transition that we still cannot manage, maybe because we have yet to find pols on the ground who have the resources to act inde-pendently. (Steve 2007)

—to which, I responded:

This consideration is itself paradoxical. I.e., our foes are the "pols on the ground" who seem quite capable of finding the resources to act independently of us. (Weeks, Steve 2007)

This is the Barnettian paradox: To the degree that nation-states and corporations continue to exercise conglomerate powers when initiating conflict, they will be the special ones. The ideal equalization cannot occur globally, and even the oxymoronic relative equalization cannot occur. So long as small groups or indeed individuals remain at the head of nation-states and corporations, those individuals will always wield greater powers with respect to everyone else within the system---they are the *super*empowered actors. (Albeit, given the distinction I have already drawn, their power may be economic more than anything else if Barnett's vision comes to fruition.)

Even despite the fact that Barnett's *super*empowered actors are few but actual, the impression that they exist in the first place creates cognitive conflict. We see the distinct case in Iraq and with the go-it-alone nation-state; but we may also infer this cognitive conflict in the growing distrust for some corporations, such as those in the military-industrial complex, pharmaceutical companies, insurance companies (viz. Katrina), and the oil industry. (For an American Rightist list, just substitute the MSM and Hollywood.)

The resolution to the Barnettian paradox is not something Barnett himself has offered: a true 5GW approach. Although he speaks in the language of co-optation, he uses the term when addressing international relations; e.g., that Iran can be co-opted. Barnett does not descend to the street level although he does support improving the lives of the persons on the street; he has yet to formulate a clear plan for co-opting the many individuals of which nations and corporations are comprised. For the most part, he seems to assume that nation-states and corporations, if they only do the right things, will be received as benevolent dictators----or, scratch that term, as benevolent *super*empowered entities.

He may be half right. Many people seek saviors of one sort or another; many are happy to delegate responsibility for the things they themselves cannot touch or do not have the time or motivation to fix themselves----or do not understand, themselves. The crux of the Barnettian paradox involves the manner and method of assigning these delegations so that the general man-on-the-street can rest easily knowing his prosperous future is assured. Even within the Core, much doubt about this process of delegation exists; various superempowerments within and without the Core threaten to upset faith in the systems of the Core.

For his theory of 5GW, Barnett needs to reduce the footprint of his preferred *super*empowered entities, and this will require a re-think about how they operate----in fact, perhaps also about who they are.

WORKING DEFINITION .91 [UPDATE] (PURPLES SLOG)

Originally published April 17, 2008, at:

http://purpleslog.wordpress.com/2008/04/17/purpleslog%E2%8 0%99s-5gw-working-definition-091/

Here is a minor update to my working description of Fifth Generation Warfare (5GW):

> 5GW is the secret deliberative manipulation of actors, networks, institutions, states or any 2GW/3GW/4GW forces to achieve a goal or set of goals across a combination of socio, economic, and political domains while attempting to avoid or minimize the retaliatory offensive or defensive actions/reactions of 2GW, 3GW and 4GW powered actors, networks, institutions, and/or states.

I just made a point of adding "institution" (per this idea) to my older definition.

[Cross-posted to Dreaming 5GW]

Update: A slight change:

> 5GW is the secret deliberative manipulation of actors, networks, institutions, states or any 0GW/1GW/2GW/3GW/4GW forces to achieve a goal or set of goals across a combination of socio, economic, and political domains while attempting to avoid or minimize the retaliatory offensive or defensive actions/reactions of 0GW/1GW/2GW/3GW/4GW powered actors, networks, institutions, and/or states.

TOWARDS A GENERAL XGW FRAMEWORK (FRANCIS EDWARD YOUNGHUSBAND)

Originally published January 6, 2009, at:

http://cominganarchy.com/2009/01/06/towardss-a-general-xgw-framework/

xGW theory has been under scrutiny in the Twitterverse, and by the usual suspects. Although xGW theory has seemed to progress in the past few years it is still a solution for a problem that we cannot seem to figure out. I have even asked, what use is xGW?

Selil offers his drawing skills to find a unified generational warfare theorem (Liles 2009). His visualizations are very inspiring-——so, in fact, that they motivated me to think about my own diagrammatical solution to the xGW problem.

Liles (2009) raises the usual problem with generational warfare theory: chronology. Abbott (The Terminology of xGW 2009) addressed this by suggesting the "G" from xGW be revised from "generation" to "grade" to deemphasize the dependence on time. I suggested returning to Boyd's original categories that served as the basis of 4GW theory and are time independent. However, that precludes any relationship between the different grades of warfare. That is a core problem of xGW: what is the relationship between the various grades (if a relationship exists at all)? It seems to me that Liles is trying to solve this problem with his pretty pictures. I also have tried to capture this problem in a series of diagrams I present to you below. Be forewarned: these diagrams represent the problem with xGW theory, not the solution. They may be a step towards the framework that makes xGW useful, a goal that Liles and I-——among others-——find worthy.

My hypothetical diagrammatical framework aims to help us think not only about what direction we should take the debate, but also the types of insights such a framework could offer. This hypothetical framework is centered upon relationships, specifically the overlaps between the various grades of warfare. Below I will present a number of examples. I offer no real-world examples to warrant my selections of the categories, and there are numerous unstated assumptions in the models. This is purely an intellectual exercise meant to engender more discussion.

Example 1: take grades 1 through 4 and assume they have an equal and overlapping relationship. The result reveals four (a, b, c, d) transitional types of war. Question: could the variously defined 5GW be found in one of these areas, or should it get its own circle?

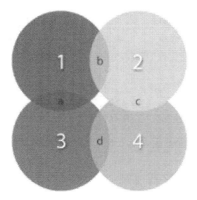

Example 2 shows a much tighter Venn diagram resulting in a much more complex set of relationships: beta, mu, omega, delta and the elusive apeiron, the singularity of conflict.

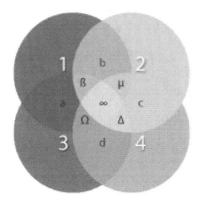

Assuming one could devise a set of stringent rules of demarcation, data could be gathered about specific conflicts, diagrammed and compared. Diagrams could be analyzed for patterns useful in decision-making.

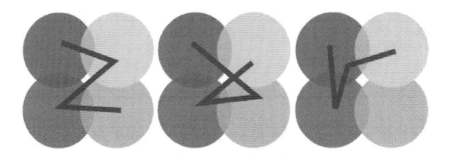

Example 3 uses Boydian categories of conflict (Attrition Warfare, Maneuver Conflict, Moral Conflict) rather than the 1 to 4 generations in fashion recently. Here we have four sub-categories of conflict: beta, mu, delta and infinity.

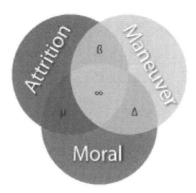

To add another layer of complexity, we could include the spectrum of conflict---from high intensity conflict (HIC) to low intensity conflict (LIC). Each of the grade circles could be gradients of the spectrum (from dark to light). In the example below the darker shades would represent HIC while lighter shades represent LIC.

This hypothetical diagram would cause us to ask the question: Are the overlapping "sub"-grades of conflict compatible with HIC? It seems only the three major types of conflict reach to the outer boundaries. That would be an interesting insight.

All said and done, this is simply speculative blue-sky engineering to get people to think about the relationships between the various grades of war. A general (and unified) framework is still needed to guide discussion of xGW, even if a use for it has yet to be discovered.

FURTHER READING

While the emergence of the xGW framework has been the most significant contribution of the 5GW literature over the past years, this framework emerged only in the context of the broader literature, whether 5GW-oriented or not. Therefore, two final resources are now presented. First, Curtis Gale Weeks's 5GW Theory Timeline is reproduced in text form. While the associated web site provides greater depth and metadata that will be of interest to historians of 5GW, the version that follows complements the Source Documents of the proceeding section. Finally, a comprehensive reference list of this volume is included. This reference list captures the universe of discourse that has encouraged the emergence of the xGW framework, and can be a guide for analysts who wish to build a library relevant for understanding 5GW and the xGW framework.

THE 5GW TIMELINE (CURTIS GALE WEEKS)

August 29, 2003: An apparent press release from OSS.net, through PRNewswire, in Windows .doc format, detailing need for fifth-generation tactics to create "the necessary new national security paradigm," as described by Robert David Steele (Steele 2003).

February 3, 2004: William S. Lind, coauthor of "The Changing Face of War: Into the Fourth Generation," which for the first time modeled modern warfare as a generational framework, and generally considered the "father" of the generational model, answers building speculation of a budding fifth generation style of warfare. In other words, the fourth generation of warfare has yet to fully materialize (or: has not been fully visualized, itself) (Lind, On War #53: Fifth Generation Warfare? 2004).

September 12, 2004: *The Sling and the Stone* book, which primarily considers 4GW, mentions 5GW briefly in three places near the end (Hammes 2004):

- First, by stating that innovative leadership training will be required "not just to deal with the seventy-year-old phenomenon of 4GW but also to deal with 5GW as it evolves" (pp. 274-275, paperback edition).
- "Only a highly flexible organization can hope to succeed in 4GW and still be prepared to deal with emerging 5GW," and "We can continue to man 3GW organizations using an 1890s personnel system. . . .Or we can accept that 4GW has arrived and that 5GW is evolving and organize ourselves accordingly" (p. 289, paperback edition).
- "Fourth-generation war has been around for more than seventy years; no doubt the fifth generation is evolving even as we attempt to deal with its predecessor. We may not recognize it as it evolves around us. Or we may look at several alternative futures and see each as fifth-generation war." The bio-attacks on Capitol Hill—anthrax in 2001in 2001 and ri-

cin in 2004in 2004-—are considered a precursor of 5GW;
Hammes emphasizes the superempowered destructive individual or small group as a viable, perhaps defining aspect of
5GW. He then reiterates his belief that the US should reor-
ganize its military and societal capability for dealing with
4GW forces and 5GW forces that may evolve-—but does
not suggest that America should develop 5GW force structures itself. I.e., 4GW and 5GW will characterize the opponent, not the US (pp. 290-291, paperback edition; last two
pages of the book).

July 17, 2005: Early and detailed consideration of aspects
which might constitute fifth generation warfare, beginning with
concepts of 4GW and building from there (Safranski, Unto the fifth
generation of war 2009).

Key trends mentioned:

- Superempowerment
- Fluidity
- Multidimensional Battlespace
- Autonomous Surrogates

Key technologies and sciences mentioned:

- Artificial Intelligence
- Genomics
- Alternative Fuels
- Quantum Computing
- Human Brain Research
- Complexity and Chaos Theory
- Nanotechnology
- String Theory

In addition, the concept of "driving deeper" is specifically
noted:

An alternative conceptualization of potential fifth generation warfare is suggested with an early reference to Thomas P. M. Barnett's "'System Administration' based Global Transaction Strategy" as a type of 5GW (Barnett, The Pentagon's new map: War and peace in the 21st century 2004).

Colonel Thomas X. Hammes's *The Sling and the Stone* is also quoted (Hammes 2004).

July 18, 2005: Building off Safranski (Unto the fifth generation of war 2009)---—"successive generations of warfare tend to drive 'deeper' into enemy territory"---—Abbott utilizes Boyd's OODA loop to show how the fifth generation of warfare "goes deeper" into the enemy's OODA cycle (Orientation and action, part I: The OODA Loop 2009).

First strong mapping of the xGW framework onto the OODA cycle.

Originally titled, "Go Deep: OODA and the Rainbow of General Warfare."

July 19, 2005: Mark Safranski (Fifth generation war in the OODA loop 2005) responds to Abbott (Orientation and action, part I: The OODA Loop 2009) of the "deeper" aspects of each succeeding generation of warfare vis-à-vis John Boyd's OODA Loop.

Whereas Mark Safranski had earlier conceived of a shift in battlespace deeper into enemy territory (Unto the fifth generation of war 2009), he now concedes that consideration of a shift in perspectives and the decision making process that is "deeper" for each succeeding generation of warfare fits the xGW framework very well.

Mark Safranski also ponders the distinct time frames associated with 4GW and, possibly, 5GW.

July 19, 2005: Early note of discussion of 5GW theory which links to Safranski (Unto the fifth generation of war 2009), Abbott (Orientation and action, part I: The OODA Loop 2009), and Safranski (Fifth generation war in the OODA loop 2005) (Younghusband, 5GW 2005).

July 20, 2005: A look at the book *Unrestricted Warfare*, which also references the blog tdaxp and links (Younghusband, 5GW 2005), which had recently noted discussion of 5GW theory at tdaxp and the blog ZenPundit (Weeks, Boot on Unrestricted Warfare 2005).

July 20, 2005: A follow-up to an earlier post which extends consideration of the "deeper" aspects of fifth generation warfare as it relates to John Boyd's OODA Loop (Safranski, The John Boyd roundtable: Debating science, strategy, and war 2008). (Abbott, Dreaming 5th generation war 2009).

A reiteration of earlier points argued—

- "5th Generation of War would focus on [the enemy's] intellectual strength."
- "a brilliantly executed 5GW might involve one side being completely ignorant that there ever was a war."

—and an exploration of them in multiple parts:

- The Uncaring War: contemplates *Fingerspitzengefuhl*, or "fingertip feeling", or a greater emphasis on the implicit (but perhaps unconscious/subconscious) than on the explicit (feelings, rational thought, morality).
- Lessons from Software Development: secrecy will require advance and precise planning; software development may provide a key for 5GW methodology: The waterfall development vs. prototyping. Conclusion: "5th Generation Wars will be created with Waterfall Development" which enables great secrecy.

- 5th Generation Networks: envisions a nonhierarchical teamwork approach to conducting 5GW; each member is equally valued by the group and equally committed to the project.
- A Boydian Approach to 5GW: on co-opting the enemy (but not phrased as such) by manipulating the enemy's OODA process so that he becomes "entangled" without being aware of what entangles him.
- A Dream of 5GW: An example of a theoretical fifth generation war is given, through the lens of a particular "Border War" involving "a highly -able team of Nativists [that] wishes to militarize the Southwest border of the United States against Mexican migrants." Two proxy groups are created by the Nativists, here called "Islamaphobes" and "Islamo-philes," which honestly believe in, and fight for, their individual causes; but the tension they create is merely a prelude to another major Islamic terrorist attack on the US, which causes the US to clamp down on all immigration. The purpose of creating the -phobes and the -philes is merely to ratchet up debate before all debate is summarily closed in a manner that also helps out the anti-Mexican-immigrants goal of the Nativist 5GW organization; and said organization is the only organization that knows exactly what has occurred.

This blog post also contains an early mention of Peter Wiggin, the brother of Ender Wiggin from (Card, Ender's Game 1985) (Card, Shadow of the Hegemon 2001).

July 21, 2005: Weeks (Interesting, Dan 2005) comments on Abbott (Dreaming 5th generation war 2009):

The comment ponders "a scenario in which multiple, seemingly unrelated events hurt one nation (or a group of nations) repeatedly, as if 'the hand of God' were behind those events" as an example of fifth generation war unfolding.

July 22, 2005: A look at how shareholder activism may be one method by which a 5GW organization can operate secretly (although said activism may also be used for 4GW) which concludes with two points (Abbott, Emerging NetWar / SecretWar Tactic: Stealth Shareholder Activism 2005). The point is also made that [shareholder activist] 5GW fighters need not influence all members of a target population but only need influence the most powerful within that population or those members of the population who are in a position to institute policy changes.

July 23, 2005: This post uses John Boyd's OODA loop to stress the importance of secrecy in fifth generation warfare efforts (Abbott, SecretWarriors Walk Without Rhythm, Won't Attract the Worm 2003). Abbott also quotes a comment left on an earlier post at tdaxp by Curtis Gale Weeks and concludes that Secret Warriors [5GWarriors] must "walk without rhythm" to avoid detection.

July 23, 2005: Among other things, Weeks's blog post (Blog Notice 2005) contemplates the changing world and whether pre-5GW styles of fighting will quickly grow cost-ineffective.

July 25, 2005: A link fest linking to many more items than can be displayed below (Safranski, 5GW Reloaded: Reflecting on 5th Generation War 2005).

Mark Safranski ponders two ideas introduced by Abbott, that 5GW will target an enemy's intellectual strength (Orientation and action, part I: The OODA Loop 2009), and that secrecy will be key in fifth generation warfare (Emerging NetWar / SecretWar Tactic: Stealth Shareholder Activism 2005).

General approval is given to these ideas for describing what is likely for fifth generation warfare, with the caveat that those two aspects of 5GW "may end up [to] be less significant than aspects of 5GW that have yet to materialize." Mark Safranski links the scope of societal changes with the advancement to 5GW in the xGW model while implying that exact predictions of what these societal changes will be are difficult to make. Indeed, future societal changes "may favor defense over offense."

Additionally, fifth generation warriors may in fact implement their changes "from above" but not as a result of revolution; rather, "by moving up through legitimate channels to implement an invisible evolution from above."

July 25, 2005: The metaphor of a "Plain Jain" who tries to kill a Yakuza Boss is utilized to argue that "randomness is very attractive" and would severely reduce the secrecy of a 5GW operation (Abbott, SecretWar: Plain Jane Tries to Kill the Yakuza Boss 2005).

I.e., where previously Abbott (SecretWarriors Walk Without Rhythm, Won't Attract the Worm 2003) argued that "walking without rhythm"--—or, with randomness-—would serve to obscure the 5GW attack, the argument is now made that the assassin (in this metaphor) would present a rhythm that is "normal" and entirely expected; she must shape the enemy's observations by presenting normalcy.

The argument is applied to a comment previously left (Weeks, Interesting, Dan 2005) concerning a succession of random events utilized to attack a nation or group of nations, with the conclusion that such a method of operation would be bad for a fifth generation warrior.

July 26, 2005: Phil's (If 5GW takes aim... 2005) guest post at the blog *tdaxp* which examines two points recently offered by two other bloggers-—

- that 5GW is a war on the enemy's "intellectual strength"
- that 5GW will go "deeper" into a target's society

----and combines them in a consideration of who, exactly, may be the fifth generation warriors. The 5GWers may in fact be citizens of the targeted population who desire that country's defeat or at least can be persuaded to act in a way that leads to that country's defeat. The thumbnail sketches are given in terms of 4GW.

The point is also made that states will have virtually no role in such warfare, since the warfare is intellectual in nature; furthermore, an early mention is made of defense against 5GW requiring the development of 5GW tactics by the defender.

July 26, 2005: A post dissecting what kind of activity the 5GWarrior would utilize. Specifically, a consideration of "rhythm" and "randomness" leads to a questioning of the secrecy aspect assumed to exist in fifth generation warfare, via a metaphor Dan tdaxp had already utilized: The female assassin that targets a Yakuza boss (Weeks, 5GW Effectors 2005):

- The Yakuza boss, when killed, would no longer appear to be alive. That is, if an action occurs, its effects are always observable, even if we don't happen to see the action itself.
- What kind of effects will a 5GW warrior desire? What kind of activity will the 5GW warrior attempt in order to obtain the results desired? Specifically, why would a 5GW warrior engage in activity the results of which are entirely unobservable; would such results truly be results, if they do not produce cascading effects or a changed reality?
- If results are observable, to what degree can the "secret" in terms such Secret War and Secret Warrior obtain or persist?

These questions lead to two alternative unfoldings for fifth generation warfare:

- Crossing the Rubicon: in which the effects caused by the fifth generation attacker may be clearly seen, but even if they are ultimately connected by the target to some enemy and understood to be a concerted effort to defeat the target, the target has already been influenced to "cross the Rubicon," unable to avoid the remaining negative effects of the fifth generation attack: "A successful 5GW will leave the target on a downward spiral into insignificance. The target's knowing it has been a victim won't save the target from the spiral."

- The Secret Warrior as Benefactor most influential members of a society able to operate with no or very limited negative suspicion are those who can promise the most benefit to that society; and, a society which believes it is moving toward a brighter future may also "cross the Rubicon"—but without realizing that the achievements it has made are in fact much less than what it might have achieved had the 5GW not occurred. Such a society might be quite happy and content with its future prospects, never even knowing that a fifth generation war had targeted them and limited them.

This post was later cross-posted to the blog Dreaming 5GW under the same name.

August 2, 2005: A blog post that considers fifth generation war waged against whole societies: what features should be considered (Weeks, Limitations of 5GW 2005)?

- Would small 5GW forces be able to defeat a large and complex society, given that a large society is also comprised of many smaller sub-sets or groups?
- "[I]f attacking the intelligence is the primary modus operandi of the 5GW force, that force would need to be, er, quite intelligent indeed in order to have any hope of success." The attacker "would need an extraordinary understanding—a fundamental comprehension—of the targeted society or force."
- Because of the complexity of a large society, the 5GW attacker would need to attack [the intelligence of] the most influential members within that society who could then

influence large portions of that society; but many others would not be so easily fooled: "the disenfranchised, the sub- and counter-cultural groups—in short: those who do not sub- scribe to the worldviews shared by most members of that so- ciety."

Conclusion:

- The 5GW attacker would "need to influence the majority and the leaders of that majority, or indeed create a majority will"; but
- "the oddball [disenfranchised] elements of a society are more likely to be sensitive to changes in the majority opi- nion than those who hold the majority opinion" and are therefore quite likely to realize something is occurring.

Early introduction of the idea of "canaries in the mine" during fifth generation war: oddball or disenfranchised elements within a society may act as signals that a 5GW is occurring.

Moreover: Those odd elements within a society might raise a defense against the 5GW attacker, but their defensive efforts may therefore seem to target the dominant elements of a society which have been influenced or co-opted by the 5GW attacker. The dominant elements, blind to the 5GW, may only see that they are being attacked by members of their own society; thus civil war may ensue—or is it possible that a main operation of 5GW that targets a whole society would be the instigation of civil war within that targeted society?

This blog post was later cross-posted to the blog Dreaming 5GW.

August 3, 2005: Alan Sullivan (Hello, Curtis 2005) suggests that 9/11 fits the prevailing description of fifth generation war. Some responses to the attack on the WTC, vis-à-vis the airline industry, were horribly bad and in fact hurt the U.S. Furthermore, such knee-jerk reactions solidified Al Qaeda's will to attack again.

August 3, 2005: Curtis Gale Weeks (Hello Alan 2005) responds to a comment left by Alan Sullivan, who suggested that 9/11 fits the description of a fifth-generation attack.

August 6, 2005: This Lane's (2005) is a PDF article which introduces 4 four elements within our modern world that will bear on the development of 5GW, followed by 3 three suggestions for defending against 5GW (Lane 2005).

Four elements promoting the shift to 5GW and/or describing 5GW:

- Technological advances which may permit very small groups or individuals to cause major effects upon the systems, mostly negative (i.e., superempowerment defined through access to technology).
- Cultural identities and cultures are weakening and may receive competition from idiosyncratic identities or individualistic ideologies. Thus, certain individuals may "see themselves and their identities writ large across the fabric of humanity and history itself."
- Targeted groups or peoples will be turned against themselves by the 5GW attacker. Specific changes in culture and ideology are not the primary goal, however; rather, such reactions within the target are "gratifying to the inside psychology of the initiating group." The subsequent results leading from reactionary responses are the primary goal.
- Factionalism will make identifying friend and foe very difficult. Reactionary factions may seek to benefit from the upheaval, thus may cause more chaos and conflict even if they are not behind the 5GW attack.

Three suggested defensive initiatives:

- Improved civic skills for managing the chaos. Those who would feed off the quick-changing conditions need to be re-directed, their activities channeled. Media will be key.
- Greater networking, or interconnection, within a society, would help identify those seeking to benefit from whatever chaos is occurring. (Those who would benefit, by latching on to the dynamics of the chaos, may not be the original in-itiators of the chaos.) Those who would benefit are not invis-ible nor particularly hidden, since they generally will come from the middle and upper-middle classes with access to the tools for effecting large changes within a society.
- Streamline infrastructure and internal systems so that they become less available as potential targets and/or potential weapons. "Remove opportunities" rather than focusing only on the individuals within the society.

Concluding thoughts/summary within the article: Superempo-werment will make possible and more likely the attempt to write one's own identity large over the society/cultural system, in particular with regard to those who are antisocial or indeed are sociopaths.

August 6, 2005: Abbott (SecretWar (5GW) 2005) responds to Weeks (Limitations of 5GW 2005) and further embellishes the idea that fifth generation war is "Secret War."

Points made:

- Economy of force improves with each succeeding generation of warfare; so 5GW targeting a society or culture will in-volve small 5GW forces able to defeat the larger societies or cultures.
- Contra CGW, these 5GW would not need to intellectually understand the targeted society in-depth, but rather will need great "fingertip feeling or *Fingerspitzengefuhl*", or good im-plicit knowledge rather than explicit knowledge of the tar-geted society.

- An open society is naturally well-defended from a 5GW attack: transparency forces the Secret Warrior to operate in the open, which risks the secrecy of the 5GW attack.
- Contra CGW (?), merely influencing the most influential members of a society should be sufficient for a 5GW attack since "Universal buy-in has never been a prerequisite for power." I.e., the dissenting voices of a small minority will be overlooked or, through transparency and general great openness, conspiracies and dissent will be laid to rest.
- Co-optation by Secret Warriors: "the President wouldn't be a Secret Warrior, but he would be a tool of the Secret Warrior."
- Operation Northwood's is referenced as a potential proto-5GW which would have purposely "created a majority will [CGW]."
- Contra CGW, small minorities such as the disenfranchised and sub-/counter-cultural elements are naturally dismissed, overlooked, their potential for warnings of 5GW attacks lost in the background noise, and thus secrecy will be maintained nonetheless: "Any real Secret War attack met with warnings that are lost in the background noise is the same as a Secret War without warning."
- If "Secret Networks", or those waging 5GW "latch on" to partisan groups, they would benefit from the disruption caused by the conflict between said partisan groups even while those groups also benefited from ratcheting up the partisan conflict, but differently.

August 7, 2005: Safranski (Revisiting 5th Generation War 2005) references Barnett (The Pentagon's new map: War and peace in the 21st century 2004) on "system perturbation" and "cascading effects" when contemplating (Lane 2005) and agreeing with Lane that geography no longer serves to define "the Logospheric state of 5GW conflict."

A consideration of Abbott (SecretWar (5GW) 2005) and Weeks (Limitations of 5GW 2005) leads to the introduction of the concept of "white noise" and 5GW. Those who hold the levers of power within a society may be influenced to act in ways which produce indirect results desired by fifth generation attackers; the actual changes or activities may not be the final goal but rather "distractors" which a) produce other indirect outcomes, or emergence, desired by the 5GW attacker, and b) enable the 5GW attacker to remain hidden.

August 9, 2005: Weeks (Personal Equals Political 2005) relates Auden (The Chimeras 1951) to 5GW.

Speculation of a label given to the effort to either preempt a 5GW attack or defend against one: "The War on Confusion."

The label is drawn from the present taxonomy being used to describe the preemption/defense against 4GW—The War on Terror.

It is suggested that either label points to the need for personal, individual development in a 4GW/5GW world, as a defense; furthermore, that superempowerment of individuals, which will figure heavily in the future dynamics of the world, correlates with the suggestion of a necessity for personal development.

It is thought that "the poem might offer deep insights into the conflicts facing us by offering insights into the very personal aspects of that conflict, the aspects of our own personal reactions and the actions of those who oppose us."

February 4, 2006: Soundless, formless, polished, leading: These are attributes of a 5GW campaign/force (Abbott, 5GW: Soundless + Formless + Polished + Leading 2006).

March 10, 2006: A consideration of Abbott (Orientation and action, part I: The OODA Loop 2009) and Abbott (5GW: Soundless + Formless + Polished + Leading 2006), followed by an alternative speculation of what will constitute fifth-generation warfare (Younghusband, Truly formless 5GW 2006).

Emergent communities, or emergent networks, may be examples of 5GW organization, particularly since these groups may form around an idea or cause but without having any actual (or at least formal) channels used for communication and coordination. This may leave them formless although their primary targets may continue to "see" a coherent operation/organization behind the attacks—thus jumping to conclusions about who is the attacker.

Keyser Soze (Singer 1995) is referenced.

March 11, 2006: From the idea that each successive generation within the xGW framework is developed to respond to, and to defeat, the previous generation, (Herring, Forgive me for being new to the 5GW discussion but I am a bit confused 2006) considers the possibility that 5GW is the next logical step of warfare.

With respect to 5GW, "the main weapon it will wield will be the idea of connectivity," and the ideas or cause which Younghusband (in the commented post) supposes may lead to the emergence of diverse and unconnected groups may rather be used in a viral way to specifically influence those groups.

March 11, 2006: Robb (I'd like to offer an alternative to the above 2006) responds to Herring's (Forgive me for being new to the 5GW discussion but I am a bit confused 2006) comment that states might use 5GW to combat 4GW networks—through the use of viral memes?—offers an alternative interpretation: fifth-generation warriors, called here by John Robb GG's (i.e., global guerrillas), may "ignore the decision making of the government entirely (their entire OODA loop) and focus directly on the population/economy."

In effect, this would shut down states as viable actors for 5GW and also leave them unable to defend against 5GW.

March 12, 2006: Responding to various other comments, and particularly considering comments left by Herring (Forgive me for being new to the 5GW discussion but I am a bit confused 2006) and Abbott (YH, the correct OODA loop can still be beautiful 2006), Weeks (A few off-the-cuff observations: 2006)suggests the necessity of reconsidering 5GW from a "nuts and bolts" perspective.

If a "fuzzy" 4GW force seeks to "sap the will" of opponents, how will a "hidden" 5GW defeat such a force without that force knowing it was the victim of 5GW? Primarily: Why would the 4GW force continue to act in a manner that becomes self-destructive—never seeing that the path is self-destructive?

Additionally, the idea is introduced that 5GW forces will utilize all prior generations of warfare fighting, when necessary, generally by co-opting or influencing prior-generation forces.

March 14, 2006: Building upon Abbott (5GW: Soundless + Formless + Polished + Leading 2006) and Younghusband (Truly formless 5GW 2006), Weeks (Initiating 5GW 2006) expands upon a comment he left on Coming Anarchy by considering how in fact 5GW forces will operate in a "nuts and bolts" fashion. Previously, most discussions of 5GW focused on the abstract or general aspects of fifth generation warfare without considering how those aspects will constrain the activities of fifth generation forces

Some "god-like" actions may have merit, e.g., Katrina-like natural disasters which entirely obsess the target of those disasters. Whether such an approach is used by a 5GW force may depend upon the sophistication of the target: Will the target have the forensic capabilities and organization which will allow it to ultimately trace back the effects to the cause, should the 5GW force directly create major disasters? Generally, the ideas that 1) all effects are observable and 2) being physical, or a matter of physics, they are traceable, means that direct kinetic activities by 5GW forces are quite dangerous for them, although given the sophistication or lack thereof of the target such activities may have some use within 5GW.

Alternatively, 5GW forces may try to frame other parties when creating major disasters, to throw off pursuit and also to set up conflict between two other parties. Preferably, these other parties who are framed will be "usual suspects"—and better yet, they will want to claim responsibility for disasters even if they had nothing to do with those disasters. Again, however, this approach may be dangerous for 5GW actors, not only because of the potential for incriminating forensic evidence but also because the framed parties may reject claims of responsibility.

However, either of the above possibilities may work even if the cause is detected or traced back to the 5GW force (or at least away from the framed party) if time-lag between the original disaster/attack and the discovery of subterfuge is great enough to have left the targets in a downward spiral from which they cannot escape or in a position of extreme weakness.

The blog post concludes from these considerations: "What things are hardest to track? Answer: memes."

Memetic engineering (though not so-called within the post) will offer the best possibility for influence and manipulation of other forces without detection. A variety of examples and possibilities are offered. The post finally answers a question implied by previous conversations on other blogs.

This blog post was later cross-posted to the blog Dreaming 5GW.

July 5, 2006: A mapping of the xGW framework onto John Boyd's OODA theory by building on his earlier work (Rethinking the OODA 2006) and (EBO is Everything in War -- Almost 2006), Weeks (Observing the Maturing World 2006) utilizes the *Revised OODA Loop*. The post has several sections:

Introduction—in which the previous post in the series, on EBO, is summarized. The limitations of EBO are thought to be a result of the difference between reason, which is informed by past experiences/learning, and concrete cause/effect chains occurring in the present. I.e., observations in the present, which EBO tries to influence, are not the sole determinant of an individual's decision to act in a particular way; thus, EBO is limited. However, no one may conduct warfare or engage in conflict without altering the present physical environment, which means that EBO, of some form, is important to modern warfare.

We Observe, We Orient, We Decide/Act—a section which examines Abbott (Orientation and action, part I: The OODA Loop 2009) and Lind et al. (The changingface of war: Into the fourth generation 1989) concerning the generational warfare model, focusing on the observational aspects of each generation. Whereas Abbott considered the way each successive generation of warfare attempts to attack the enemy's decision process by "going deeper" into the enemy's OODA, and William Lind focused on the technological and tactical differences between each succeeding generation, both approaches may be seen to reflect changes in observational capability due to changing technology and changing societal forces.

Going Deeper into OODA—in which Abbott (Orientation and action, part I: The OODA Loop 2009), in light of the previous sections of the post, reiterates of the importance of EBO as characterized in the previous post in the series.

And Deeper... ...—in which a new mapping of xGW is offered, but onto the Revised OODA designed by CGW, followed by notes explaining the implications and variations upon previous mappings:

September 26, 2006: Langbert (Fifth Generation Warfare: 4GW No Longer Applies 2006) seems to envision 5GW as the evolution of nationalistic 4GW (Mao, Ho Chi Min) to that of the purely ideologically driven (Al Qaeda, the Arab Mujahadeen) 4GW (or, in Langbert's view, 5GW). In essence the absence of jingoism and the introduction of ideology as a cause of guerrilla resistance amount to 5GW. Further affecting this evolution are the introduction of new technologies unavailable during the time of Mao or Ho Chi Min; specifically mentioned are cellular communication and the Internet.

October 7, 2006: Robb (JOURNAL: Can Georgie become a MicroPower? 2006) states that "the idea is that small states can protect themselves if they are willing to use economic systems disruption as a strategic weapon." Said systems disruption, and the Global Guerrilla dynamic (Robb, Brave New War: The Next Stage of Terrorism and the End of Globalization 2007), are called fifth-generation warfare. Scenarios involving the Ukraine, Georgia, and Russia are considered. Such methods may work to influence the target down a predetermined path (in this case, retreat?).

October 8, 2006: Building from the *SysAdmin* concept (Barnett, The Pentagon's new map: War and peace in the 21st century 2004), Abbott (Dreaming 5th generation war 2009), Younghusband (Truly formless 5GW 2006), and a comment by "RevG," Thomas P. M. Barnett (The sandwhich generations-of-war strategy 2006) discusses the importance the 3GW Leviathan.

The advent of nuclear weapons failed to achieve a new generation of war, although it did focus the development of war into 1) limited warfare and 2) proxy warfare and 4GW. This manner of conducting conflict was "defensible in the go-go 90s, when globalization was going to do all the heavy lifting for us and didn't need a bodyguard," but is no longer enough and will not work for "the Long War."

However, with respect to Abbott (Orientation and action, part I: The OODA Loop 2009), Barnett counters that although a too-upfront and obvious approach to shaping the Gap may seem to be a weakness, in truth, transparency is the key to success, since it opposes the status quo of authoritarian regimes.

Essentially, then, the 5GW "sandwich" strategy would mean that the 5GW sandwich works after the 3GW Leviathan force has successfully built a space for the SysAdmin to operate, not only holding off potential 3GW opponent peer competitors but also by keeping 4GW opponents from being able to expand beyond the Gap.

October 8, 2006: An exploration of ideas from Barnett (The sandwhich generations-of-war strategy 2006), with agreement than the US Leviathan helps to keep Old Core and New Core powers from reinaugurating the era of great 3GW war between powers; i.e., that the US force keeps 3GW power primarily for itself and operates as a closing book-end to 3GW dynamics (Safranski, A Strategic Dagwood 2006).

Globalization has become the premiere economic model for the world, as a consequence, by forcing methods other than autarky for organizing economic systems. "Offensively shaping the battlespace and . . . ...defensively bring the Gap into the light."—a characterization of the 5GW aspects of Thomas Barnett's strategy; however, with connectivity comes new dangers. *Development-in-a-Box* is a necessary response to present circumstances.

October 8, 2006: Abbott (5GW and Ruleset Automation 2006) considers ideas found in Barnett (The sandwhich generations-of-war strategy 2006), although does not actually link to it. *Development-in-a-Box* "has its limitations." Rather than "automated rulesets" and "implicit rulesets," what are required are "functional rulesets." A consideration of Sharia law, Communist rule in China, and American federalism implies that each is a functional ruleset for those who follow it.

October 9, 2006: Robb (Lots of discussion of what 5GW is 2006) cites Safranski (A Strategic Dagwood 2006) and writes that "It's clear we are in a phase transition from classic 4GW guerrilla warfare to something worse." That something worse is "the super-empowered individual that can use the technologies of self-replication to collapse/kill on a grand scale"—which John Robb calls the defining aspect of 5GW.

October 9, 2006: Building off Robb's (Lots of discussion of what 5GW is 2006) claim that the destructive technologically superempowered fighter defines fifth-generation warfare, Vaidya (5GW and Beyond 2006) offers his reasons why this will be so while offering a glimpse at "6GW" and "7GW":

Technological Singularity Track—5GW marks where "the human body becomes the limitation"; 6GW will occur when humans have replaced their human body (except for brain?) with technology; and 7GW will occur "when brains are made obsolete by machines."

OODA Loop Track—With consideration of Abbott (Orientation and action, part I: The OODA Loop 2009): "The human decision cycle becomes irrelevant." Presumably, this will apply to 7GW, previously described.

October 9, 2006: Inaugural post of the blog Dreaming 5GW (Weeks, Dreaming 5GW in Surround Sound 2006).

An initial consideration of secrecy leads into a broad outline of how fifth generation warfare may play out, building upon the idea of memetic engineering:

This consideration, along with Abbott (5GW and Ruleset Automation 2006), Barnett (The sandwhich generations-of-war strategy 2006), and Safranski (A Strategic Dagwood 2006), lead the author to wonder "that Thomas Barnett's PNM theory is very 5GWish." Both 5GW and PNM have violent and nonviolent features. A previous conversation at the blog *PurpleSlog* (Slog and al., Bizarro Fred Phelps and 5GW Sepculation 2006) had considered the possibility that Thomas Barnett's PNM theory might be a type of fifth generation warfare.

Barnett (The sandwhich generations-of-war strategy 2006) is considered; but Weeks believes Thomas Barnett is wrong to assume that "we deny evolution toward 5GW in those parts of the Gap we deny to our enemies" (TPMB). Rather, the triumph of US 3GW in the Gap would only produce opponents who would necessarily be forced to operate at the next generational level; stopping the development of 4GW in the Gap with a superior 3GW (assuming that would be possible) would force our enemies to develop a 5GW strategy.

However, "the idealized version of Barnett's system would likely produce—it is hoped—a world view paradigm shift within a significant portion of the Gap populace that would serve to preempt opposition...."

Even so, the attempt to create that paradigm shift openly, as prescribed by Thomas Barnett, would keep it from being 5GW.

The post concludes by quoting Safranski (A Strategic Dagwood 2006) —citing increased connectivity and openness as a potential vehicle for empowering Global Guerrillas (Robb, Brave New War: The Next Stage of Terrorism and the End of Globalization 2007)— and then considering the possibility that so many millions within the gap may be greatly influenced by a handful of superempowered individuals.

October 14, 2006: A blog post considering how "micropowers" might utilize 5GW to conduct warfare in the future (Weeks, Micropowers and the Art of 5GW 2006).

The post begins with a look at Robb (JOURNAL: Can Georgie become a MicroPower? 2006) and others, concerning the issue of micropowers and how Georgia (the nation) might be able to thwart Russian influence.

John Robb suggests systempunkt attacks; system disruption could coerce Russia to back down. This approach would not be 5GW, but 4GW (even though John Robb has called it fifth-generation), for two reasons:

- "Directly hiring terrorists/mercenaries to carry out the opera-tion may be old school very shortly. It allows too much op-portunity for tracing the activity back to the employer, threatens the very secrecy necessary for running a successful 5GW operation."
- "Again, we have the standard GG and 4GW 'negativity' approach, of merely: disruption, chaos, confusion, destruc-tion. 5GW may indeed use these things, but the ultimate goal is not so much systempunkt as the creation of new orders that will continue to operate long after the 5GW force has fi-nished its operations."

The post continues with a consideration of how micropowers, which seem to be forming on the world stage, may be setting the stage for 5GW. First, they are too small to directly attack (by whatever means, kinetic or non-kinetic) much larger nations; retaliations would be swift and probably decisive. Second, the "power" in "micropowers" may translate to a great capacity for influence if not control on the world stage: thus, a 5GW paradigm which greatly differs from pre-5GW paradigms.

October 16, 2006: Thomas P. M. Barnett (My own personal 5GW dream 2006) lays out his own personal 5GW dream, building from Weeks (Dreaming 5GW in Surround Sound 2006).

Rather than develop 5GW theory, he decides to approach the subject of fifth generation warfare that he has "essentially laid out in both books" which he has already written, "namely, the use of

System Perturbations to alter existing rule sets or to replace them entirely with new ones."

System perturbations may well appear quite negative at the beginning, but not be.

Utilizing 5GW against the Gap will produce 5GW responses, since "first responses are typically symmetrical." Aggressive 5GW offenses in the Gap will disorient authoritarian types while shaping the observations of those within the Gap wanting to escape the status quo.

The point is made that 9/11 was "Osama's reach for 5GW-level strategy"—but did not actually achieve a 5GW level.

Barnett gives an xGW perspective on his two published books while offering a look at the still-as-yet-unwritten third book, which eventually became (Barnett, Great Powers: America and the World After Bush 2009).

Finally, a 5GW scenario is suggested, in which America takes a false "beating in Afghanistan and Iraq" as long as a strategic alliance can be built with China: by withdrawing in seeming defeat, America cannot only force China to take a stand in helping to "shrink the Gap," but allow China to become an "alternative" to America in the eyes of those living in the Gap—even if in reality America and China have very common goals with respect to the Gap.

October 16, 2006: Citing Lind et al. (1989), Robb (THE CHANGING FACE OF WAR: Into the 5th Generation (5GW) 2006) expands the xGW framework from Lind's stopping point and into consideration of fifth generation warfare.

Three key elements appear to be emerging:

- Open Source Warfare—"This new structure doesn't only radically expand the number of potential participants, it shrinks the group size well below any normal measures of viability."

- Systems Disruption—broad-spectrum sabotage, perhaps often occurring as a Black Swan, may "undermine and reorder global systems."
- Virtual States—"black globalization", or "military/economic integration" outside the normal channels protected by nation-states, may enable diverse non-state groups "to gain greater degrees of independence and financial wealth through the warfare they conduct."

The author adds a concluding note: "NOTE: Whether you call these developments 4GW on steroids or the start of a 5th generation, it just doesn't matter."

October 16, 2006: Robb (Totally unreal 2006) believes Barnett (My own personal 5GW dream 2006) "is trying to refashion global guerrillas as his big idea," after the latter discussed his previous works, *The Pentagon's New Map* (2004) and *Blueprint for Action* (2005) as his own type of 5GW.

October 17, 2006: Responding to Robb's (Totally unreal 2006) accusation that he is attempting "to refashion global guerrillas as his big idea," Barnett (A thousand flowers will bloom on 5GW, and countless more weeds 2006) affirms that he did not "employ" 5GW in his books but thought that his own published ideas correlate with some contemporary, blogospheric discussion of fifth generation warfare.

The claim is made that John Robb's sensitivity—"since he offers his own, particularly striking definition of 5GW"—may be related to the fact that John Robb's book is nearing publication; also, that his own (Barnett's) attempt to fit his ideas within the framework of 5GW has come as a result of having his own ideas already discussed within that context by other bloggers.

Although appreciating John Robb's exploration of the dynamic of Global Guerrillas—"specifically some of his descriptions of the dynamics we'll meet from non-state actors in coming years"— Thomas Barnett does not believe the GG phenomenon constitutes a new form of warfare, nor that the threats explored by John Robb are as serious as John Robb describes them.

Finally, TPMB considers the "Long War" and notes that much more friction will occur within the Gap.

October 17, 2006: An attack on John Robb's concept of Global Guerrillas, particularly on Robb (THE CHANGING FACE OF WAR: Into the 5th Generation (5GW) 2006), Abbott (5GW is Closed Source (and Global Guerillas Theory is Incoherent) 2006) responds, "5GW is not open source. 5GW is closed source." Primarily, secrecy–which will be important for fifth generation operations–means that, unlike the *open source warfare* suggested by Robb, fifth-generation warfare will necessarily be *closed source.*

October 17, 2006: Weeks (Barnett and Rob 2006) considers Robb (THE CHANGING FACE OF WAR: Into the 5th Generation (5GW) 2006) and Barnett (My own personal 5GW dream 2006) in the context of exploration of fifth generation warfare.

On Barnett::

- "Not very secret, is it?"— It would inspire domestic and foreign opposition; this is a nod to the idea that 5GW requires secrecy.
- "I wish he would stop thinking about other countries for a bit and think about the American psyche" — referring to Thomas Barnett's idea that America could welcome a "false" defeat in order to shape views in China and the Gap; the implication is that shaping domestic memes is also very important.

- "I do like Barnett's thinking, however, and he's far more right than wrong."

On Robb: "His method is disingenuous, to say the least."

However, with respect to John Robb, "Robb may be more right than wrong, at least on some particulars." That follows a consideration of the role of non-state actors, or what John Robb calls "Global Guerrillas," which concludes with the assertion that John Robb has failed to consider the role of "angels" in the system who might naturally oppose the "demons" he has drawn for us to consider.

October 30, 2006: Abbott (Against William Lind, Against John Robb, in favor of 5GW 2006) argues the xGW framework needs to be approached scientifically.

First introduction of that conceptual framework of "G," or that the relation of "G" to intensity of kinetics within any generation, should be a guide when contemplating xGW theory.

Two alternative approaches are given at the introduction to the post: William Lind's "Hegelian-Marxist-Dialectic [nonsense]" and another which co-opts the terminology of "5GW" for reasons which may be unrelated to the actual intent behind using the xGW model for understanding warfare.

November 12, 2006: A consideration of the "next generation of analysts and collectors which must confront these challenges" arising with the advent of 5GW (Imperative 2006).

The view is circumspect as the author contemplates previous contemplation inspired by various others writing about fifth generation warfare:

August 23, 2007: An alleged secret plan to overthrow the Soviet government through ideological manipulation. Does it relate to 5GW (Slog, Found on Wikipedia: "The Dulles Plan" 2007)?

May 22, 2008: Through several stages, the blog author examines whether fifth generation warfare can be called "warfare" (Boland, 5GWhat? The Meaning of "Warfare" in 2008 2008).

"Is blogging warfare?" The author mentions the DoD concept of information operations, answering affirmatively. "Is activism warfare?" The author alludes to the White House at "war" with liberal activism. Also, the author makes reference to "low intensity conflict." Again, the answer is affirmative. "Are domestic law enforcement operations warfare?" Drawing parallels between domestic law enforcement and foreign counter-insurgency, the author again answers affirmatively.

Summing up the blog post, the author confutes conflates "conflict" with "war" further by considering how expanding populations, resource conflict, homicide, and even super-empowered individuals—"from Al Gore to Vladimir Putin to Hugo Chavez to George Bush" to the individual on the ground—may ultimately be responsible for the outcomes of many conflicts. However, quoting a blog comment left elsewhere by "Smitten Eagle," the blog author promises a follow-up post which would tie the Uncertainty Principle into the consideration (given the large scope of so many actors involved in conflict?).

May 23, 2008: Abbott (5GW as the Event Horizon 2008) links to Boland (Henry Okah and MEND 2008), where it is pondered if fifth generation warfare will be a blending of warfare with "everything else."

Seizing upon the idea that 5GW will be an "event horizon for warfare theory," Abbott agrees, "with one change: 5GW is the event horizon, beyond which the xGW framework breaks down as violence is dispersed and action indirect enough that the study of war becomes the study of politics."

A lively discussion ensues, during which William Lind's "generations of modern warfare" (GMW)— an important precursor to study of 5GW — is distinguished from "xGW," to which 5GW belongs. 0GW-5GW are more properly seen to exist through the framework of xGW than through Lind's GMW.

WORKS CITED

Abbott, Daniel H. "5GW and Ruleset Automation." *tdaxp*. October 8, 2006. http://www.tdaxp.com/archive/2006/10/08/5gw-and-ruleset-automation.html (accessed May 8, 2009).

—. "5GW as the Event Horizon." *tdaxp*. May 23, 2008. http://www.5gw.phaticcommunion.com/2008/05/5gw_as_the_event_horizon.php (accessed May 8, 2009).

—. "5GW is Closed Source (and Global Guerillas Theory is Incoherent)." *tdaxp*. October 17, 2006. http://www.5gw.phaticcommunion.com/2007/09/5gw_is_closed_source_and_globa.php (accessed May 8, 2009).

—. "5GW: Soundless + Formless + Polished + Leading." *tdaxp*. February 4, 2006. http://www.tdaxp.com/archive/2006/02/04/5gw-soundless-formless-polished-leading.html (accessed May 8, 2009).

Abbott, Daniel H. "A history of the OODA loop." In *The John Boyd Roundtable: Debating Science, Strategy, and War*, edited by Mark Safranski, 1-5. Ann Arbor, MI: Nimble, 2008.

—. "Against William Lind, Against John Robb, in favor of 5GW." *Dreaming 5GW*. October 30, 2006. http://dreaming5gw.com/2006/10/against_william_lind_against_j.php (accessed May 8, 2009).

—. "Brave New War, Aftermath: Mountainrunner's Review." *tdaxp*. June 10, 2007. http://www.tdaxp.com/archive/2007/06/10/brave-new-war-aftermath-mountainrunners-review.html (accessed May 11, 2009).

Abbott, Daniel H. "Dreaming 5th generation war." In *The handbook of 5GW: A fifth generation of war?*, by Daniel H. Abbott. Ann Arbor, MI: Nimble Books, 2009.

—. "Emerging NetWar / SecretWar Tactic: Stealth Shareholder Activism." *tdaxp.* July 22, 2005. http://www.tdaxp.com/archive/2005/07/22/emerging-netwar-secretwar-tactic-stealth-shareholder-activism.html (accessed May 8, 2009).

Abbott, Daniel H. "Orientation and action, part I: The OODA Loop." In *The handbook of 5GW: A fifth generation of war?*, by Daniel H. Abbott. Ann Arbor, MI: Nimble Books, 2009.

—. *Revolutionary strategies in early Christianity.* Ann Arbor, MI: Nimble Books, 2008.

—. *Revolutionary Strategies in Early Christianity.* Ann Arbor, MI: Nimble Books, 2008.

—. "SecretWar (5GW)." *tdaxp.* August 6, 2005. http://www.tdaxp.com/archive/2005/08/06/secretwar-5gw.html (accessed May 8, 2009).

—. "SecretWar: Plain Jane Tries to Kill the Yakuza Boss." *tdaxp.* July 25, 2005. http://www.tdaxp.com/archive/2005/07/25/secretwar-plain-jane-tries-to-kill-the-yakuza-boss.html (accessed May 8, 2009).

—. "SecretWarriors Walk Without Rhythm, Won't Attract the Worm." *tdaxp.* July 23, 2003. http://www.tdaxp.com/archive/2005/07/23/secretwarriors-walk-without-rhythm-wont-attract-the-worm.html (accessed May 8, 2009).

Abbott, Daniel H. "The Terminology of xGW." In *The handbook of xGW: A Fifth generation of war?*, by Daniel H. Abbott. Ann Arbor, MI: Nimble Books, 2009.

Abbott, Daniel H. "The xGW Framework." In *The Handbook of 5GW: A fifth generation of war?*, edited by D.H. Abbott. Ann Arbor, MI: Nimble Books, 2009.

—. "YH, the correct OODA loop can still be beautiful." *Coming Anarchy.* March 12, 2006.

http://cominganarchy.com/2006/03/10/truly-formless-5gw/#comment-73378 (accessed May 8, 2009).

Adams IV, Nathan A. "Creating clones, kids, and chimera: Liberal democratic compromise at the crossroads." *Issues in Law and Medicine* 20, no. 3 (2004): 2-69.

Anderson, Brian C. "Identity crisis." *National Review* 54, no. 10 (2002): 41-45.

Answers.com. *grade: Definition, Synonyms from Answers.com.* http://www.answers.com/grade&r=67 (accessed May 27, 2008).

Armstrong, Karen. *Muhammad: A Biography of the Prophet.* San Francisco, CA: HarperSanFrancisco, 1993.

Armstrong, Matt. "Book Review: Brave New War." *MountainRunner.* June 8, 2007. http://mountainrunner.us/2007/06/book_review_brave_new_war.html (accessed May 11, 2009).

Arquilla, John, interview by Harry Kreisler. *International relations in the information age: The structure of networks* (March 17, 2003).

Arquilla, John, and David Ronfeldt. *Cyberwar is coming!* Santa Monica, CA: RAND, 1996.

—. *In Athena's Camp: Preparing for conflicts in this information rage.* Santa Monica, CA: RAND, 1997.

—. *Networks and Netwars.* Santa Monica, CA: RAND, 2001.

Auden, W.H. "The Chimeras." *The Times Literary Supplement*, 1951.

Auer, Catherine. "Super snacks for super soldiers." *Bulletin of the Atomic Scientists* 60, no. 3 (2004).

Axe, David. "Piracy, human security, and 5GW in Somalia." In *The Handbook of 5GW: A fifth generation of war?*, edited by Daniel H. Abbott. Ann Arbor, MI: Nimble Books, 2009.

Bailey, Ronald. "Transhumanism: The most dangerous idea?" *Reason Online.* August 24, 2004.

http://www.reason.com/news/show/34867.html (accessed February 26, 2008).

Barabasi, Albert-Laslo, and Eric Bonabeau. "Scale-free networks." *Scientific American* 288 (2003): 60-69.

Barabási, Albert-László. *Linked: The New Science of Networks.* Cambridge, MA: Perseus Publishing, 2002.

Barnett, Thomas P.M. "A thousand flowers will bloom on 5GW, and countless more weeds." *Thomas P.M. Barnett :: Weblog.* October 17, 2006. http://www.thomaspmbarnett.com/weblog/2006/10/a_thousand _flowers_will_bloom.html (accessed May 8, 2009).

—. *Blueprint for Action: A Future Worth Creating.* New York: Putnam Adult, 2005.

—. *Great Powers: America and the World After Bush.* New York: Putnam Adult, 2009.

—. "My own personal 5GW dream." *Thomas P.M. Barnett ::* *Weblog.* October 16, 2006. http://www.5gw.phaticcommunion.com/2007/09/my_own_per sonal_5gw_dream_1.php (accessed May 8, 2009).

—. *The Pentagon's new map: War and peace in the 21st century.* New York: G.P. Putnam, 2004.

—. "The sandwhich generations-of-war strategy." *Thomas P.M. Barnett :: Weblog.* October 8, 2006. http://www.thomaspmbarnett.com/weblog/2006/10/the_sandwi ch_generationsofwar.html (accessed May 8, 2009).

Bay, Austin. *GEN Petraeus' Chief Counter-Insurgency Adviser on "Iraqi Narratives".* May 25, 2007. http://austinbay.net/blog/?p=1805 (accessed May 7, 2009).

Beam, Louis. "Leaderless Resistance." *The Seditionist*, 1992.

Biernan, Ben. *1996.* New Haven, CT: Yale University Press, The Pol Pot Regime.

Bigelow, R.S. *The dawn warriors: Man's evolution toward peace.* London: Hutchinson, 1970.

The Incredibles. Directed by Brad Bird. 2004.

Boehm, Barry W. "A spiral model of software development and enhancement." *Computer* 21, no. 5 (1988): 61-72.

Boesche, Roger. *The First Great Political Realist: Kautilya and his Arthashastra.* Lanham: Lexington Books, 2003.

Boland, Justin. "5GWhat? The Meaning of "Warfare" in 2008." *Skilluminati Research.* May 22, 2008. http://www.skilluminati.com/research/entry/5gwhat_the_meaning_of_warfare_in_2008 (accessed May 8, 2009).

—. "Henry Okah and MEND." *Skilluminati.* May 23, 2008. http://www.skilluminati.com/research/entry/5gwhat_the_meaning_of_warfare_in_2008/#C_610 (accessed May 8, 2009).

Bostrom, Nick. "In defense of posthuman dignity." *Bioethics* 19, no. 3 (2005): 202-214.

—. *Transhumanist FAQ.* 2008. http://www.transhumanism.org/index.php/WTA/faq21/46/ (accessed February 16, 2008).

—. *Transhumanist FAQ 1.2.* http://www.transhumanism.org/index.php/WTA/faq21/56/ (accessed February 16 2008).

Boyd, John. "A discourse of winning and losing." 1995.

Boyd, John. *Patterns of Conflict.* 1981.

Bush, George W. *Address to a Joint Session of Congress and the American People.* September 20, 2001. http://www.dhs.gov/xnews/speeches/speech_0016.shtm (accessed May 7, 2009).

Canton, James. "NBIC convergent technologies and the innovation economy: Challenges and opportunities in the 21st century." In *Managing nano-bio-info-cogno innovations: Converging technologies in society,* by Bainbridge, William Simms and Mihail C. Roco. Washington, DC: Springer, 2005.

Card, Orson Scott. *Ender's Game.* New York: Tor, 1985.

—. *Shadow of the Hegemon.* New York: Tor, 2001.

Cebrowski, Arthur K, and Thomas P.M. Barnett. "The American way of war." *Proceedings,* 2003.

Conquest, Robert. *The Great Terror: A Reassessment.* New York: Oxford University Press, 1991.

Creswell, J.A. *Research design: Qualitative, quantitative, and mixed methods approaches.* 3rd. Thousand Oaks, CA: Sage, 2008.

Creswell, J.W., and V. Plano Clark. *Designing and conducting mixed methods research.* Thousand Oaks, CA: Sage, 2007.

Creswell, J.W., W.E. Hanson, V.L. Plano Clark, and A. Morales. "Qualitative research designs: Selection and implementation." *The Counseling Psychologist* 35, no. 2 (2007): 236-264.

Deichman, Shane. "Battling for perception." In *The handbook of 5GW: A fifth generation of war?*, by Daniel H. Abbott. Ann Arbor, MI: Nimble Books, 2009.

Dubner, S., and S. Levitt. *Freakonomics: A rogue economist explores the hidden side of everything.* New York: Harper Collins, 2005.

Eibl-Eibesfeldt, Iraneus. "Evolution of destructive aggression." *Aggressive Behavior* 3, no. 2 (1977): 127-144.

Elkus, Adam. "5GW as information-aged networked politics." In *The handbook of 5GW: A fifth generation of war?*, by Daniel H. Abbott. Ann Arbor, MI: Nimble Books, 2009.

Elliot, C. "Humanity 2.0." *Wilson Quarterly* 27, no. 4 (2003): 13-21.

Evans, Woody. "Singularity warfare: A bibliometric survey of militarized transhumanism." *Journal of Evolution and Technology* 16, no. 1 (2007): 161-165.

Federal News Service, Inc. "Department of Defense Roundtable with Rear Admiral Terry McKnight." *United States Department of Defense.* January 29, 2009. http://www.defense.gov/DODCMSShare/BloggerAssets/2009-01/012909114913200090129_RearAdmMcKnight_transcript.pdf (accessed July 7, 2010).

"France accused in Rwanda Genocide." *BBC News.* August 5, 2008. http://news.bbc.co.uk/2/hi/africa/7542418.stm (accessed May 7, 2009).

Friedman, Thomas L. "Longitudes and Attitudes." *Thomas L. Friedman.* 2002. http://www.thomaslfriedman.com/bookshelf/longitudes-and-attitudes/prologue (accessed March 9, 2008).

Fukuyama, Francis. *Our transhuman future: Consequences of the biotechnology revolution.* New York: Farrar, Straus, and Giroux, 2002.

Garreau, Joel. "Perfecting the human." *Fortune* 151, no. 11 (2005): 101-108.

Gibson, William, interview by Brooke Gladstone. "The science of science fiction." *Talk of the Nation.* (November 30, 1999).

Girifalco, Louis A. *Dynamics of technological change.* New York: Van Nostrand Reinhold, 1991.

Goldblatt, Michael. "DARPA's programs in enhancing human performance." In *Converging technologies for improving human performance*, by Mihail C. Roco and William Sims Bainbridge. Arlington, VA: National Science Foundation, 2002.

Gorman, M.E., and J. Groves. "Collaboration on converging technologies: Education and practice." In *Managing nano-bio-info-cogno innovations: Converging technologies in society*, edited by W.S. Bainbridge and M.C. Roco, 71-87. Washington, DC: Spengler, 2005.

Grace, Brent. "The War for Robert Taylor." In *The Handbook of 5GW: A fifth generation of war?*, edited by Daniel H. Abbott. Ann Arbor, MI: Nimble Books, 2009.

Green, Lexington. "I am going to have to write something..." *Zenpundit.* January 13, 2009. http://zenpundit.com/?p=2987#comment-10014 (accessed July 30, 2009).

Hammes, Thomas X. *The Sling and the stone: On war in the 21st century.* Saint Paul, MN: Zenith Press, 2004.

Hashim, Ahmed. *Insurgency and counterinsurgency in Iraq.* Ithaca, NY: Cornell University Press, 2006.

Hatch, J.A. *Doing qualitative research in educational settings.* Albany, NY: State University of New York Press, 2001.

Herring, Adam. "Forgive me for being new to the 5GW discussion but I am a bit confused." *Coming Anarchy.* March 11, 2006. http://cominganarchy.com/2006/03/10/truly-formless-5gw/#comment-73227 (accessed May 8, 2009).

Herring, Adam. "Searching for 5GW." In *The handbook of 5GW: A fifth generation of war?*, by Daniel H. Abbott. Ann Arbor, MI: Nimble Books, 2009.

Herring, Adam. "Working definition v. 2.3." In *The handbook of 5GW: A fifth generation of war?*, by Daniel Hebbert Abbott. Ann Arbor, MI: Nimble Books, 2009.

Hudson, Valerie M., and Andrea M. Den Boer. *Bare branches: The security implications of Asia's surplus male population.* Boston: MIT Press, 2005.

Imperative, Kent's. "War in the next generation." *Kent's Imperative.* November 12, 2006. http://kentsimperative.blogspot.com/2006/11/war-in-next-generation.html (accessed May 8, 2009).

"Interviews: Gourevitch." *Frontline: The Triumph of Evil.* 2008. http://www.pbs.org/wgbh/pages/frontline/shows/evil/interviews/gourevitch.html (accessed May 7, 2009).

Jenkins, Brian. *International terrorism: A new kind of warfare.* Santa Monica, CA: RAND Corporation, 1974.

Johnson, Steven, interview by David Sims and Rael Dornfest. *Steven Johnson on "Emergence"* (February 22, 2005).

Kautilya. *The Arthashastra.* Translated by L.N. Rangarian. New Delhi: Pengium Books, 1992.

Keohane, Robert O. *After hegemony.* Princeton, NJ: Princeton University Press, 1984.

Kilcullen, David. "Anatomy of a tribal revolt." *Small Wars Journal Blog.* August 29, 2007. http://smallwarsjournal.com/blog/2007/08/anatomy-of-a-tribal-revolt/ (accessed May 6, 2009).

Knaus, Gerhard, and Felix Martin. "Travails of the European Raj." *Journal of Democracy* 14, no. 3 (2003): 60-74.

Kohalyk, Chad. "5GW as Netwar 2.0." In *The handbook of 5GW: A fifth generation of war?*, by Daniel H. Abbott. Ann Arbor, MI: Nimble Books, 2009.

Krebs, Valdis. "Social network analysis of the 911 terrorist network." *orgnet.com.* 2008. http://orgnet.com/hijackers.html (accessed August 8, 2009).

Lane, Bryce. "On "Fifth Generation" Warfare?" *Defense and the National Interest.* August 6, 2005. http://www.d-n-i.net/fcs/pdf/lane_fifth_gen.pdf (accessed May 8, 2009).

Langbert, Mitchell. "Fifth Generation Warfare: 4GW No Longer Applies." *Democracy Project.* September 26, 2006. http://www.democracy-project.com/archives/002814.html (accessed May 8, 2009).

Lawrence, T.E. *Seven pillars of wisdom: A triumph.* New York: Anchor Books, 1991.

—. "The Evolution of a Revolt." *The Army Quarterly and Defence Journal*, October 1920.

Levvit, S., and S. Venkatesh. "Growing up in the projects: The economic lives of a cohort of men who came of age in Chicago Public Housing." *The American Economic Review* 91, no. 2 (2001).

Levy, D., and M. Gallagher. *HOPE VI and neighborhood revitilization.* Washington, DC: The Urban Institute, 2007.

Liles, Samuel. "Unified Generational Warfare." In *The handbook of 5GW: A fifth generation of war?*, by Daniel H. Abbott. Ann Arbor, MI: Nimble Books, 2009.

Lind, William S. "On War #53: Fifth Generation Warfare?" *Defense in the National Interest.* February 3, 2004. http://www.d-n-i.net/lind/lind_2_03_04.htm (accessed May 8, 2009).

—. "On War #90: The Sling and the Stone." *Defense and the National Interest.* November 6, 2004. www.d-n-i.net/lind/lind_11_05_04.htm (accessed 10 2009, May).

Lind, William S., Keith Nightengale, John F. Schmitt, Joseph W. Sutton, and Gary I. Wilson. "The changingface of war: Into the fourth generation." *Marine Corps Gazetta*, October 1989: 22-26.

Lovecraft, H.P. "The Dream-Quest of Unknown Kadath." In *The Dreams in the Witch House: And Other Weird Stories*, by S.T. Joship, 155-251. New York: Penguin Classics, 2004.

Malkasian, Carter. "Did the United States need more forces in Iraq? Evidence from al Al Anbar." *Defense Studies* 8, no. 1 (2008): 78-107.

Mao, Zedong. *On Guerrilla Warfare*. Translated by Samuel Griffith. New York: Praeger, 1961.

McFarland, Sean, and Neil Smith. "Anbar awakens: The tipping point." *Military Review*, 2008: 41-52.

Mead, George Herbert. *Mind, Self, and Society*. Edited by Charles W. Morris. Chicago, IL: University of Chicago Press, 1934.

Michaelson, Evan S. "Measuring the merger: Examining the onset of emerging technologies." In *Managing nano-bio-info-cogno innovations: Converging technologies in society*, by William Simms Bainbridge and Mihail C. Roco. Washington, DC: Springer, 2005.

Micheals Development Company. *Legends South (Formerly Known as Robert Taylor Homes)*. Chicago, IL: Micheals Development Company, 2003.

Montefiore, Simon S. *Stalin: The Court of the Red Tsar*. New York: Vintage Books, 2003.

Nagl, John. *U.S. Army / Marine Corps Counterinsurgency Field Manual*. Chicago, IL: University of Chicago Press, 2007.

National Commission on Terrorist Attacks Upon the United States. *Final Report of the National Commission on Terrorist Attacks Upon the United States*. July 22, 2004. http://www.gpoaccess.gov/911/Index.html (accessed 7 2009, May).

Odom, Thomas P. "Book Review - Conspiracy to Murder: The Rwanda Genocide." *Small Wars Journal*. August 4, 2008.

http://smallwarsjournal.com/blog/2008/08/book-review-conspiracy-to-murd/ (accessed May 7, 2009).

Osborne, Joseph E. "Beyond Irregular Warfare." *Small Wars Journal.* February 19, 2009. http://smallwarsjournal.com/blog/2009/02/beyond-irregular-warfare/ (accessed May 7, 2009).

Osinga, Frans. *Science, strategy, and war: The strategic theory of John Boyd.* New York: Routledge, 2006.

Pampinella, Stephen. "The construction of 5GW." In *The handbook of 5GW: A fifth generation of war?*, by Daniel H. Abbott. Ann Arbor, MI: Nimble Books, 2009.

Pattinson, Shaun D, and Timothy Caulfield. "Variations and voids: The regulation of human cloning around the world." *BMC Medical Ethics* 5, no. 9 (2004).

Phil. "If 5GW takes aim..." *tdaxp.* July 27, 2005. http://www.tdaxp.com/archive/2005/07/26/5th-generation-thumbnail-sketches.html#comment-12636 (accessed May 8, 2009).

Phillips, T.R. *Roots of strategy.* Harrisburg, PA: Stackpole Books, 1985.

Popper, K. "Science: Conjectures and Refutations." In *Conjectures and Refutations*, by K. Popper, 33-59. New York, NY: Routledge, 1963.

Power, Samantha. *A Problem from Hell: America in the Age of Genocide.* New York: Basic Books, 2002.

Rees, L.C. "The End of the Rainbow: Implications of 5GW for a General Theory of War." In *The handbook of 5GW: A fifth generation of war?*, by Daniel H. Abbott. Ann Arbor, MI: Nimble Books, 2009.

Richards, Chet. *If We Can Keep It: A National Security Manifesto for the Next Administration.* Washington, DC: Center for Defense Information, 2008.

Ricks, Thomas E. *Fiasco: The American military adventure in Iraq.* New York: Penguin, 2006.

Robb, John. *Brave New War: The Next Stage of Terrorism and the End of Globalization.* Hoboken, NJ: John Wiley & Sons, 2007.

—. "I'd like to offer an alternative to the above." *Coming Anarchy.* March 11, 2006. http://cominganarchy.com/2006/03/10/truly-formless-5gw/#comment-73234 (accessed May 8, 2009).

—. "JOURNAL: Can Georgie become a MicroPower?" *Global Guerrillas.* October 7, 2006. http://globalguerrillas.typepad.com/globalguerrillas/2006/10/journal_the_noo.html (accessed May 8, 2009).

—. "Lots of discussion of what 5GW is." *John Robb's Weblog.* October 9, 2006. http://globalguerrillas.typepad.com/johnrobb/2006/10/lots_of_discuss.html (accessed May 8, 2009).

—. "THE CHANGING FACE OF WAR: Into the 5th Generation (5GW)." *Global Guerrillas.* October 16, 2006. http://globalguerrillas.typepad.com/globalguerrillas/2006/10/the_changing_fa.html (accessed May 8, 2009).

—. "Totally unreal." *John Robb's Weblog.* October 16, 2006. http://www.5gw.phaticcommunion.com/2007/09/totally_unreal.php (accessed May 8, 2009).

Robinett, Warren. "The consequences of fully understanding the brain." In *Converging technologies for improving human performance*, by Mihail C. Roco and William Sims Bainbridge. Arlington, VA: National Science Foundation, 2002.

Roco, M.C., and W.S. Bainbridge. *Managing nano-bio-info-cogno innovations: Converging technologies for improving human performance.* Arlington, VA: NSF, 2002.

Ronfeldt, David, and Danielle Varda. *The prospects for cyberocracy.* December 1, 2008. http://papers.ssrn.com/sol3/papers.cfm?abstract_id=1325809 (accessed May 5, 2009).

Safranski, Mark. "5GW Reloaded: Reflecting on 5th Generation War." *Zenpundit.* July 25, 2005. http://www.5gw.phaticcommunion.com/2007/08/5gw_reloaded_reflecting_on_5th.php (accessed May 8, 2009).

Safranski, Mark. "5GW: Into the heart of darkness." In *The handbook of 5GW: A fifth generation of war?*, by Daniel H. Abbott. Ann Arbor, MI: Nimble Books, 2009.

—. "A Strategic Dagwood." *Zenpundit.* October 8, 2006. http://zenpundit.blogspot.com/2006/10/strategic-dagwood-dr.html (accessed May 8, 2009).

—. *Fifth generation war in the OODA loop.* July 19, 2005. http://zenpundit.blogspot.com/2005/07/fifth-generation-war-in-ooda-loop-dan.html (accessed May 7, 2009).

—. "Revisiting 5th Generation War." *Zenpundit.* August 7, 2005. http://zenpundit.blogspot.com/2005/08/revisiting-5th-generation-war.html (accessed May 8, 2009).

—. *The expert informed me that my drawing...* July 20, 2005. http://www.tdaxp.com/archive/2005/07/20/ooda-loop-as-flowchart-try-2.html#comment-12585 (accessed May 7, 2009).

Safranski, Mark, ed. *The John Boyd roundtable: Debating science, strategy, and war.* Ann Arbor, MI: Nimble Books, 2008.

Safranski, Mark. "Unto the fifth generation of war." In *The handbook of 5GW: A fifth generation of war?*, by Daniel H. Abbott. Ann Arbor, MI: Nimble Books, 2009.

Sageman, Marc. *Understanding terror networks.* Philadelphia: University of Pennsylvania Press, 2004.

Schumpeter, Joseph A. *Capitalism, socialism, and democracy.* London: Routledge, 2006.

Sententia, Wyre. "Cognitive enhancement and the neuroethics of memory drugs." In *Managing nano-bio-info-cogno innovations: Converging technologies in society*, by William Sims Bainbridge and Mihail C. Roco. Washington, DC: Springer, 2005.

Sfranski, Richard. "Neocortical warfare? The acme of skill." *Military Review*, November 1994: 41-55.

The Usual Suspects. Directed by Bryan Singer. 1995.

Slog, Purple. "5GW working definition .091." In *The handbook of 5GW: A fifth generation of war?*, by Daniel H. Abbott. Ann Arbor, MI: Nimble Books, 2009.

—. "Found on Wikipedia: "The Dulles Plan"." *Purpleslog.* August 23, 2007. http://purpleslog.wordpress.com/2007/08/23/found-on-wikipedia-the-dulles-plan/ (accessed May 8, 2009).

Slog, Purple, and et al. "Bizarro Fred Phelps and 5GW Sepculation." *PurpleSlog.* September 9, 2006. http://purpleslog.wordpress.com/2006/09/09/bizzaro-fred-phelps-and-5gw-speculation/ (accessed May 8, 2009).

Snow, David A., and Robert D. Benford. "Ideology, frame resonance, and participant mobilization." *International Social Movement Journal* 1 (1988).

Steele, Robert. "FIFTH GENERATION WARFARE WITH PEACEFUL PREVENTIVE INVESTMENTS IS THE NECESSARY NEW NATIONAL SECURITY PARADIGM, NATIONAL SECURITY EXPERT SAYS." *PRNEWSWIRE.* August 19, 2003. http://www.oss.net/dynamaster/file_archive/040126/0edbc426d03357fb9970806bd01dca56/A041-5th%20Generation%20Warfare.doc (accessed May 8, 2009).

Steve. "Curtis, I think both the freedom to be responsible and freedom from responsibility are complimentary forms of empowerment." *Dreaming 5GW.* May 30, 2007. http://www.dreaming5gw.com/2007/05/kilcullen_on_narratives_in_ira.php#comment-406 (accessed May 11, 2009).

Sullivan, Alan. "Hello, Curtis." *Phatic Communion.* August 3, 2005. http://www.phaticcommunion.com/archives/2005/08/limitations_of.php#comment-286 (accessed May 8, 2009).

Tabachnick, B.G., Fidell, and L.S. *Using multivariate statistics.* 5th. Boston, MA: Allyn & Bacon, 2006.

Trinquier, Roger. *Modern warfare: A French view of counterinsurgency.* Translated by Daniel Lee. London: Pall Mall Press, 1964.

Tucker, Robert C. *Stalin in Power*. New York: W.W. Norton & Company, 1990.

Vaidya, Shlok. "5GW and Beyond." *Shlok Vaidya's Thinking*. October 9, 2006. http://www.shloky.com/?p=337 (accessed May 8, 2009).

Van Crevald, Martin. *The changing face of war*. New York: Presidio Press, 2006.

—. *The transformation of war*. New York: Free Press, 1991.

Venkatesh, S. A. *American project*. Cambridge, MA: Harvard University Press, 2002.

—. *Gang leader for a day: A rogue sociologist takes to the streets*. New York: Penguin Press, 2008.

von Clausewitz, C. *On war*. Translated by M. Howard and P. Paret. Princeton, NJ: Princeton University Press., 1989.

von Clausewitz, Carl. *On war*. Translated by Michael Howard and Peter Paret. Princeton, NJ: Princeton University Press, 1989.

Waltz, Kenneth. *Theory of international politics*. New York: McGraw-Hill, 1979.

Weeks, Curtis Gale. "5GW Effectors." *Phatic Communion*. July 26, 2005. http://www.phaticcommunion.com/archives/2005/07/5gw_effe ctors.php (accessed May 8, 2009).

—. "A few off-the-cuff observations:." *Coming Anarchy*. March 12, 2006. http://cominganarchy.com/2006/03/10/truly-formless-5gw/#comment-73431 (accessed May 8, 2009).

—. "Barnett and Rob." *Dreaming 5GW*. October 17, 2006. http://dreaming5gw.com/2006/10/barnett_and_robb.php (accessed May 8, 2009).

—. "Blog Notice." *Phatic Communion*. July 23, 2005. http://www.5gw.phaticcommunion.com/2007/08/blog_notice_ 1.php (accessed May 8, 2009).

—. "Boot on Unrestricted Warfare." *Phatic Communion*. July 20, 2005.

http://www.phaticcommunion.com/archives/2005/07/boot_on_
unrestr.php (accessed May 8, 2009).

—. "Dreaming 5GW in Surround Sound." *Dreaming 5GW*.
October 9, 2006.
http://dreaming5gw.com/2006/10/dreaming_5gw_in_surround
_sound.php (accessed May 8, 2009).

—. "EBO is Everything in War -- Almost." *Phatic Communion*.
July 2, 2006.
http://www.phaticcommunion.com/archives/2006/07/ebo_is_e
verythi.php (accessed May 8, 2009).

—. "Empires of the Mind." *Dreaming 5GW*. March 21, 2007.
http://www.dreaming5gw.com/2007/03/empires_of_the_mind.
php (accessed May 11, 2009).

—. "Global Guerillas as 5GW Warriors." *Dreaming 5GW*. October
19, 2006.
http://www.dreaming5gw.com/2006/10/global_guerrillas_as_5
gw_warri.php (accessed May 11, 2009).

—. "Hello Alan." *Phatic Communion*. August 3, 2005.
http://www.phaticcommunion.com/archives/2005/08/limitation
s_of.php#comment-287 (accessed May 8, 2009).

—. "Initiating 5GW." *Phatic Communion*. March 14, 2006.
http://www.phaticcommunion.com/archives/2006/03/initiating
_5gw.php (accessed May 8, 2009).

—. "Interesting, Dan." *tdaxp*. July 21, 2005.
http://www.tdaxp.com/archive/2005/07/20/dreaming-5th-
generation-war.html#comment-12573 (accessed May 8, 2009).

Weeks, Curtis Gale. "Kilcullen narratives on Iraq." In *The
handbook of 5GW: A fifth generation of war?*, edited by Daniel
H. Abbott. Ann Arbor, MI: Nimble Books, 2009.

—. "Limitations of 5GW." *Phatic Communion*. August 2, 2005.
http://www.phaticcommunion.com/archives/2005/08/limitation
s_of.php (accessed May 8, 2009).

—. "Micropowers and the Art of 5GW." *Dreaming 5GW*. October
14, 2006.
http://www.fifthgeneration.phaticcommunion.com/archives/20

06/10/micropowers_and_the_art_of_5gw.php (accessed May 8, 2009).

—. "Observing the Maturing World." *Phatic Communion.* July 5, 2006.
http://www.phaticcommunion.com/archives/2006/07/observing_the_m.php (accessed May 8, 2009).

Weeks, Curtis Gale. "On the Barnettian 5GW." In *The handbook of 5GW: A fifth generation of war?*, edited by Daniel H. Abbott. Ann Arbor, MI: Nimble Books, 2009.

—. "Personal Equals Political ." *Phatic Communion.* August 9, 2005.
http://www.phaticcommunion.com/archives/2005/08/personal_equals.php (accessed May 8, 2009).

—. "Rethinking the OODA." *Phatic Communion.* June 26, 2006.
http://www.phaticcommunion.com/archives/2006/06/rethinking_the.php (accessed May 8, 2009).

—. "Steve." *Dreaming 5GW.* June 10, 2007.
http://www.dreaming5gw.com/2007/05/kilcullen_on_narratives_in_ira.php#comment-409 (accessed May 11, 2009).

Weinberger, S. *Imaginary Weapons.* New York: Nation Books, 2006.

Wendt, Alexander. *Social theory of international politics.* Cambridge, UK: Cambridge University Press, 1999.

West, Bing. *The strongest tribe: War, politics, and the endgame in Iraq.* New York: Random House, 2008.

World Transhumanist Association. *Transhumanist FAQ.* 2008.
http://www.transhumanism.org/index.php/WTA/faq21 (accessed February 16, 2008).

Younghusband, Francis Edward. "5GW." *Coming Anarchy.* July 19, 2005. http://cominganarchy.com/2005/07/19/5gw/ (accessed May 8, 2009).

Younghusband, Francis Edward. "Towards a General xGW Framework." In *The handbook of xGW: A fifth generation of war?*, by Daniel H. Abbott. Ann Arbor, MI: Nimble Books, 2009.

—. "Truly formless 5GW." *Coming Anarchy*. March 10, 2006.
http://cominganarchy.com/2006/03/10/truly-formless-5gw/
(accessed May 8, 2009).

Made in the USA
Middletown, DE
30 March 2022